$\frac{10}{62}$

10/6

EVERYMAN'S LIBRARY

52

Everyman, I will go with thee, and be thy guide,
In thy most need to go by thy side

ROBERT SOUTHEY, born at Bristol in 1774.
Educated at Oxford. Visited Spain, 1795;
Portugal, 1800. Settled at Greta Hall, Keswick,
1803. Poet Laureate, 1813. Died in 1843.

ROBERT SOUTHEY

LIFE OF NELSON

INTRODUCTION BY
CAROLA OMAN

LONDON   J. M. DENT & SONS LTD
NEW YORK   E. P. DUTTON & CO INC

© Introduction, J. M. Dent and Sons Ltd, 1962
Made in Great Britain
at the
Aldine Press · Letchworth · Herts
for
J. M. DENT & SONS LTD
Aldine House · Bedford Street · London
First published in Everyman's Library 1906
Last reprinted 1962

INTRODUCTION

ROBERT SOUTHEY, when he undertook as 'task-work' instructions to write what has been generally acclaimed as his
masterpiece, was, in his own words, struggling to feed many
mouths 'out of one inkstand'.

He was born in 1774, the second son of a family deep-
rooted in west country soil, but diminished in prestige and
income. His father pined as a Bristol linen-draper. When
Robert was three, his parents delivered him to the imperious
charge of a much older, spinster, half-sister of his mother.
They seem to have acted from sheer weakness. The event
proved formative in Southey's career, for he became one of
the best fathers in literary history; nor was fate kind to him,
for in addition to his own beloved brood, he got all of
Coleridge's, as permanent residents, and had also to provide
for three sons of his sailor brother Tom, boys remorsefully
noted by him as unattractive.

Unprovided with companions of his own age, Southey,
according to his own account of his almost joyless infancy,
had read by the age of eight all the plays in the library of his
aunt (who included him in her theatre-going) and had himself begun dramatic composition. His story, up to the time
when he was obliged to write for a living, was mainly one
of rebellion. An uncle, who was chaplain to the British fac-
tory at Lisbon, paid for his education. Southey had been at
Westminster School one year when the Fall of the Bastille
marked, in popular reckoning, the beginning of the French
Revolution, with which he was an ardent sympathizer.
When he had been there four years he was expelled for
writing an essay against flogging; but by then he had collected two lifelong friends in Charles Watkin Williams Wynn
and Grosvenor Bedford. He went on to Balliol (Christ Church
having refused to have him), and it was there, in 1794, that a
friend brought round to his rooms a Unitarian who was
on a walking tour from Cambridge to North Wales, Samuel
Taylor Coleridge. The poets (for Southey had already completed an epic, *Joan of Arc*), together with some other
enthusiasts, planned an American Utopia, on the banks of
the Susquehanna. Twelve male emigrants were to till the
soil while a dozen females cooked, cleaned and looked after

their offspring. Four years were still to pass before William
Wordsworth wrote that:

> Bliss was it in that dawn to be alive,
> But to be young was very heaven!

Robert Lovell, an original member of the Pantisocracy, as
they called it, had already found a wife ready to emigrate, in
Mary Fricker, one of the six fatherless daughters of an
unsuccessful manufacturer of sugar-pans. Mrs Southey
employed the Fricker girls on sewing, in her home. Coleridge,
after hesitation, married Sara, to whom he was tempera-
mentally unsuited. Southey seems to have proposed to
Edith, who was always sickly, mainly through pity. The
circumstances of their wedding were wildly romantic. It took
place on a November morning in one of the most beautiful
of English churches, St Mary Redcliffe, Bristol, and after
the ceremony the bride returned to the Lovell's house, wore
her wedding-ring round her neck, on a string, out of sight,
and resumed her maiden name. Southey's aunt had turned
him out of her house when he told her of his engagement.
She said she would never look upon his face again, and she
kept her word. He would not be a surgeon, and he could not
be a parson, for together with Pantisocracy he had adopted
Unitarianism. He set off on a visit to his Lisbon uncle, with
the intention of writing his first travel-book. On his return,
Joseph Cottle, the Bristol bookseller, gave him £50 for
Joan of Arc, and Wynn settled upon him an annuity of £160.
He then began to read for the Bar. The Chancellor of the
Exchequer for Ireland endured him, for a short spell, as
private secretary. But Southey, who 'had a mimosa sensi-
bility', seemed to be able to persevere only as an author.

In 1803, after much wandering and ill health, he arrived at
Greta Hall, Keswick, where Coleridge had said that there was
room for both their families. It was to be Southey's home
for the rest of his life—nearly forty years. Between 1807
and 1816 he was at the height of his powers. His appearance
was striking. He was five feet eleven inches, an inch taller
than his neighbour Wordsworth, very thin and agile, with a
high nose, dark curly hair and eyes that were hazel and
hawk-like. De Quincey thought that Southey in his normal
Westmorland costume of nankeen pantaloons and short
jacket rather resembled a Tyrolese mountaineer.

As a regular contributor to the *Quarterly Review*, edited by
William Gifford and published by John Murray, he produced
the first sketch of his *Life of Nelson* within six years of

Trafalgar. The parcel from the *Quarterly* offices delivered
by the carrier at Keswick, for Greta Hall, included four
recently published books (on which Southey was to write an
article of forty-four pages), and a fifth, *Authentic Narrative
of the Death of Lord Nelson* by William Beatty, M.D., surgeon in the *Victory*. The books for review were *Memoirs of
Lord Viscount Nelson* by John Charnock, an enthusiastic
naval volunteer who entirely failed to communicate his
enthusiasm, a negligible Life by Thomas Churchill, another
(but containing some new information) by James Harrison
(employed by Lady Hamilton to exalt her claims to a
Government pension), and finally the semi-official *Life
and Services*, by James Clarke, chaplain to the Prince of
Wales, and John M'Arthur, who had been secretary to Lord
Hood. Both had been afloat in the royal service, and had
known Nelson well. Clarke and M'Arthur's two quarto
volumes weigh nearly twenty-three pounds, and as Southey
soon found, their contents were equally solid. The authors
had been both helped and impeded by being given every
assistance by the Nelson family. They had therefore deemed
it prudent as far as possible to avoid any mention of Lady
Hamilton, explaining that for the last four years of their
hero's life they had devoted their attention to 'his more
splendid public character'. Southey could not know that
they had failed in the first principles of editorship, and had not
only deleted passages from letters, but had run many together
and even corrected Nelson's characteristic lively prose. But
his possession of Beatty's publication enabled him to judge
how they had presumed to tamper with that noble simplicity.

John Murray instantly saw, from Southey's review, des-
pite the ferocious cuts made by Gifford, that there was now
a market for what Southey described as 'Such a life of
Nelson as shall be put into the hands of every youth destined
for the Navy—a five-shilling volume, for which he will give
me a hundred guineas'. He set to work.

The surroundings in which he wrote his life of Nelson were
well suited to a lofty theme. Greta Hall still stands, essentially unchanged, a plain-faced Georgian house, with pillars
and a pediment at the front door, and some windows in the
style known as Venetian at the sides, and with the slightly
staring look of stark reality noticeable in houses which find
themselves in remote situations of peculiar beauty. Southey's
first-floor study, which held 14,000 volumes, had a view of
immense skies, and atmospheric effects, often of unimagin-
able majesty. Derwentwater was backed by the waters of

Borrowdale; to the right lay Bassenthwaite, and beyond
Skiddaw. Of it Southey wrote: 'There is something in this
place more like the scenes of enchantment in the books of
chivalry than any thing in our ordinary world.'

To Walter Scott, who had encouraged him, Southey
described his new task as: 'Not self-chosen, and out of my
way, but executed *con amore*.' He realized that he was not an
expert on naval matters, and his letters to his brother Tom,
who had been in action at Copenhagen, display an almost
morbid fear of error. (He had perhaps another rich source of
naval lore in the retired sailor, a veteran of the Battle of
the Saints, now the best barber in Keswick.) 'I am such a
sad lubber,' mourned Southey. 'I walk among sea-terms as
a cat does in a china-pantry.' He did, naturally, make some
mistakes, even when trusting to Clarke and M'Arthur to
save him from the perils of the deep. No modern examinee,
questioned on the tactics of the battles of Cape St Vincent
and the Nile, or the strategy of the Trafalgar campaign,
would do wisely to quote Southey. But his work was the
first on naval history since Hakluyt's *Traffics and Discoveries* to pass at once, unchallenged, into English literature.

The printer's estimate had been misleading. Southey's
Nelson had to be issued in two volumes, but each small
enough to slip into the pocket—4 by 6½ inches. It was well
received, and a second impression followed within a year, but
nothing further was called for for twelve years. In all, six
impressions were issued during the author's lifetime, and he
made revisions for an 1830 'new edition', as several works of
importance bearing on his subject had appeared since 1813.

In the autumn of 1813, on the death of the minor poet Pye,
Scott was offered the laureateship. He declined, and begged
leave to suggest the name of Southey, who therefore became
poet laureate in the same year that his most famous book
was published. He never himself rated his life of Nelson as
highly as his lives of Cowper and Wesley, which came later.
In his own opinion his *History of Brazil* was his *magnum
opus.* His predeliction for the chronicle shows in his life of
Nelson, where the reader's attention is suddenly deflected,
first by an account of polar exploration and presently by a
history of Corsica. He was much too close a contemporary to
present a reasonable view of Bonaparte, and although he did
not follow Clarke and M'Arthur in ignoring Lady Hamilton,
he did worse. He repeated damaging anecdotes about her,
which succeeding generations have believed, some of which
have been proved false. But he had a personal reason for

this. Lady Nelson was a deserted wife, and Coleridge's deserted wife faced Southey at every meal. He was truly gallant, however, in his references to Lady Nelson.

The fact remains that since Southey's death there has been a constant call for his life of Nelson, and the 1813 edition (which is that here presented) remains a classic. In 1846 came the Bible of Nelson biographers, the seven-volume collection of his letters and dispatches edited by Sir Harris Nicolas. Admiral Mahan, in 1897, produced *Nelson, the embodiment of the sea-power of Great Britain.* No student can ignore this Nelson Monument, but it cannot compare with Southey in popular favour. In 1922 Sir Geoffrey Callender edited an annotated edition of Southey's *Nelson* (based on the 1830 version) giving many interesting and valuable corrections of detail.

Southey, who 'lifted' Clarke and M'Arthur's ponderous volumes into literature, was very well qualified to do so. He was a disciplined accomplished writer; he could tell a tale with convincing clarity. Even Byron admitted 'Southey's prose is perfect'. He painted the portrait of a national hero in glowing colours, and the Nelson who would be recognized by the man in the street today is still Southey's Nelson. There is one piece of amusing evidence that he knew his hero through and through. In 1814 there appeared the anonymously printed *Letters of Lord Nelson to Lady Hamilton.* These seemed to Southey to confirm some judgments made by him in 1813, and he quoted copiously from them in his 1830 edition. The letters had been for long denounced by admirers of the admiral as forgeries, and Southey was severely criticized. The originals arrived at the National Maritime Museum, Greenwich, in 1946. One more reason may be suggested for Southey's success as the biographer of Nelson. Southey also was what was called in his day 'a man of courage'. Ghastly and unmerited afflictions crowded upon him in his later years. He lost his most gifted son, just when the boy was at an age to appreciate the model biography his father had written. He long devoted every hour, except those when he must write, to the care of a wife who had lost her reason. He never ceased, while he could, to produce an immense quantity of work which was distinguished also for high quality. He brought greatness to his great task; and of this the reader becomes aware the moment he opens Southey's *Nelson.*

CAROLA OMAN.

1961.

SELECT BIBLIOGRAPHY

POETRY. *The Fall of Robespierre. An Historic Drama*, 1794; *Poems* (R. Lovell and Southey), 1795; *Joan of Arc. An Epic Poem*, 1796; *Poems*, 2 vols., 1797–9; *Thalaba the Destroyer*, 2 vols., 1801; *Madoc, a Poem in two parts*, 1805; *The Curse of Kehama*, 1810; *Roderick, the Last of the Goths*, 1814; *Odes to His Royal Highness the Prince Regent*, etc., 1814; *The Poet's Pilgrimage to Waterloo*, 1816; *The Lay of the Laureate, Carmen Nuptiale*, 1816; *Wat Tyler. A Dramatic Poem*, 1817; *A Vision of Judgement*, 1821; *A Tale of Paraguay*, 1825; *All for Love; and the Pilgrim to Compostella*; *The Devil's Walk, a poem by Professor Porson*, 1830.

There is a ten-volume edition of the Poetical Works, collected by Southey himself, 1837–8, and often reprinted.

PROSE. *The Flagellant*, 9 nos., 1st March–26th April 1792; *Letters written during a short residence in Spain and Portugal*, 1797; *Letters from England: by Don Manuel Alvarez Espriella*, 3 vols., 1807; ed. with introduction by J. Simons, 1951; *History of Brazil*, 3 parts, 1810–29; *Omniana, or Horae Otiosiores*, 2 vols., 1812; *The Life of Nelson*, 2 vols., 1813; with Southey's corrections, 1831; ed. G. A. R. Callender, 1922; ed. Sir H. Newbolt, 1925; *The Life of Wesley; and the Rise and Progress of Methodism*, 2 vols., 1820; *History of the Peninsular War*, 3 vols., 1823–32; *The Book of the Church*, 2 vols., 1824; *Vindiciae Ecclesiae Anglicanae*, 1826; *Sir Thomas More: or, Colloquies on the Progress and Prospects of Society*, 2 vols., 1829; *Lives of the British Admirals*, 5 vols., 1833–40; *The Doctor*, 7 vols., 1834–47; edited by his son-in-law, J. W. Warter, 1848; abridged version, ed. M. Fitzgerald, 1930; *The Life of the Reverend Andrew Bell. Comprising the History of the Rise and Progress of the System of Mutual Tuition*, 3 vols., 1844; *Southey's Common Place Book*, ed. J. W. Warter, 4 series, 1849–1851; 1876; *Journal of a Tour in the Netherlands in the Autumn of 1815*, ed. Sir W. R. Nicoll, 1903; *Journal of a Tour in Scotland in 1819*, ed. C. H. Herford, 1929.

EDITIONS AND TRANSLATIONS. *The Annual Anthology*, 2 vols. (ed. and partly written by Southey), 1799–1800; *Amadis of Gaul* (trans.), 1803; *The Works of Thomas Chatterton* (ed. by J. Cottle and Southey), 3 vols., 1803; *Chronicle of the Cid* (trans.), 1808; *The Byrth, Lyf and Actes of Kyng Arthur* (Introduction and notes by Southey), 2 vols., 1817; *Select Works of the British Poets, from Chaucer to Jonson*, 1831; *The Works of William Cowper*, 15 vols., 1835–7.

BIOGRAPHY AND CRITICISM. C. C. Southey (ed.), *The Life and Correspondence of the late Robert Southey*, 6 vols., 1849–50; C. T. Browne, *Life of Robert Southey*, 1854; E. Dowden, *Southey* (English Men of Letters series), 1874; W. Haller, *The Early Life of Robert Southey*, 1917; J. Simmons, *Robert Southey*, 1945.

THE LIFE OF NELSON

CHAPTER I

HORATIO, son of Edmund and Catherine Nelson, was born September 29, 1758, in the parsonage house of Burnham Thorpe, a village in the county of Norfolk, of which his father was rector. The maiden name of his mother was Suckling: her grandmother was an elder sister of Sir Robert Walpole, and this child was named after his godfather, the first Lord Walpole. Mrs. Nelson died in 1767, leaving eight, out of eleven, children. Her brother, Captain Maurice Suckling, of the Navy, visited the widower upon this event, and promised to take care of one of the boys. Three years afterwards, when Horatio was only twelve years of age, being at home during the Christmas holidays, he read in the county newspaper that his uncle was appointed to the *Raisonnable*, of 64 guns. "Do, William," said he to a brother who was a year and a half older than himself, "write to my father, and tell him that I should like to go to sea with Uncle Maurice." Mr. Nelson was then at Bath, whither he had gone for the recovery of his health: his circumstances were straitened and he had no prospect of ever seeing them bettered: he knew that it was the wish of providing for himself by which Horatio was chiefly actuated, and did not oppose his resolution; he understood also the boy's character, and had always said, that in whatever station he might be placed, he would climb, if possible, to the very top of the tree. Accordingly Captain Suckling was written to. "What," said he in his answer, "has poor Horatio done, who is so weak, that he, above all the rest, should be sent to rough it out at sea? But let him come, and the first time we go into action, a cannon-ball may knock off his head, and provide for him at once."

It is manifest from these words, that Horatio was not the boy whom his uncle would have chosen to bring up in his own profession. He was never of a strong body; and the ague, which at that time was one of the most common diseases in England, had greatly reduced his strength; yet he had already given proofs of that resolute heart and nobleness of mind, which, during his whole career of labour and of glory, so eminently distinguished him. When a mere child, he strayed birds-nesting from his mother's house in company with a cow-boy: the dinner-hour elapsed; he was absent, and could not be found; and the alarm of the family became very great, for they apprehended that he might have been carried off by the gipsies. At length, after search had been made for him in various directions, he was discovered alone, sitting composedly by the side of a brook, which he could not get over. "I wonder, child," said the old lady when she saw him, "that hunger and fear did not drive you home." "Fear! grandmamma," replied the future hero, "I never saw fear: what is it?" Once, after the winter holidays, when he and his brother William had set off on horseback to return to school, they came back because there had been a fall of snow; and William, who did not much like the journey, said it was too deep for them to venture on. "If that be the case," said the father, "you certainly shall not go; but make another attempt, and I will leave it to your honour. If the road is dangerous you may return: but remember, boys, I leave it to your honour."

The snow was deep enough to have afforded them a reasonable excuse; but Horatio was not to be prevailed upon to turn back. "We must go on," said he; "remember, brother, it was left to our honour!" There were some fine pears growing in the schoolmaster's garden, which the boys regarded as lawful booty, and in the highest degree tempting; but the boldest among them were afraid to venture for the prize. Horatio volunteered upon this service: he was lowered down at night from the bed-room window by some sheets, plundered the tree, was drawn up with the pears, and then distributed them among his school-fellows, without reserving any for himself. "He only took them," he said, "because every other boy was afraid."

Early on a cold and dark spring morning Mr. Nelson's servant arrived at this school at North Walsham with the expected summons for Horatio to join his ship. The parting from his brother William, who had been for so many years his playmate and bedfellow, was a painful effort, and was the beginning of those privations which are the sailor's lot through life. He accompanied his father to London. The *Raisonnable* was lying in the Medway. He was put into the Chatham stage, and on its arrival was set down with the rest of the passengers, and left to find his way on board as he could. After wandering about in the cold, without being able to reach the ship, an officer observed the forlorn appearance of the boy, questioned him, and happening to be acquainted with his uncle, took him home, and gave him some refreshments. When he got on board, Captain Suckling was not in the ship, nor had any person been apprised of the boy's coming. He paced the deck the whole remainder of the day, without being noticed by any one; and it was not till the second day that somebody, as he expressed it, "took compassion on him." The pain which is felt when we are first transplanted from

our native soil—when the living branch is cut from
the parent tree—is one of the most poignant which we
have to endure through life.   There are after-griefs
which wound more deeply, which leave behind them
scars never to be effaced, which bruise the spirit, and
sometimes break the heart : but never, never do we
feel so keenly the want of love, the necessity of being
loved, and the sense of utter desertion, as when we
first leave the haven of home, and are, as it were,
pushed off upon the stream of life.   Added to these
feelings, the sea-boy has to endure physical hardships,
and the privation of every comfort, even of sleep.
Nelson had a feeble body and an affectionate heart,
and he remembered through life his first days of
wretchedness in the service.

The *Raisonnable* having been commissioned on
account of the dispute respecting the Falkland Islands,
was paid off as soon as the difference with the Court
of Spain was accommodated, and Captain Suckling
was removed to the *Triumph*, 74, then stationed as a
guard-ship in the Thames.   This was considered as
too inactive a life for a boy, and Nelson was therefore
sent a voyage to the West Indies in a merchant-ship,
commanded by Mr. John Rathbone, an excellent seaman, who had served as master's-mate under Captain
Suckling in the *Dreadnought*.   He returned a prac-
tical seaman, but with a hatred of the king's service,
and a saying then common among the sailors—"Aft
the most honour ; forward, the better man."   Rathbone had probably been disappointed and disgusted in
the navy ; and, with no unfriendly intentions, warned
Nelson against the profession which he himself had
found hopeless.   His uncle received him on board the
Triumph on his return, and discovering his dislike to
the navy, took the best means of reconciling him to
it.   He held it out as a reward, that if he attended
well to his navigation, he should go in the cutter and
decked longboat, which was attached to the commanding officer's ship at Chatham.   Thus he became

a good pilot for vessels of that description from Chatham to the Tower, and down the Swin Channel to the North Foreland, and acquired a confidence among rocks and sands of which he often felt the value.

Nelson had not been many months on board the *Triumph*, when his love of enterprise was excited by hearing that two ships were fitting out for a voyage of discovery toward the North Pole. In consequence of the difficulties which were expected on such a service, these vessels were to take out effective men, instead of the usual number of boys. This, however, did not deter him from soliciting to be received, and by his uncle's interest he was admitted as coxswain under Captain Lutwidge, second in command. The voyage was undertaken in compliance with an application from the Royal Society. The Hon. Captain Constantine John Phipps, eldest son of Lord Mulgrave, volunteered his services. The *Racehorse* and *Carcass* bombs were selected, as the strongest ships, and therefore best adapted for such a voyage; and they were taken into dock and strengthened, to render them as secure as possible against the ice. Two masters of Greenlandmen were employed as pilots for each ship. No expedition was ever more carefully fitted out; and the First Lord of the Admiralty, Lord Sandwich, with a laudable solicitude, went on board himself, before their departure, to see that everything had been completed to the wish of the officers. The ships were provided with a simple and excellent apparatus for distilling fresh from salt water, the invention of Dr. Irving, who accompanied the expedition. It consisted merely in fitting a tube to the ship's kettle, and applying a wet mop to the surface as the vapour was passing. By these means from thirty-four to forty gallons were produced every day.

They sailed from the Nore on the 4th of June: on the 6th of the following month they were in lat. 79° 56' 39"; long. 9° 43' 30" E. The next day, about the place where most of the old discoverers had been stopped, the *Racehorse* was beset with ice; but they heaved her through with ice-anchors. Captain Phipps continued ranging along the ice northward and westward till the 24th : he then tried to the eastward. On the 30th he was in lat. 80° 13'; long. 18° 48' E. among the islands and in the ice, with no appearance of an opening for the ships. The weather was exceedingly fine, mild, and unusually clear. Here they were becalmed in a large bay, with three apparent openings between the islands which formed it; but everywhere, as far as they could see, surrounded with ice. There was not a breath of air; the water perfectly smooth; the ice covered with snow, low and even, except a few broken pieces near the edge; and the pools of water in the middle of the ice-fields just crusted over with young ice. On the next day the ice closed upon them, and no opening was to be seen anywhere, except a hole, or lake, as it might be called, of about a mile and a half in circumference, where the ships lay fast to the ice with their ice-anchors. They filled their casks with water from these ice-fields, which was very pure and soft. The men were playing on the ice all day : but the Greenland pilots, who were farther than they had ever been before, and considered that the season was advancing, were alarmed at being thus beset.

The next day there was not the smallest opening, the ships were within less than two lengths of each other, separated by ice, and neither having room to turn. The ice, which yesterday had been all flat, and almost level with the water's edge, was now in many places forced higher than the mainyard, by the pieces squeezing together. A day of thick fog followed : it was succeeded by clear weather; but the passage by which the ships had entered from the westward was closed, and no open water was in sight either in that or any other quarter. By the pilots' advice the men were set to work to cut a passage and warp through the small openings to the westward. They sawed through pieces twelve feet thick; and this labour con-

tinued the whole day, during which their utmost
efforts did not move the ships above three hundred
yards; while they were driven, together with the ice,
far to the N. E. and E. by the current. Sometimes a
field of several acres square would be lifted up between
two larger islands, and incorporated with them : and
thus these larger pieces continued to grow by aggre-
gation. Another day passed, and there seemed no
probability of getting the ships out, without a strong
E. or N.E. wind. The season was far advanced, and
every hour lessened the chance of extricating themselves. Young as he was, Nelson was appointed to
command one of the boats which were sent out to
explore a passage into the open water. It was the
means of saving a boat belonging to the *Racehorse*
from a singular but imminent danger. Some of the
officers had fired at and wounded a walrus. As no
other animal has so human-like an expression in its
countenance, so also is there none that seems to
possess more of the passions of humanity. The
wounded one dived immediately, and brought up a
number of its companions; and they all joined in an
attack upon the boat. They wrested an oar from one
of the men; and it was with the utmost difficulty that
the crew could prevent them from staving or upsetting
her, till the *Carcass's* boat came up : and the walruses,
finding their enemies thus reinforced, dispersed.
Young Nelson exposed himself in a more daring
manner. One night, during the mid-watch, he stole
from the ship with one of his comrades, taking
advantage of a rising fog, and set out over the ice in
pursuit of a bear. It was not long before they were
missed. The fog thickened, and Captain Lutwidge
and his officers became exceedingly alarmed for their
safety. Between three and four in the morning the
weather cleared, and the two adventurers were seen,
at a considerable distance from the ship, attacking a
huge bear. The signal for them to return was
immediately made; Nelson's comrade called upon him

to obey it, but in vain; his musket had flashed in the pan; their ammunition was expended; and a chasm in the ice, which divided him from the bear, probably preserved his life. "Never mind," he cried; "do but let me get a blow at this devil with the butt-end of my musket, and we shall have him." Captain Lutwidge, however, seeing his danger, fired a gun, which had the desired effect of frightening the beast; and the boy then returned, somewhat afraid of the consequences of his trespass. The captain reprimanded him sternly for conduct so unworthy of the office which he filled, and desired to know what motive he could have for hunting a bear. "Sir," said he, pouting his lip, as he was wont to do when agitated, "I wished to kill the bear, that I might carry the skin to my father."

A party were now sent to an island, about twelve miles off (named Walden's Island in the charts, from the midshipman who was intrusted with this service), to see where the open water lay. They came back on the 6th, with information that the ice, though close all about them, was open to the westward, round the point by which they came in. They said also, that upon the island they had had a fresh east wind. This intelligence considerably abated the hopes of the crew, for where they lay it had been almost calm, and their main dependence had been upon the effect of an easterly wind in clearing the bay. There was but one alternative: either to wait the event of the weather upon the ships, or to betake themselves to the boats. The likelihood that it might be necessary to sacrifice the ships had been foreseen; the boats accordingly were adapted, both in number and size, to transport, in case of emergency, the whole crew; and there were Dutch whalers upon the coast, in which they could all be conveyed to Europe. As for wintering where they were, that dreadful experiment had been already tried too often. No time was to be lost; the ships had driven into shoal water, having but fourteen fathoms. Should

they, or the ice to which they were fast, take the
ground, they must inevitably be lost : and at this time
they were driving fast toward some rocks on the N.E.
Captain Phipps sent for the officers of both ships, and
told them his intention of preparing the boats for
going away. They were immediately hoisted out, and
the fitting began. Canvas bread-bags were made, in
case it should be necessary suddenly to desert the
vessels; and men were sent with the lead and line to
the northward and eastward, to sound wherever they
found cracks in the ice, that they might have notice
before the ice took the ground; for, in that case, the
ships must instantly have been crushed, or overset.

On the 7th they began to haul the boats over the ice,
Nelson having command of the four-oared cutter.
The men behaved excellently well, like true British
seamen : they seemed reconciled to the thought of
leaving the ships, and had full confidence in their
officers. About noon, the ice appeared rather more
open near the vessels; and as the wind was easterly,
though there was but little of it, the sails were set,
and they got about a mile to the westward. They
moved very slowly, and were not now nearly so far to
the westward as when they were first beset. However, all sail was kept upon them, to force them
through whenever the ice slacked the least. Whatever exertions were made, it could not be possible to
get the boats to the water edge before the 14th; and
if the situation of the ships should not alter by that
time, it would not be justifiable to stay longer by
them. The commander therefore resolved to carry on
both attempts together, moving the boats constantly,
and taking every opportunity of getting the ships
through. A party was sent out next day to the westward, to examine the state of the ice : they returned
with tidings that it was very heavy and close, consisting chiefly of large fields. The ships, however,
moved something, and the ice itself was drifting westward. There was a thick fog, so that it was im-

possible to ascertain what advantage had been gained.
It continued on the 9th; but the ships were moved a
little through some very small openings: the
mist cleared off in the afternoon; and it was
then perceived that they had driven much more
than could have been expected to the westward,
and that the ice itself had driven still farther. In
the course of the day they got past the boats, and
took them on board again. On the morrow the
wind sprang up to the N.N.E. All sail was set,
and the ships forced their way through a great deal of
very heavy ice. They frequently struck, and with
such force, that one stroke broke the shank of the
Racehorse's best bower anchor: but the vessels made
way; and by noon they had cleared the ice, and were
out at sea. The next day they anchored in Smeeren-
berg Harbour, close to that island of which the
westernmost point is called Hakluyt's Headland, in
honour of the great promoter and compiler of our
English voyages of discovery.

Here they remained a few days, that the men might
rest after their fatigue. No insect was to be seen in
this dreary country, nor any species of reptile, not
even the common earthworm. Large bodies of ice,
called icebergs, filled up the valleys between high
mountains, so dark as, when contrasted with the
snow, to appear black. The colour of the ice was a
lively light green. Opposite to the place where they
fixed their observatory was one of these icebergs,
above three hundred feet high: its side towards the
sea was nearly perpendicular, and a stream of water
issued from it. Large pieces frequently broke off, and
thundered down into the sea. There was no thunder
nor lightning during the whole time they were in these
latitudes. The sky was generally loaded with hard
white clouds, from which it was never entirely free,
even in the clearest weather. They always knew
when they were approaching the ice long before they
saw it, by a bright appearance near the horizon, which

the Greenlandmen called the blink of the ice. The season was now so far advanced, that nothing more could have been attempted, if indeed anything had been left untried : but the summer had been unusually favourable, and they had carefully surveyed the wall of ice extending for more than twenty degrees between the latitudes of 80° and 81°, without the smallest appearance of any opening.

The ships were paid off shortly after their return to England; and Nelson was then placed, by his uncle, with Captain Farmer, in the *Seahorse*, of 20 guns, then going out to the East Indies in the squadron under Sir Edward Hughes. He was stationed in the foretop at watch and watch. His good conduct attracted the attention of the master (afterwards Captain Surridge), in whose watch he was; and, upon his recommendation, the captain rated him as midshipman. At this time his countenance was florid, and his appearance rather stout and athletic; but, when he had been about eighteen months in India, he felt the effects of that climate, so perilous to European constitutions. The disease baffled all power of medicine; he was reduced almost to a skeleton; the use of his limbs was for some time entirely lost; and the only hope that remained was from a voyage home. Accordingly he was brought home by Captain Pigot, in the *Dolphin*; and had it not been for the attentive and careful kindness of that officer on the way, Nelson would never have lived to reach his native shores. He had formed acquaintance with Sir Charles Pole, Sir Thomas Trowbridge, and other distinguished officers, then, like himself, beginning their career; he had left them pursuing that career in full enjoyment of health and hope, and was returning from a country in which all things were to him new and interesting, with a body broken down by sickness, and spirits which had sunk with his strength. Long afterwards, when the name of Nelson was known as widely as that of England itself, he spoke of the feelings which he at this time endured. "I felt impressed," said he, "with a feeling that I should never rise in my profession. My mind was staggered with a view of the difficulties I had to surmount, and the little interest I possessed. I could discover no means of reaching the object of my ambition. After a long and gloomy reverie, in which I almost wished myself overboard, a sudden glow of patriotism was kindled within me, and presented by king and country as my patron. Well, then," I exclaimed, "I will be a hero! and, confiding in Providence, I will brave every danger!" Long afterwards Nelson loved to speak of the feeling of that moment; and from that time, he often said, a radiant orb was suspended in his mind's eye, which urged him onward to renown. The state of mind in which these feelings began, is what the mystics mean by their season of darkness, of aridity, and of desertion. If the animal spirits of coarser enthusiasts fail, they represent it as an actual temptation, a snare of Satan. The enthusiasm of Nelson's nature had taken a different direction, but in its essence it was the same. He knew to what the previous state of dejection was to be attributed; that an enfeebled body, and a mind depressed, had cast this shade over his soul; but he always seemed willing to believe, that the sunshine which succeeded bore with it a prophetic glory, and that the light which led him on was "light from heaven."

His interest, however, was far better than he imagined. During his absence, Captain Suckling had been made Comptroller of the Navy; his health had materially improved upon the voyage; and, as soon as the *Dolphin* was paid off, he was appointed acting lieutenant in the *Worcester*, 64, Captain Mark Robinson, then going out with convoy to Gibraltar. Soon after his return, on the 8th of April 1777, he passed his examination for a lieutenancy. Captain Suckling sat at the head of the board, and when the examination had ended, in a manner highly honourable to

Nelson, rose from his seat, and introduced him to the examining captains as his nephew. They expressed their wonder that he had not informed them of this relationship before; he replied that he did not wish the younker to be favoured; he knew his nephew would pass a good examination, and he had not been deceived. The next day Nelson received his commission as second lieutenant of the *Lowestoffe* frigate, Captain William Locker, then fitting out for Jamaica.

American and French privateers, under American colours, were at that time harassing our trade in the West Indies: even a frigate was not sufficiently active for Nelson, and he repeatedly got appointed to the command of one of the *Lowestoffe's* tenders. During one of their cruises the *Lowestoffe* captured an American letter-of-marque: it was blowing a gale, and a heavy sea running. The first lieutenant being ordered to board the prize, went below to put on his hanger. It happened to be mislaid; and, while he was seeking it, Captain Locker came on deck. Perceiving the boat still alongside, and in danger every moment of being swamped, and being extremely anxious that the privateer should be instantly taken in charge, because he feared that it would otherwise founder, he exclaimed, " Have I no officer in the ship who can board the prize? " Nelson did not offer himself immediately, waiting, with his usual sense of propriety, for the first lieutenant's return; but hearing the master volunteer, he jumped into the boat, saying, " It is my turn now; and if I come back, it is yours." The American, who had carried a heavy press of sail in hope of escaping, was so completely water-logged that the *Lowestoffe's* boat went in on deck, and out again, with the sea.

About this time he lost his uncle. Captain Locker, however, who had perceived the excellent qualities of Nelson, and formed a friendship for him, which continued during his life, recommended him warmly to Sir Peter Parker, then commander-in-chief upon that

station. In consequence of this recommendation he
was removed into the *Bristol* flagship, and Lieutenant
Cuthbert Collingwood succeeded him in the *Lowestoffe*. He soon became first lieutenant; and on the 8th
of December, 1778, was appointed commander of the
Badger brig : Collingwood again succeeding him in
the *Bristol*. While the *Badger* was lying in Montego
Bay, Jamaica, the *Glasgow,* of 20 guns, came in and
anchored there, and in two hours was in flames, the
steward having set fire to her while stealing rum out
of the after-hold. Her crew were leaping into the
water, when Nelson came up in his boats, made them
throw their powder overboard, and point their guns
upward; and, by his presence of mind and personal
exertions, prevented the loss of life which would otherwise have ensued. On the 11th of June, 1779, he was
made post into the *Hinchinbrook,* of 28 guns, an
enemy's merchant-man, sheathed with wood, which
had been taken into the service. A short time after he
left the *Lowestoffe,* that ship, with a small squadron,
stormed the fort of St. Fernando de Omoa, on the
south side of the bay of Honduras, and captured some
register ships which were lying under its guns. Two
hundred and fifty quintals of quicksilver, and three
millions of piastres, were the reward of this enterprise :
and it is characteristic of Nelson, that the chance by
which he missed a share in such a prize is never mentioned in any of his letters; nor is it likely that it ever
excited even a momentary feeling of vexation.

Nelson was fortunate in possessing good interest at
the time when it could be most serviceable to him; his
promotion had been almost as rapid as it could be;
and before he had attained the age of twenty-one he
had gained that rank which brought all the honours of
the service within his reach. No opportunity, indeed,
had yet been given him of distinguishing himself; but
he was thoroughly master of his profession, and his
zeal and ability were acknowledged wherever he was
known. Count d'Estaing, with a fleet of 125 sail,

men-of-war and transports, and a reputed force of five-and-twenty thousand men, threatened Jamaica from St. Domingo. Nelson offered his services to the Admiral and to Governor-General Dalling, and was appointed to command the batteries of Fort Charles, at Port Royal. Not more than seven thousand men could be mustered for the defence of the island,—a number wholly inadequate to resist the force which threatened them. Of this Nelson was so well aware, that when he wrote to his friends in England, he told them they must not be surprised to hear of his learning to speak French. D'Estaing, however, was either not aware of his own superiority, or not equal to the command with which he was intrusted; he attempted nothing with this formidable armament; and General Dalling was thus left to execute a project which he had formed against the Spanish colonies.

This project was to take Fort San Juan, on the river of that name, which flows from Lake Nicaragua into the Atlantic; make himself master of the lake itself, and of the cities of Granada and Leon; and thus cut off the communication of the Spaniards between their northern and southern possessions in America. Here it is that a canal between the two seas may most easily be formed—a work more important in its consequences than any which has ever yet been effected by human power. Lord George Germaine, at that time Secretary of State for the American Department, approved the plan: and as discontents at that time were known to prevail in the Nuevo Reyno, in Popayan, and in Peru, the more sanguine part of the English began to dream of acquiring an empire in one part of America more extensive than that which they were on the point of losing in another. General Dalling's plans were well formed; but the history and the nature of the country had not been studied as accurately as its geography. The difficulties which occurred in fitting out the expedition delayed it till the season was too far advanced; and the men were thus sent to adventure themselves, not so much against an enemy whom they would have beaten, as against a climate which would do the enemy's work.

Early in the year 1780, five hundred men, destined for this service, were convoyed by Nelson from Port Royal to Cape Gracias a Dios, in Honduras. Not a native was to be seen when they landed : they had been taught that the English came with no other intent than that of enslaving them, and sending them to Jamaica. After a while, however, one of them ventured down, confiding in his knowledge of one of the party ; and by his means the neighbouring tribes were conciliated with presents, and brought in. The troops were encamped on a swampy and unwholesome plain, where they were joined by a party of the 79th Regiment, from Black River, who were already in a deplorable state of sickness. Having remained here a month, they proceeded, anchoring frequently, along the Mosquito shore, to collect their Indian allies, who were to furnish proper boats for the river, and to accompany them. They reached the river San Juan, March 24th ; and here, according to his orders, Nelson's services were to terminate ; but not a man in the expedition had ever been up the river, or knew the distances of any fortification from its mouth : and he, not being one who would turn back when so much was to be done, resolved to carry the soldiers up. About two hundred, therefore, were embarked in the Mosquito shore craft, and in two of the *Hinchingbrook's* boats, and they began their way. It was the latter end of the dry season, the worst time for such an expedition ; the river was consequently low. Indians were sent forward through narrow channels between shoals and sandbanks ; and the men were frequently obliged to quit the boats, and exert their utmost strength to drag or thrust them along. The labour continued for several days, then they came into deeper water ; but then they had sometimes currents and rapids to contend with, which would have been insurmountable had

it not been for the skill of the Indians in such difficulties. The brunt of the labour was borne by them,
and by the sailors—men never accustomed to stand
aloof when any exertion of strength or hardihood is
required. The soldiers, less accustomed to rely upon
themselves, were of little use. But all equally endured
the violent heat of the sun, rendered more intense by
being reflected from the white shoals, and because the
high woods on both sides of the river were frequently
so close as to prevent all refreshing circulation of air ;
and during the night all were equally exposed to the
heavy and unwholesome dews.

On the 9th of April they reached an island in the
river called St. Bartolomeo, which the Spaniards had
fortified as an outpost, with a small semicircular battery, mounting nine or ten swivels, and manned with
sixteen or eighteen men. It commanded the river in
a rapid and difficult part of the navigation. Nelson,
at the head of a few of his seamen, leaped upon the
beach. The ground upon which he sprang was so
muddy that he had some difficulty in extricating himself, and lost his shoes : barefooted, however, he advanced, and, in his own phrase, boarded the battery.
In this resolute attempt he was bravely supported by
Despard, who was at that time a captain in the army,
and whose after fate was so disastrous. The Castle
of St. Juan is situated about sixteen miles higher up :
the stores and ammunition, however, were landed a
few miles below the castle, and the men had to march
through woods almost impassable. One of the men
was bitten under the eye by a snake, which darted
upon him from the bough of a tree. He was unable
to proceed for the violence of the pain ; and when,
after a short while, some of his comrades were sent
back to assist him, he was dead, and the body already
putrid. Nelson himself narrowly escaped a similar
fate. He had ordered his hammock to be slung under
some trees, being excessively fatigued, and was sleeping when a monitory lizard passed across his face.

The Indians happily observed the reptile, and, knowing what it indicated, awoke him. He started up, and found one of the deadliest serpents of the country coiled up at his feet. He suffered from poison of another kind; for, drinking at a spring in which some boughs of the manchineel had been thrown, the effects were so severe, as, in the opinion of some of his friends, to inflict a lasting injury upon his constitution.

The Castle of St. Juan is thirty-two miles below the Lake of Nicaragua, from which it issues, and sixty-nine from the mouth of the river. Boats reach the sea from thence in a day and a half; but their navigation back, even when unladen, is the labour of nine days. The English appeared before it on the eleventh, two days after they had taken St. Bartolomeo. Nelson's advice was, that it should instantly be carried by assault; but Nelson was not the commander, and it was thought proper to observe all the formalities of a siege. Ten days were wasted before this could be commenced: it was a work more of fatigue than of danger; but fatigue was more to be dreaded than the enemy. The rains set in; and could the garrison have held out a little longer, disease would have rid them of their invaders. Even the Indians sunk under it, the victims of unusual exertion and of their own excesses. The place surrendered on the 24th. But victory procured to the conquerors none of that relief which had been expected; the castle was worse than a prison; and it contained nothing which could contribute to the recovery of the sick, or the preservation of those who were yet unaffected. The huts, which served for hospitals, were surrounded with filth and with the putrefying hides of slaughtered cattle—almost sufficient of themselves to have engendered pestilence; and when at last orders were given to erect a convenient hospital, the contagion had become so general that there were none who could work at it; for, besides the few who were able to perform garrison duty, there

were not orderly men enough to assist the sick.
Added to these evils, there was the want of all needful
remedies; for though the expedition had been amply
provided with hospital stores, river-craft enough had
not been procured for transporting the requisite baggage; and when much was to be left behind, provision for sickness was that which of all things men in
health would be most ready to leave. Now, when
these medicines were required, the river was swollen
and so turbulent that its upward navigation was almost impracticable. At length even the task of bury-
ing the dead was more than the living could perform,
and the bodies were tossed into the stream, or left for
beasts of prey, and for the gallinazos—those dreadful
carrion-birds, which do not always wait for death
before they begin their work. Five months the
English persisted in what may be called this war
against nature; they then left a few men, who seemed
proof against the climate, to retain the castle till the
Spaniards should choose, when the fit season arrived,
to retake it and make them prisoners. The rest abandoned their baleful conquest. Eighteen hundred men
were sent to different posts upon this wretched expedition; not more than three hundred and eighty ever
returned. The *Hinchinbrook's* complement consisted
of two hundred men; eighty-seven took to their beds
in one night, and of the whole crew not more than ten
survived.

Nelson himself was saved by a timely removal. In
a few days after the commencement of the siege he
was seized with the prevailing dysentery: meantime
Captain Glover (son of the author of *Leonidas*) died,
and Nelson was appointed to succeed him in the *Janus,*
of 44 guns. He returned to the harbour the day
before St. Juan surrendered, and immediately sailed
for Jamaica in the sloop which brought the news of his
appointment. He was, however, so greatly reduced
by the disorder, that when they reached Port Royal
he was carried ashore in his cot; and finding himself,

after a partial amendment, unable to retain the command of his new ship, he was compelled to ask leave to return to England, as the only means of recovery. Captain (afterwards Admiral) Cornwallis took him home in the *Lion*; and to his care and kindness Nelson believed himself indebted for his life. He went immediately to Bath, in a miserable state; so helpless that he was carried to and from his bed; and the act of moving him produced the most violent pain. In three months he was recovered, and immediately he hastened to London, and applied for employment. After an interval of about four months he was appointed to the *Albemarle*, of 28 guns, a French merchantman which had been purchased from the captors for the king's service.

His health was not yet thoroughly re-established; and while he was employed in getting his ship ready, he again became so ill as hardly to be able to keep out of bed. Yet in this state, still suffering from the fatal effect of a West Indian climate, as if, it might almost be supposed, he said, to try his constitution, he was sent to the North Seas, and kept there the whole winter. The asperity with which he mentioned this so many years afterwards evinces how deeply he resented a mode of conduct equally cruel to the individual and detrimental to the service. It was during the armed neutrality, and when they anchored off Elsineur, the Danish admiral sent on board, desiring to be informed what ships had arrived, and to have their force written down. "The *Albemarle*," said Nelson to the messenger, "is one of His Britannic Majesty's ships. You are at liberty, sir, to count the guns as you go down the side; and you may assure the Danish admiral that, if necessary, they shall all be well served." During this voyage he gained a considerable knowledge of the Danish coast and its soundings, greatly to the advantage of his country in after times. The *Albemarle* was not a good ship, and was several times nearly overset, in consequence of the masts having been made much too long for her. On her return to England they were shortened, and some other improvements made, at Nelson's suggestion. Still he always insisted that her first owners, the French, had taught her to run away, as she was never a good sailer, except when going directly before the wind.

On their return to the Downs, while he was ashore visiting the senior officer, there came on so heavy a gale, that almost all the vessels drove, and a storeship came athwarthawse of the *Albemarle*. Nelson feared she would drive on the Goodwin Sands : he ran to the beach ; but even the Deal boatmen thought it impossible to get on board, such was the violence of the storm. At length some of the most intrepid offered to make the attempt for fifteen guineas ; and, to the astonishment and fear of all the beholders, he embarked during the height of the tempest. With great difficulty and imminent danger he succeeded in reaching her. She lost her bowsprit and foremast, but escaped further injury. He was now ordered to Quebec, where his surgeon told him he would certainly be laid up by the climate. Many of his friends urged him to represent this to Admiral Keppel; but, having received his orders from Lord Sandwich, there appeared to him an indelicacy in applying to his successor to have them altered.

Accordingly he sailed for Canada. During her first cruise on that station, the *Albemarle* captured a fishing schooner, which contained in her cargo nearly all the property that her master possessed, and the poor fellow had a large family at home, anxiously expecting him. Nelson employed him as a pilot in Boston Bay, then restored him the schooner and cargo, and gave him a certificate to secure him against being captured by any other vessel. The man came off afterwards to the *Albemarle*, at the hazard of his life, with a present of sheep, poultry, and fresh provisions. A most valuable supply it proved, for the scurvy was raging on

board; this was in the middle of August, and the
ship's company had not had a fresh meal since the
beginning of April. The certificate was preserved at
Boston in memory of an act of unusual generosity;
and now that the fame of Nelson has given interest
to everything connected with his name, it is regarded
as a relic. The *Albemarle* had a narrow escape upon
this cruise. Four French sail of the line and a frigate
which had come out of Boston harbour, gave chase to
her; and Nelson, perceiving that they beat him in
sailing, boldly ran among the numerous shoals of St.
George's Bank, confiding in his own skill in pilotage.
Captain Salter, in the *St. Margaretta*, had escaped the
French fleet, by a similar manœuvre, not long before.
The frigate alone continued warily to pursue him; but
as soon as he perceived that this enemy was unsupported, he shortened sail, and hove to: upon which
the Frenchman thought it advisable to give over the
pursuit, and sail in quest of his consorts.

At Quebec Nelson became acquainted with Alexander Davison, by whose interference he was prevented from making what would have been called an
imprudent marriage. The *Albemarle* was about to
leave the station, her captain had taken leave of his
friends, and was gone down the river to the place of
anchorage; when the next morning, as Davison was
walking on the beach, to his surprise he saw Nelson
coming back in his boat. Upon inquiring the cause
of this reappearance, Nelson took his arm to walk towards the town, and told him he found it utterly impossible to leave Quebec without again seeing the
woman whose society had contributed so much to his
happiness there, and offering her his hand. " If you
do," said his friend, " your utter ruin must inevitably
follow." " Then let it follow," cried Nelson, " for I
am resolved to do it." " And I," replied Davison,
" am resolved you shall not." Nelson, however, upon
this occasion was less resolute than his friend, and
suffered himself to be led back to the boat.

The *Albemarle* was under orders to convoy a fleet of transports to New York. " A very pretty job," said her captain, " at this late season of the year " (October was far advanced), " for our sails are at this moment frozen to the yards." On his arrival at Sandy Hook he waited on the commander-in-chief, Admiral Digby, who told him he was come on a fine station for making prize-money. " Yes, sir," Nelson made answer; " but the West Indies is the station for honour." Lord Hood, with a detachment of Rodney's victorious fleet, was at that time at Sandy Hook : he had been intimate with Captain Suckling; and Nelson, who was desirous of nothing but honour, requested him to ask for the *Albemarle*, that he might go to that station where it was most likely to be obtained. Admiral Digby reluctantly parted with him. His professional merit was already well known; and Lord Hood, on introducing him to Prince William Henry, as the Duke of Clarence was then called, told the prince, if he wished to ask any questions respecting naval tactics, Captain Nelson could give him as much information as any officer in the Fleet. The Duke, who, to his own honour, became from that time the firm friend of Nelson, describes him as appearing the merest boy of a captain he had ever seen, dressed in a full-laced uniform, an old-fashioned waistcoat with long flaps, and his lank unpowdered hair tied in a stiff Hessian tail of extraordinary length ; making, altogether, so remarkable a figure, " that," says the Duke, " I had never seen anything like it before, nor could I imagine who he was, nor what he came about. But his address and conversation were irresistibly pleasing ; and when he spoke on professional subjects, it was with an enthusiasm that showed he was no common being."

It was expected that the French would attempt some of the passages between the Bahamas : and Lord Hood, thinking of this, said to Nelson, " I suppose, sir, from the length of time you were cruising among

the Bahama Keys, you must be a good pilot there."
He replied, with that constant readiness to render
justice to every man which was so conspicuous in all
his conduct through life, that he was well acquainted
with them himself, but that in that respect his second
lieutenant was far his superior. The French got into
Puerto Cabello on the coast of Venezuela. Nelson
was cruising between that port and La Guayra, under
French colours, for the purpose of obtaining information; when a king's launch, belonging to the
Spaniards, passed near, and being hailed in French,
came alongside without suspicion, and answered all
questions that were asked concerning the number and
force of the enemy's ships. The crew, however, were
not a little surprised when they were taken on board,
and found themselves prisoners. One of the party
went by the name of the Count de Deux Ponts. He
was, however, a prince of the German empire, and
brother to the heir of the electorate of Bavaria : his
companions were French officers of distinction, and
men of science, who had been collecting specimens in
the various branches of natural history. Nelson having entertained them with the best his table could
afford, told them they were at liberty to depart with
their boat and all that it contained. He only required
them to promise that they would consider themselves
as prisoners, if the commander-in-chief should refuse
to acquiesce in their being thus liberated,—a circumstance which was not by any means likely to happen.
Tidings soon arrived that the preliminaries of peace
had been signed, and the *Albemarle* returned to England, and was paid off. Nelson's first business after
he got to London, even before he went to see his
relations, was to attempt to get the wages due to his
men, for the various ships in which they had served
during the war. " The disgust of seamen to the
navy," he said, " was all owing to the infernal plan
of turning them over from ship to ship; so that men
could not be attached to the officers, nor the officers

care the least about the men." Yet he himself was so
beloved by his men, that his whole ship's company
offered, if he could get a ship, to enter for her immediately. He was now, for the first time, presented
at court. After going through this ceremony, he
dined with his friend Davison, at Lincoln's Inn. As
soon as he entered the chambers, he threw off what
he called his iron-bound coat; and, putting himself at
ease in a dressing-gown, passed the remainder of the
day in talking over all that had befallen them since
they parted on the shore of the river St. Lawrence.

CHAPTER II

" I HAVE closed the war," said Nelson, in one of his
letters, " without a fortune; but there is not a speck in
my character. True honour, I hope, predominates in
my mind far above riches." He did not apply for a
ship, because he was not wealthy enough to live on
board in the manner which was then become cus-
tomary. Finding it, therefore, prudent to economise
on his half-pay during the peace, he went to France,
in company with Captain Macnamara, of the navy,
and took lodgings at St. Omer's. The death of his
favourite sister, Anne, who died in consequence of
going out of the ballroom, at Bath, when heated with
dancing, affected his father so much that it had nearly
occasioned him to return in a few weeks. Time, however, and reason and religion, overcame this grief in
the old man; and Nelson continued at St. Omer's
long enough to fall in love with the daughter of an
English clergyman. This second attachment appears
to have been less ardent than the first; for, upon
weighing the evils of a straitened income to a married
man, he thought it better to leave France, assigning
to his friends something in his accounts as the cause.
This prevented him from accepting an invitation from
the Count of Deux Ponts to visit him at Paris, couched

in the handsomest terms of acknowledgment for the
treatment which he had received on board the *Albemarle.*

The self-constraint which Nelson exerted in subduing this attachment made him naturally desire to be
at sea; and when, upon visiting Lord Howe at the
Admiralty, he was asked if he wished to be employed,
he made answer that he did.   Accordingly, in March,
he was appointed to the *Boreas,* 28 guns, going to the
Leeward Islands, as a cruiser, on the peace establishment.   Lady Hughes and her family went out with
him to Admiral Sir Richard Hughes, who commanded
on that station.   His ship was full of young midshipmen, of whom there were not less than thirty on
board : and happy were they whose lot it was to be
placed with such a captain.   If he perceived that a boy
was afraid at first going aloft, he would say to him,
in a friendly manner : " Well, sir, I am going a race
to the mast-head, and beg that I may meet you there."
The poor little fellow instantly began to climb, and
got up how he could,—Nelson never noticed in what
manner ; but, when they met in the top, spoke cheerfully to him ; and would say, how much any person
was to be pitied who fancied that getting up was
either dangerous or difficult.   Every day he went into
the schoolroom, to see that they were pursuing their
nautical studies ; and at noon he was always the first on
deck with his quadrant.   Whenever he paid a visit of
ceremony some of these youths accompanied him : and
when he went to dine with the governor at Barbadoes,
he took one of them in his hand and presented him,
saying, " Your Excellency must excuse me for bringing one of my midshipmen.   I make it a rule to introduce them to all the good company I can, as they have
few to look up to, besides myself, during the time
they are at sea."

When Nelson arrived in the West Indies he found
himself senior captain, and, consequently, second in
command on that station.   Satisfactory as this was, it

soon involved him in a dispute with the admiral, which a man less zealous for the service might have avoided. He found the *Latona* in English Harbour, Antigua, with a broad pendant hoisted; and upon inquiring the reason, was presented with a written order from Sir R. Hughes, requiring and directing him to obey the orders of Resident Commissioner Moutray, during the time he might have occasion to remain there; the said Resident Commissioner being in consequence authorised to hoist a broad pendant on board any of His Majesty's ships in that port that he might think proper. Nelson was never at a loss how to act in any emergency. " I know of no superior officers," said he, " beside the Lords Commissioners of the Admiralty, and my seniors on the post list." Concluding, therefore, that it was not consistent with the service for a Resident Commissioner, who held only a civil situation, to hoist a broad pendant, the moment that he had anchored he sent an order to the captain of the *Latona* to strike it, and return it to the dockyard. He then went on shore the same day, dined with the Commissioner, to show him that he was actuated by no other motive than a sense of duty, and gave him the first intelligence that his pendant had been struck. Sir Richard sent an account of this to the Admiralty; but the case could admit of no doubt, and Captain Nelson's conduct was approved.

He displayed the same promptitude on another occasion. While the *Boreas*, after the hurricane months were over, was riding at anchor in Nevis Road, a French frigate passed to leeward, close along shore. Nelson had obtained information that this ship was sent from Martinique, with two general officers and some engineers on board, to make a survey of our sugar islands. This purpose he was determined to prevent them from executing, and therefore he gave orders to follow them. The next day he came up with them at anchor in the roads of St. Eustatia, and anchored at about two cables' length on the frigate's

quarter. Being afterwards invited by the Dutch
governor to meet the French officers at dinner, he
seized that occasion of assuring the French captain
that, understanding it was his intention to honour
the British possessions with a visit, he had taken the
earliest opportunity in his power to accompany him,
in His Majesty's ship the *Boreas*, in order that such
attention might be paid to the officers of his Most
Christian Majesty, as every Englishman in the islands
would be proud to show. The French, with equal
courtesy, protested against giving him this trouble;
especially, they said, as they intended merely to cruise
round the islands, without landing on any. But
Nelson, with the utmost politeness, insisted on paying
them this compliment, followed them close, in spite
of all their attempts to elude his vigilance, and never
lost sight of them; till finding it impossible either to
deceive or escape him, they gave up their treacherous
purpose in despair, and beat up for Martinico.

A business of more serious import soon engaged
his attention. The Americans were at this time
trading with our islands, taking advantage of the
register of their ships, which had been issued while
they were British subjects. Nelson knew that, by the
Navigation Act, no foreigners, directly or indirectly,
are permitted to carry on any trade with these possessions : he knew also, that the Americans had made
themselves foreigners with regard to England; they
had broken the ties of blood and language, and acquired the independence which they had been provoked
to claim, unhappily for themselves, before they were
fit for it; and he was resolved that they should derive
no profit from those ties. Foreigners they had made
themselves, and as foreigners they were to be treated.
" If once," said he, " they are admitted to any kind
of intercourse with our islands, the views of the
loyalists, in settling at Nova Scotia, are entirely done
away; and when we are again embroiled in a French
war, the Americans will first become the carriers of

these colonies, and then have possession of them.
Here they come, sell their cargoes for ready money,
go to Martinico, buy molasses, and so round and
round. The loyalist cannot do this, and, consequently,
must sell a little dearer. The residents here are
Americans by connection and by interest, and are
inimical to Great Britain. They are as great rebels
as ever were in America, had they the power to show
it." In November, when the squadron, having arrived
at Barbadoes, was to separate, with no other orders
than those for examining anchorages, and the usual
inquiries concerning wood and water, Nelson asked his
friend Collingwood, then captain of the *Mediator,*
whose opinions he knew upon the subject, to accompany him to the commander-in-chief, whom he then
respectfully asked, Whether they were not to attend
to the commerce of the country, and see that the Navigation Act was respected? that appearing to him to
be the intent of keeping men-of-war upon this station
in time of peace. Sir Richard Hughes replied, he had
no particular orders, neither had the Admiralty sent
him any Acts of Parliament. But Nelson made answer
that the Navigation Act was included in the statutes of
the Admiralty, with which every captain was furnished,
and that Act was directed to admirals, captains, etc.,
to see it carried into execution. Sir Richard said he
had never seen the book. Upon this Nelson produced
the statutes, read the words of the Act, and apparently convinced the commander-in-chief that men-of-
war, as he said, " were sent abroad for some other
purpose than to be made a show of." Accordingly,
orders were given to enforce the Navigation Act.

General Sir Thomas Shirley was at this time
governor of the Leeward Islands; and when Nelson
waited on him to inform him how he intended to act,
and upon what grounds, he replied that " old generals
were not in the habit of taking advice from young
gentlemen."—" Sir," said the young officer, with that
confidence in himself which never carried him too far,

and always was equal to the occasion, " I am as old
as the Prime Minister of England, and think myself
as capable of commanding one of His Majesty's ships
as that minister is of governing the state." He was
resolved to do his duty, whatever might be the opinion
or conduct of others; and when he arrived upon his
station at St. Kitt's he sent away all the Americans,
not choosing to seize them before they had been well
apprised that the Act would be carried into effect,
lest it might seem as if a trap had been laid for them.
The Americans, though they prudently decamped from
St. Kitt's, were emboldened by the support they met
with, and resolved to resist his orders, alleging that
king's ships had no legal power to seize them without
having deputations from the customs. The planters
were to a man against him; the governors and the
presidents of the different islands, with only a single
exception, gave him no support; and the admiral,
afraid to act on either side, yet wishing to oblige the
planters, sent him a note, advising him to be guided
by the wishes of the President of the Council. There
was no danger in disregarding this, as it came un-
officially, and in the form of advice. But scarcely a
month after he had shown Sir Richard Hughes the
law, and, as he supposed, satisfied him concerning it,
he received an order from him, stating that he had
now obtained good advice upon the point, and the
Americans were not to be hindered from coming, and
having free egress and regress, if the governor chose
to permit them. An order to the same purport had
been sent round to the different governors and presidents; and General Shirley and others informed him,
in an authoritative manner, that they chose to admit
American ships, as the commander-in-chief had left
the decision to them. These persons, in his own
words he soon " trimmed up, and silenced "; but it
was a more delicate business to deal with the admiral.
" I must either," said he, " disobey my orders or
disobey Acts of Parliament. I determined upon the

former, trusting to the uprightness of my intentions, and believing that my country would not let me be ruined for protecting her commerce.'' With this determination he wrote to Sir Richard, appealed again to the plain, literal, unequivocal sense of the Navigation Act; and in respectful language told him he felt it his duty to decline obeying these orders till he had an opportunity of seeing and conversing with him. Sir Richard's first feeling was that of anger, and he was about to supersede Nelson; but having mentioned the affair to his captain, that officer told him he believed all the squadron thought the orders illegal, and therefore did not know how far they were bound to obey them. It was impossible, therefore, to bring Nelson to a court-martial composed of men who agreed with him in opinion upon the point in dispute; and, luckily, though the admiral wanted vigour of mind to decide upon what was right, he was not obstinate in wrong, and had even generosity enough in his nature to thank Nelson afterwards for having shown him his error.

Collingwood, in the *Mediator,* and his brother, Winefred Collingwood, in the *Rattler,* actively co-operated with Nelson. The custom-houses were informed, that after a certain day all foreign vessels found in the ports would be seized; and many were, in consequence, seized, and condemned in the Admiralty Court. When the *Boreas* arrived at Nevis, she found four American vessels deeply laden, and with what are called the island colours flying—white, with a red cross. They were ordered to hoist their proper flag, and depart within eight and forty hours; but they refused to obey, denying that they were Americans. Some of their crews were then examined in Nelson's cabin, where the judge of the Admiralty happened to be present. The case was plain; they confessed that they were Americans, and that the ships, hull, and cargo were wholly American property —upon which he seized them. This raised a storm:

the planters, the custom-house, and the governor were
all against him. Subscriptions were opened, and presently filled, for the purpose of carrying on the cause
in behalf of the American captains : and the admiral,
whose flag was at that time in the roads, stood neutral.
But the Americans and their abettors were not content
with defensive law. The marines whom he had sent
to secure the ships had prevented some of the masters
from going ashore; and those persons, by whose
depositions it appeared that the vessels and cargoes
were American property, declared that they had given
their testimony under bodily fear, for that a man with
a drawn sword in his hand had stood over them the
whole time. A rascally lawyer, whom the party
employed, suggested this story; and as the sentry at
the cabin-door was a man with a drawn sword, the
Americans made no scruple of swearing to this ridicu-
lous falsehood, and commencing prosecutions against
him accordingly. They laid their damages at the
enormous amount of £40,000; and Nelson was obliged
to keep close on board his own ship, lest he should
be arrested for a sum for which it would have been
impossible to find bail. The marshal frequently came
on board to arrest him, but was always prevented by
the address of the first lieutenant, Mr. Wallis. Had he
been taken, such was the temper of the people, that
it was certain he would have been cast for the whole
sum. One of his officers, one day, in speaking of the
restraint which he was thus compelled to suffer, happened to use the word *pity!* "Pity!" exclaimed
Nelson; "Pity! did you say? I shall live, sir, to be
envied! and to that point I shall always direct my
course." Eight weeks he remained under this state
of duresse. During that time the trial respecting
these detained ships came on in the Court of
Admiralty. He went on shore under a protection for
the day from the judge; but, notwithstanding this, the
marshal was called upon to take that opportunity of
arresting him, and the merchants promised to indem-

nify him for so doing. The judge, however, did his duty, and threatened to send the marshal to prison if he attempted to violate the protection of the court. Mr. Herbert, the president of Nevis, behaved with singular generosity upon this occasion. Though no man was a greater sufferer by the measures which Nelson had pursued, he offered in court to become his bail for £10,000, if he chose to suffer the arrest. The lawyer whom he had chosen proved to be an able as well as an honest man; and, notwithstanding the opinions and pleadings of most of the counsel of the different islands, who maintained that ships of war were not justified in seizing American vessels without a deputation from the customs, the law was so explicit, the case so clear, and Nelson pleaded his own cause so well, that the four ships were condemned. During the progress of this business he sent a memorial home to the king: in consequence of which, orders were issued that he should be defended at the expense of the Crown. And upon the representations which he made at the same time to the Secretary of State, and the suggestions with which he accompanied it, the Register Act was framed. The sanction of Government, and the approbation of his conduct which it implied, were highly gratifying to him; but he was offended, and not without just cause, that the Treasury should have transmitted thanks to the commander-in-chief for his activity and zeal in protecting the commerce of Great Britain. "Had they known all," said he, "I do not think they would have bestowed thanks in that quarter, and neglected me. I feel much hurt that, after the loss of health and risk of fortune, another should be thanked for what I did against his orders. I either deserved to be sent out of the service, or at least to have had some little notice taken of what I had done. They have thought it worthy of notice, and yet have neglected me. If this is the reward for a faithful discharge of my duty, I shall be careful, and never stand forward again.

But I have done my duty, and have nothing to accuse myself of."

The anxiety which he had suffered from the harassing uncertainties of law is apparent from these expressions. He had, however, something to console him, for he was at this time wooing the niece of his friend the president, then in her eighteenth year, the widow of Dr. Nisbet, a physician. She had one child, a son, by name Josiah, who was three years old. One day Mr. Herbert, who had hastened, half-dressed, to receive Nelson, exclaimed, on returning to his dressing-room, "Good God! if I did not find that great little man, of whom everybody is so afraid, playing in the next room, under the dining-table, with Mrs. Nisbet's child!" A few days afterwards, Mrs. Nisbet herself was first introduced to him, and thanked him for the partiality which he had shown to her little boy. Her manners were mild and winning; and the captain, whose heart was easily susceptible of attachment, found no such imperious necessity for subduing his inclinations as had twice before withheld him from marrying. They were married on March 11, 1787; Prince William Henry, who had come out to the West Indies the preceding winter, being present, by his own desire, to give away the bride. Mr. Herbert, her uncle, was at this time so much displeased with his only daughter, that he had resolved to disinherit her, and leave his whole fortune, which was very great, to his niece. But Nelson, whose nature was too noble to let him profit by an act of injustice, interfered, and succeeding in reconciling the president to his child.

"Yesterday," said one of his naval friends, the day after the wedding, "the navy lost one of its greatest ornaments by Nelson's marriage. It is a national loss that such an officer should marry: had it not been for this, Nelson would have become the greatest man in the service." The man was rightly estimated; but he who delivered this opinion did not understand the effect of domestic love and duty upon a mind of the true heroic stamp. " We are often separate," said Nelson in a letter to Mrs. Nisbet, a few months before their marriage; " but our affections are not by any means on that account diminished. Our country has the first demand for our services; and private convenience or happiness must ever give way to the public good. Duty is the great business of a sea officer : all private considerations must give way to it, however painful." " Have you not often heard," says he, in another letter, " that salt water and absence always wash away love? Now I am such a heretic as not to believe that faith; for, behold, every morning I have had six pails of salt water poured upon my head, and instead of finding what seamen say to be true, it goes on so contrary to the prescription, that you must, perhaps, see me before the fixed time." More frequently his correspondence breathed a deeper strain. " To write letters to you," says he, " is the next greatest pleasure I feel to receiving them from you. What I experience when I read such as I am sure are the pure sentiments of your heart, my poor pen cannot express; nor, indeed, would I give much for any pen or head which could express feelings of that kind. Absent from you, I feel no pleasure : it is you who are everything to me. Without you, I care not for this world; for I have found, lately, nothing in it but vexation and trouble. These are my present sentiments. God Almighty grant they may never change! Nor do I think they will. Indeed there is, as far as human knowledge can judge, a moral certainty that they cannot : for it must be real affection that brings us together; not interest or compulsion." Such were the feelings, and such the sense of duty, with which Nelson became a husband.

During his stay upon this station he had ample opportunity of observing the scandalous practices of the contractors, prize-agents, and other persons in the

West Indies connected with the naval service. When
he was first left with the command, and bills were
brought him to sign for money which was owing for
goods purchased for the navy, he required the original
voucher, that he might examine whether those goods
had been really purchased at the market price; but
to produce vouchers would not have been convenient,
and therefore was not the custom. Upon this Nelson
wrote to Sir Charles Middleton, then Comptroller of
the Navy, representing the abuses which were likely
to be practised in this manner. The answer which he
received seemed to imply that the old forms were
thought sufficient: and thus having no alternative, he
was compelled, with his eyes open, to submit to a
practice originating in fradulent intentions. Soon
afterwards two Antigua merchants informed him that
they were privy to great frauds which had been committed upon Government in various departments—at
Antigua, to the amount of nearly £500,000; at Lucie,
£300,000; at Barbardoes, £250,000; at Jamaica, upwards of a million. The informers were both shrewd,
sensible men of business : they did not affect to be
actuated by a sense of justice, but required a per-
centage upon so much as Government should actually
recover through their means. Nelson examined the
books and papers which they produced, and was convinced that Government had been most infamously
plundered. Vouchers, he found, in that country were
no check whatever; the principle was, that "a thing
was always worth what it would bring"; and the
merchants were in the habit of signing vouchers for
each other, without even the appearance of looking at
the articles. These accounts he sent home to the
different departments which had been defrauded; but
the peculators were too powerful, and they succeeded
not merely in impeding inquiry, but even in raising
prejudices against Nelson at the Board of Admiralty,
which it was many years before he could subdue.
Owing, probably, to these prejudices, and the in-

fluence of the peculators, he was treated, on his return to England, in a manner which had nearly driven him from the service. During the three years that the *Boreas* had remained upon a station which is usually so fatal, not a single officer or man of her whole complement had died. This almost unexampled instance of good health, though mostly, no doubt, imputable to a healthy season, must, in some measure, also be ascribed to the wise conduct of the captain. He never suffered the ships to remain more than three or four at a time at any of the islands; and when the hurricane months confined him to English Harbour, he encouraged all kinds of useful amusements : music, dancing, and cudgelling among the men; theatricals among the officers,—anything which could employ their attention and keep their spirits cheerful. The *Boreas* arrived in England in June. Nelson, who had many times been supposed to be consumptive when in the West Indies, and perhaps was saved from consumption by that climate, was still in a precarious state of health; and the raw wet weather of one of our ungenial summers brought on cold and sore throat and fever : yet his vessel was kept at the Nore from the end of June till the end of November, serving as a sloop and receiving ship. This unworthy treatment, which more probably proceeded from intention than from neglect, excited in Nelson the strongest indignation. During the whole five months he seldom or never quitted the ship, but carried on the duty with strict and sullen attention. On the morning when orders were received to prepare the *Boreas* for being paid off, he expressed his joy to the senior officer in the *Medway,* saying, " It will release me for ever from an ungrateful service, for it is my firm and unalterable determination never again to set my foot on board a king's ship. Immediately after my arrival in town I shall wait on the First Lord of the Admiralty, and resign my commission." The officer to whom he thus communicated his intentions behaved in the wisest

and most friendly manner; for, finding it in vain to
dissuade him in his present state of feeling, he secretly
interfered with the First Lord to save him from a step
so injurious to himself, little foreseeing how deeply
the welfare and honour of England were at that
moment at stake. This interference produced a letter
from Lord Howe, the day before the ship was paid off,
intimating a wish to see Captain Nelson as soon as
he arrived in town; when, being pleased with his conversation, and perfectly convinced, by what was then
explained to him, of the propriety of his conduct, he
desired that he might present him to the king on the
first levee-day: and the gracious manner in which
Nelson was then received effectually removed his
resentment.

Prejudices had been, in like manner, excited against
his friend, Prince William Henry. "Nothing is
wanting, sir," said Nelson in one of his letters, "to
make you the darling of the English nation, but truth.
Sorry I am to say, much to the contrary has been dispersed." This was not flattery; for Nelson was no
flatterer. The letter in which this passage occurs
shows in how wise and noble a manner he dealt with
the prince. One of his royal highness's officers had
applied for a court-martial upon a point in which he
was unquestionably wrong. His royal highness,
however, while he supported his own character and
authority, prevented the trial, which must have been
injurious to a brave and deserving man. "Now that
you are parted," said Nelson, "pardon me, my prince,
when I presume to recommend that he may stand in
your royal favour as if he had never sailed with you,
and that at some future day you will serve him. There
only wants this to place your conduct in the highest
point of view. None of us are without failings; his
was being rather too hasty: but that, put in compe-
tition with his being a good officer, will not, I am bold
to say, be taken in the scale against him. More able
friends than myself your royal highness may easily

find, and of more consequence in the state; but one more attached and affectionate is not so easily met with. Princes seldom, very seldom, find a disinterested person to communicate their thoughts to : I do not pretend to be that person : but of this be assured, by a man who, I trust, never did a dishonourable act, that I am interested only that your royal highness should be the greatest and best man this country ever produced.''

Encouraged by the conduct of Lord Howe, and by his reception at court, Nelson renewed his attack upon the peculators with fresh spirit. He had interviews with Mr. Rose, Mr. Pitt, and Sir Charles Middleton; to all of whom he satisfactorily proved his charges. In consequence, it is said, these very extensive public frauds were at length put in a proper train to be provided against in future : his representations were attended to and every step which he recommended was adopted : the investigation was put into a proper course, which ended in the detection and punishment of some of the culprits : an immense saving was made to Government, and thus its attention was directed to similar peculation in other parts of the Colonies. But it is said, also, that no mark of commendation seems to have been bestowed upon Nelson for his exertion. And it is justly remarked, that the spirit of the navy cannot be preserved so effectually by the liberal honours bestowed on officers when they are worn out in the service, as by an attention to those who, like Nelson at this part of his life, have only their integrity and zeal to bring them into notice. A junior officer, who had been left with the command at Jamaica, received an additional allowance, for which Nelson had applied in vain. Double pay was allowed to every artificer and seaman employed in the naval yard. Nelson had superintended the whole business of that yard with the most rigid exactness, and he complained that he was neglected. '' It was most true,'' he said, '' that the trouble which he took to detect the fraudulent practices then carried on was no more than his duty; but he little thought that the expenses attending his frequent journeys to St. John's, upon that duty (a distance of twelve miles), would have fallen upon his pay as captain of the *Boreas*." Nevertheless, the sense of what he thought this unworthy usage did not diminish his zeal. " I," said he, " must still buffet the waves in search of—What? Alas! that they called honour is now thought of no more. My fortune, God knows, has grown worse for the service: so much for serving my country. But the devil, ever willing to tempt the virtuous, has made me offer, if any ships should be sent to destroy his Majesty of Morocco's ports, to be there; and I have some reason to think that, should any more come of it, my humble services will be accepted. I have invariably laid down, and followed close, a plan of what ought to be uppermost in the breast of an officer,— that it is much better to serve an ungrateful country than to give up his own fame. Posterity will do him justice. An uniform course of honour and integrity seldom fails of bringing a man to the goal of fame at last."

The design against the Barbary pirates, like all other designs against them, was laid aside; and Nelson took his wife to his father's parsonage, meaning only to pay him a visit before they went to France—a project which he had formed for the sake of acquiring a competent knowledge of the French language. But his father could not bear to lose him thus unnecessarily. Mr. Nelson had long been an invalid, suffering under paralytic and asthmatic affections, which for several hours after he rose in the morning, scarcely permitted him to speak. He had been given over by his physicians for this complaint nearly forty years before his death; and was, for many of his last years, obliged to spend all his winters at Bath. The sight of his son, he declared, had given him new life. " But, Horace," said he, " it would have been better that I had not been thus cheered, if I am so soon to be bereaved of you again. Let me, my good son, see you whilst I can. My age and infirmities increase, and I shall not last long." To such an appeal there could be no reply. Nelson took up his abode at the parsonage, and amused himself with the sports and the occupations of the country. Sometimes he busied himself with farming the glebe; sometimes spent the greater part of the day in the garden, where he would dig as if for the mere pleasure of wearying himself. Sometimes he went bird-nesting, like a boy; and in these expeditions Mrs. Nelson always, by his express desire, accompanied him. Coursing was his favourite amusement. Shooting, as he practised it, was far too dangerous for his companions; for he carried his gun upon the full cock, as if he were going to board an enemy; and the moment a bird rose, he let fly, without ever putting the fowling-piece to his shoulder. It is not, therefore, extraordinary, that his having once shot a partridge should be remembered by his family among the remarkable events of his life.

But his time did not pass away thus without some vexatious cares to ruffle it. The affair of the American ships was not yet over, and he was again pestered with threats of prosecution. " I have written them word," said he, " that I will have nothing to do with them, and they must act as they think proper. Government, I suppose, will do what is right, and not leave me in the lurch. We have heard enough lately of the consequence of the Navigation Act to this country. They may take my person: but if sixpence would save me from a prosecution, I would not give it." It was his great ambition at this time to possess a pony; and having resolved to purchase one, he went to a fair for that purpose. During his absence two men abruptly entered the parsonage and inquired for him: they then asked for Mrs. Nelson; and after they had made her repeatedly declare that she was really and truly the captain's wife, presented her with a

writ, or notification on the part of the American captains, who now laid their damages at £20,000, and
they charged her to give it to her husband on his
return. Nelson having bought his pony, came home
with it in high spirits. He called out his wife to
admire the purchase, and listen to all its excellencies :
nor was it till his glee had in some measure subsided
that the paper could be presented to him. His indignation was excessive : and in the apprehension that
he should be exposed to the anxieties of the suit, and
the ruinous consequences which might ensue, he
exclaimed, "This affront I did not deserve! But I'll
be trifled with no longer. I will write immediately to
the Treasury; and if Government will not support me,
I am resolved to leave the country." Accordingly, he
informed the Treasury that if a satisfactory answer
were not sent him by return of post, he should take
refuge in France. To this he expected he should be
driven, and for this he arranged everything with his
characteristic rapidity of decision. It was settled that
he should depart immediately, and Mrs. Nelson follow
under the care of his elder brother, Maurice, ten days
after him. But the answer which he received from
Government quieted his fears : it stated that Captain
Nelson was a very good officer, and needed to be
under no apprehension, for he would assuredly be
supported.

Here his disquietude upon this subject seems to have
ended. Still he was not at ease; he wanted employment, and was mortified that his applications for it
produced no effect. "Not being a man of fortune,"
he said, "was a crime which he was unable to get
over, and therefore none of the great cared about
him." Repeatedly he requested the Admiralty that
they would not leave him to rust in indolence. During
the armament which was made upon occasion of the
dispute concerning Nootka Sound he renewed his
application : and his steady friend, Prince William,
who had then been created Duke of Clarence, recom-

mended him to Lord Chatham. The failure of this recommendation wounded him so keenly that he again thought of retiring from the service in disgust : a resolution from which nothing but the urgent remonstrances of Lord Hood induced him to desist.

Hearing that the *Raisonnable*, in which he had commenced his career, was to be commissioned, he asked for her. This also was in vain : and a coolness ensued, on his part, toward Lord Hood, because that excellent officer did not use his influence with Lord Chatham upon this occasion. Lord Hood, however, had certainly sufficient reason for not interfering ; for he ever continued his steady friend. In the winter of 1792, when we were on the eve of the Anti-Jacobin war, Nelson once more offered his services, earnestly requested a ship, and added, that if their lordships should be pleased to appoint him to a cockle-boat he should feel satisfied. He was answered in the usual official form : " Sir, I have received your letter of the 5th instant, expressing your readiness to serve, and have read the same to my Lords Commissioners of the Admiralty." On the 12th of December he received this dry acknowledgment. The fresh mortification did not, however, affect him long ; for, by the joint interest of the Duke and Lord Hood, he was appointed, on the 30th of January following, to the *Agamemnon*, of 64 guns.

CHAPTER III

" THERE are three things, young gentleman," said Nelson to one of his midshipmen, " which you are constantly to bear in mind. First, you must always implicitly obey orders, without attempting to form any opinion of your own respecting their propriety. Secondly, you must consider every man your enemy who speaks ill of your king; and thirdly, you must hate a Frenchman as you do the devil.'' With these feelings he engaged in the Anti-Jacobean war. Josiah, his step-son, went with him as a midshipman.

The *Agamemnon* was ordered to the Mediterranean, under Lord Hood. The fleet arrived in those seas at a time when the South of France would willingly have formed itself into a separate republic, under the protection of England. But good principles had been at that time perilously abused by ignorant and profligate men; and, in its fear and hatred of democracy, the English Government leagued itself with despotism, —a miserable error, of which the consequences will long be to be deplored : for had not England, in an unhappy hour, interfered, the rotten governments of the Continent would then have fallen; and the Continental nations, acquiring a revolutionary impulse and strength, at the same time as France, would now have been the rivals of France, instead of her prey. Lord Hood could not take advantage of the fair occasion which presented itself; and which, if it had been seized with vigour, might have ended in dividing France; but he negotiated with the people of Toulon to take possession provisionally of their port and city, which, fatally for themselves, was accordingly done. Before the British fleet entered, Nelson was sent with despatches to Sir William Hamilton, our envoy to the court of Naples. Sir William, after his first interview with him, told Lady Hamilton he was about to introduce a little man to her, who could not boast of being very handsome, but such a man as, he believed, would one day astonish the world. "I have never before,'' he continued, "entertained an officer at my house; but I am determined to bring him here. Let him be put in the room prepared for Prince Augustus.'' Thus that acquaintance began which ended in the destruction of Nelson's domestic happiness. It seemed to threaten no such consequences at its commencement. He spoke of Lady Hamilton, in a letter to his wife, as a young woman of amiable manners, who did honour to the station to which she had been raised: and he remarked, that she had been exceedingly kind to Josiah. The activity with which the envoy exerted himself in procuring troops from Naples to assist in garrisoning Toulon, so delighted him that he is said to have exclaimed: "Sir William, you are a man after my own heart!—you do business in my own way": and then to have added, "I am now only a captain: but I will, if I live, be at the top of the tree." Here, also, that acquaintance with the Neapolitan court commenced, which led to the only blot upon Nelson's public character. The king, who was sincere at that time in his enmity to the French, called the English the saviours of Italy, and of his dominions in particular. He paid the most flattering attentions to Nelson, made him dine with him, and seated him at his right hand.

Having accomplished this mission, Nelson received orders to join Commodore Linzee at Tunis. On the way, five sail of the enemy were discovered off the coast of Sardinia, and he chased them. They proved to be three 44 gun frigates, with a corvette of 24, and a brig of 12. The *Agamemnon* had only 345 men at quarters, having landed part of her crew at Toulon, and others being absent in prizes. He came near enough one of the frigates to engage her, but at great disadvantage, the Frenchman manœuvring well, and sailing greatly better. A running fight of three hours ensued; during which the other ships, which were at some distance, made all speed to come up. By this time the enemy was almost silenced, when a favourable change of wind enabled her to get out of reach of the *Agamemnon's* guns; and that ship had received so much damage in the rigging that she could not follow her. Nelson expecting that this was but the forerunner of a far more serious engagement, called his officers together, and asked them if the ship was fit to go into action against such a superior force,

without some small refit, and refreshment for the
men.   Their answer was, that she certainly was not.
He then gave these orders : " Veer the ship, and lay
her head to the westward : let some of the best men
be employed refitting the rigging, and the carpenter
getting crows and capstan-bars to prevent our
wounded spars from coming down ; and get the wine
up for the people, with some bread, for it may be
half an hour good before we are again in action."
But when the French came up, their comrade made
signals of distress, and they all hoisted out their boats
to go to her assistance, leaving the *Agamemnon*
unmolested.

Nelson found Commodore Linzee at Tunis, where
he had been sent to expostulate with the dey upon
the impolicy of his supporting the revolutionary
Government of France.   Nelson represented to him
the atrocity of that Government.   Such arguments
were of little avail in Barbary : and when the dey was
told that the French had put their sovereign to death,
he dryly replied, that " Nothing could be more
heinous ; and yet, if historians told the truth, the English had once done the same."   This answer had
doubtless been suggested by the French about him :
they had completely gained the ascendency, and all
negotiation on our part proved fruitless.   Shortly
afterward Nelson was detached with a small squadron
to co-operate with General Paoli and the Anti-Gallican
party in Corsica.

Some thirty years before this time, the heroic
patriotism of the Corsicans, and of their leader Paoli,
had been the admiration of England.   The history
of these brave people is but a melancholy tale.   The
island which they inhabit has been abundantly blessed
by nature : it has many excellent harbours ; and though
the *malaria*, or pestilential atmosphere, which is so
deadly in many parts of Italy, and of the Italian
islands, prevails on the eastern coast, the greater part
of the country is mountainous and healthy.   It is about

150 miles long, and from 40 to 50 broad; in circumference, some 320,—a country large enough, and sufficiently distant from the nearest shores, to have subsisted in an independent state, if the welfare and happiness of the human race had ever been considered as the end and aim of policy. The Moors, the Pisans, the kings of Aragon, and the Genoese, successively attempted, and each for a time effected its conquest. The yoke of the Genoese continued longest, and was the heaviest. These petty tyrants ruled with an iron rod; and when at any time a patriot rose to resist their oppressions, if they failed to subdue him by force, they resorted to assassination. At the commencement of the last century they quelled one revolt by the aid of German auxiliaries, whom the Emperor Charles VI. sent against a people who had never offended him, and who were fighting for whatever is most dear to man. In 1734 the war was renewed; and Theodore, a Westphalian baron, then appeared upon the stage. In that age men were not accustomed to see adventurers play for kingdoms, and Theodore became the common talk of Europe. He had served in the French armies; and having afterwards been noticed both by Ripperda and Alberoni, their example, perhaps, inflamed a spirit as ambitious and as unprincipled as their own. He employed the whole of his means in raising money and procuring arms; then wrote to the leaders of the Corsican patriots, to offer them considerable assistance, if they would erect Corsica into an independent kingdom, and elect him king. When he landed among them, they were struck with his stately person, his dignified manners, and imposing talents; they believed the magnificent promises of foreign assistance which he held out, and elected him king accordingly. Had his means been as he represented them, they could not have acted more wisely than in thus at once fixing the government of their country, and putting an end to those rivalries among the leading families, which had so often proved

pernicious to the public weal. He struck money, conferred titles, blocked up the fortified towns which were
held by the Genoese, and amused the people with
promises of assistance for about eight months; then,
perceiving that they cooled in their affections towards
him, in proportion as their expectations were disappointed, he left the island, under the plea of ex-
pediting himself the succours which he had so long
awaited. Such was his address that he prevailed upon
several rich merchants in Holland, particularly the
Jews, to trust him with cannon and warlike stores to
a great amount. They shipped these under the charge
of a supercargo. Theodore returned with this supercargo to Corsica, and put him to death on his arrival,
as the shortest way of settling the account. The
remainder of his life was a series of deserved afflictions. He threw in the stores which he had thus
fraudulently obtained; but he did not dare to land, for
Genoa had now called in the French to their assistance, and a price had been set upon his head. His
dreams of royalty were now at an end: he took refuge
in London, contracted debts, and was thrown into the
King's Bench. After lingering there many years, he
was released under an act of insolvency; in consequence of which, he made over the kingdom of Corsica
for the use of his creditors, and died shortly after his
deliverance.

The French, who have never acted a generous part
in the history of the world, readily entered into the
views of the Genoese, which accorded with their own
policy: for such was their ascendency at Genoa, that
in subduing Corsica for these allies, they were in fact
subduing it for themselves. They entered into the
contest, therefore, with their usual vigour and their
usual cruelty. It was in vain that the Corsicans
addressed a most affecting memorial to the court of
Versailles; that remorseless Government persisted in
its flagitious project. They poured in troops; dressed
a part of them like the people of the country, by which

means they deceived and destroyed many of the
patriots; cut down the standing corn, the vines and
the olives; set fire to the villages, and hung all the
most able and active men who fell into their hands.
A war of this kind may be carried on with success
against a country so small and so thinly peopled as
Corsica. Having reduced the island to perfect servi-
tude, which they called peace, the French withdrew
their forces. As soon as they were gone, men, women
and boys rose again against their oppressors. The
circumstances of the times were now favourable to
them; and some British ships, acting as allies of Sardinia, bombarded Bastia and San Fiorenzo, and
delivered them into the hands of the patriots. This
service was long remembered with gratitude; the impression made upon our own countrymen was less
favourable. They had witnessed the heart-burning
of rival chiefs, and the dissensions among the
patriots; and perceiving the state of barbarism to
which continual oppression, and habits of lawless
turbulence, had reduced the nation, did not recollect
that the vices of the people were owing to their unhappy circumstances; but that the virtues which they
displayed arose from their own nature. This feeling,
perhaps, influenced the British Court, when, in 1746,
Corsica offered to put herself under the protection of
Great Britain: an answer was returned, expressing
satisfaction at such a communication, hoping that the
Corsicans would preserve the same sentiments, but
signifying also that the present was not the time for
such a measure.

These brave islanders then formed a government
for themselves, under two leaders, Gaffori and Matra,
who had the title of Protectors. The latter is represented as a partisan of Genoa, favouring the views of
the oppressors of his country by the most treasonable
means. Gaffori was a hero worthy of old times. His
eloquence was long remembered with admiration. A
band of assassins was once advancing against him:

he heard of their approach, went out to meet them;
and with a serene dignity which overawed them,
requested them to hear him : then spake to them so
forcibly of the distresses of their country, her intoler-
able wrongs, and the hopes and views of their brethren
in arms, that the very men who had been hired to
murder him, fell at his feet, implored his forgiveness,
and joined his banner.   While he was besieging the
Genoese in Corte, a party of the garrison perceiving
the nurse with his eldest son, then an infant in arms,
straying at a little distance from the camp, suddenly
sallied out and seized them.   The use they made of
their persons was in conformity to their usual exe-
crable conduct.   When Gaffori advanced to batter the
walls, they held up the child directly over that part
of the wall at which the guns were pointed.   The
Corsicans stopped : but Gaffori stood at their head
and ordered them to continue the fire.   Providentially
the child escaped, and lived to relate, with becoming
feeling, a fact so honourable to his father.   That
father conducted the affairs of the island till 1753,
when he was assassinated by some wretches, set on,
it is believed, by Genoa; but certainly pensioned by
that abominable government after the deed.   He left
the country in such a state that it was enabled to continue the war two years after his death without a
leader : then they found one worthy of their cause in
Pasquale de Paoli.

Paoli's father was one of the patriots who effected
their escape from Corsica when the French reduced
it to obedience.   He retired to Naples, and brought up
this his youngest son in the Neapolitan service.   The
Corsicans heard of young Paoli's abilities, and
solicited him to come over to his native country and
take the command.   He did not hesitate long : his
father, who was too far advanced in years to take an
active part himself, encouraged him to go; and when
they separated, the old man fell on his neck and kissed
him, and gave him his blessing.   "My son," said he,

"perhaps I may never see you more; but in my mind
I shall ever be present with you. Your design is
great and noble; and I doubt not but God will bless
you in it. I shall devote to your cause the little
remainder of my life, in offering up my prayers for
your success." When Paoli assumed the command,
he found all things in confusion; he formed a demo-
cratical government, of which he was chosen chief;
restored the authority of the laws; established an
university; and took such measures, both for repress-
ing abuses and moulding the rising generation, that,
if France had not interfered, upon its wicked and
detestable principle of usurpation, Corsica might, at
this day, have been as free and flourishing and happy
a commonwealth as any of the Grecian states in the
days of their prosperity. The Genoese were at this
time driven out of their fortified towns, and must in
a short time have been expelled. France was indebted
some millions of livres to Genoa : it was not convenient
to pay this money; so the French minister proposed to
the Genoese that she should discharge the debt by
sending six battalions to serve in Corsica for four
years. The indignation which this conduct excited in
all generous hearts, was forcibly expressed by Rousseau, who, with all his errors, was never deficient
in feeling for the wrongs of humanity. "You Frenchmen," said he, writing to one of that people, "are a
thoroughly servile nation, thoroughly sold to tyranny,
thoroughly cruel, and relentless in persecuting
the unhappy. If they knew of a freeman at the other
end of the world, I believe they would go thither for
the mere pleasure of extirpating him."

The immediate object of the French happened to
be purely mercenary : they wanted to clear off their
debt to Genoa; and as the presence of their troops in
the island effected this, they aimed at doing the people
no further mischief. Would that the conduct of England had been at this time free from reproach ! but
a proclamation was issued by the English Government,

after the Peace of Paris, prohibiting any intercourse with the rebels of Corsica. Paoli said, he did not expect that from Great Britain. This great man was deservedly proud of his country :—" I defy Rome, Sparta, or Thebes," he used to say, " to show me thirty years of such patriotism as Corsica can boast ! " Availing himself of the respite which the inactivity of the French, and the weakness of the Genoese, allowed, he prosecuted his plans of civilising the people. He used to say that, though he had an unspeakable pride in the prospect of the fame to which he aspired, yet, if he could but render his countrymen happy, he could be content to be forgotten. His own importance he never affected to under-value. " We are now to our country," said he, " like the prophet Elisha, stretched over the dead child of the Shunammite—eye to eye, nose to nose, mouth to mouth. It begins to recover warmth, and to revive : I hope it will yet regain full health and vigour."

But when the four years were expired, France purchased the sovereignty of Corsica from the Genoese for forty millions of livres ; as if the Genoese had been entitled to sell it ; as if any bargain and sale could justify one country in taking possession of another against the will of the inhabitants, and butchering all who oppose the usurpation ! Among the enormities which France has committed, this action seems but as a speck ; yet the foulest murderer that ever suffered by the hand of the executioner has infinitely less guilt upon his soul than the statesman who concluded this treaty, and the monarch who sanctioned and confirmed it. A desperate and glorious resistance was made ; but it was in vain ; no power interposed in behalf of these injured islanders, and the French poured in as many troops as were required. They offered to confirm Paoli in the supreme authority, only on condition that he would hold it under their Government. His answer was, that " the rocks which surrounded him should melt away before he would betray a cause which

he held in common with the poorest Corsican." This
people then set a price upon his head. During two
campaigns he kept them at bay : they overpowered
him at length : he was driven to the shore, and, having escaped on shipboard, took refuge in England. It
is said that Lord Shelburne resigned his seat in the
Cabinet, because the Ministry looked on without
attempting to prevent France from succeeding in this
abominable and important act of aggrandisement. In
one respect, however, our country acted as became
her. Paoli was welcomed with the honours which he
deserved, a pension of £1,200 was immediately
granted him ; and provision was liberally made for
his elder brother and his nephew.

Above twenty years Paoli remained in England, enjoying the friendship of the wise and the admiration
of the good. But when the French Revolution began,
it seemed as if the restoration of Corsica was at hand.
The whole country, as if animated by one spirit, rose
and demanded liberty ; and the National Assembly
passed a decree, recognising the island as a department of France, and therefore entitled to all the privi-
leges of the new French constitution. This satisfied
the Corsicans, and it satisfied Paoli also. He resigned his pension in the year 1790, and appeared at
the bar of the Assembly with the Corsican deputies,
when they took the oath of fidelity to France. But
the course of events in France soon dispelled those
hopes of a new and better order of things, which
Paoli, in common with so many of the friends of
humankind, had indulged : and perceiving, after the
execution of the king, that a civil war was about to
ensue, of which no man could foresee the issue, he
prepared to break the connection between Corsica and
the French Republic. The Convention, suspecting
such a design, and perhaps occasioning it by their
suspicions, ordered him to their bar. That way, he
well knew, led to the guillotine; and returning a respectful answer, he declared that he would never be

found wanting in his duty, but pleaded age and infirmity as a reason for disobeying the summons. Their second order was more summary : and the French troops who were in Corsica, aided by those of the natives, who were either influenced by hereditary party feelings, or who were sincere in Jacobinism, took the field against him. But the people were with him. He repaired to Corte, the capital of the island, and was again invested with the authority which he had held in the noon-day of his fame. The Convention upon this denounced him as a rebel, and set a price upon his head. It was not the first time that France had proscribed Paoli.

Paoli now opened a correspondence with Lord Hood, promising, if the English would make an attack upon St. Fiorenzo from the sea, he would, at the same time, attack it by land. This promise he was unable to perform : and Commodore Linzee, who, in reliance upon it, was sent upon this service, was repulsed with some loss. Lord Hood, who had now been compelled to evacuate Toulon, suspected Paoli of intentionally deceiving him. This was an injurious suspicion. Shortly afterward he despatched Lieutenant-Colonel (afterwards Sir John) Moore and Major Koehler to confer with him upon a plan of operations. Sir Gilbert Elliot accompanied them : and it was agreed upon that, in consideration of the succours, both military and naval, which His Britannic Majesty should afford for the purpose of expelling the French, the island of Corsica should be delivered into the immediate possession of His Majesty, and bind itself to acquiesce in any settlement he might approve of concerning its government and its future relation with Great Britain. While this negotiation was going on, Nelson cruised off the island with a small squadron, to prevent the enemy from throwing in supplies. Close to St. Fiorenzo the French had a storehouse of flour, near their only mill : he watched an opportunity, and landed 120 men, who threw the flour into the sea, burnt the mill, and re-embarked before 1,000 men, who were sent against him, could occasion them the loss of a single man. While he exerted himself thus, keeping out all supplies, intercepting despatches, attacking their outposts and forts, and cutting out vessels from the bay,—a species of warfare which depresses the spirit of an enemy even more than it injures them, because of the sense of individual superiority which it indicates in the assailants,—troops were landed, and St. Fiorenzo was besieged. The French, finding themselves unable to maintain that post, sank one of their frigates, burnt another, and retreated to Bastia. Lord Hood submitted to General Dundas, who commanded the land forces, a plan for the reduction of this place : the general declined co-operating, thinking the attempt impracticable without a reinforcement of 2,000 men, which he expected from Gibraltar. Upon this Lord Hood determined to reduce it with the naval force under his command ; and leaving part of his fleet off Toulon, he came with the rest to Bastia.

He showed a proper sense of respect for Nelson's services, and of confidence in his talents, by taking care not to bring with him any older captain. A few days before their arrival, Nelson had had what he called a brush with the enemy. " If I had had with me five hundred troops," he said, " to a certainty I should have stormed the town ; and I believe it might have been carried. Armies go so slow that seamen think they never mean to get forward : but I daresay they act on a surer principle, although we seldom fail." During this partial action our army appeared upon the heights ; and having reconnoitred the place, returned to St. Fiorenzo. " What the general could have seen to make a retreat necessary," said Nelson, " I cannot comprehend. A thousand men would certainly take Bastia ; with five hundred and *Agamemnon* I would attempt it. My seamen are now what British seamen ought to be, almost invincible. They really mind shot no more than peas." General Dundas had

not the same confidence. "After mature consideration," said he in a letter to Lord Hood, "and a personal inspection for several days of all circumstances,
local as well as others, I consider the siege of Bastia,
with our present means and force, to be a most
visionary and rash attempt ; such as no officer would
be justified in undertaking." Lord Hood replied, that
nothing would be more gratifying to his feelings than
to have the whole responsibility upon himself ; and
that he was ready and willing to undertake the reduction of the place at his own risk, with the force
and means at present there. General D'Aubant, who
succeeded at this time to the command of the army,
coincided in opinion with his predecessor, and did not
think it right to furnish his lordship with a single
soldier, cannon, or any stores. Lord Hood could only
obtain a few artillerymen ; and ordering on board that
part of the troops who, having been embarked as
marines, were borne on the ships' books as part of
their respective complements, he began the siege with
1,183 soldiers, artillerymen, and marines, and 250
sailors. "We are but few," said Nelson, " but of
the right sort ; our general at St. Fiorenzo not giving
us one of the five regiments he has there lying idle."

These men were landed on the 4th of April, under
Lieutenant-Colonel Villettes and Nelson, who had now
acquired from the army the title of brigadier. Guns
were dragged by the sailors up heights where it appeared almost impossible to convey them—a work of
the greatest difficulty ; and which Nelson said could
never, in his opinion, have been accomplished by any
but British seamen. The soldiers, though less dex-
terous in such service, because not accustomed, like
sailors, to habitual dexterity, behaved with equal
spirit. "Their zeal," said the brigadier, " is almost
unexampled. There is not a man but considers himself as personally interested in the event ; and, deserted by the general, it has, I am persuaded, made
them equal to double their numbers." This is one

proof, of many, that for our soldiers to equal our seamen, it is only necessary for them to be equally well commanded. They have the same heart and soul, as well as the same flesh and blood. Too much may, indeed, be exacted from them in a retreat; but set their face toward a foe, and there is nothing within the reach of human achievement which they cannot perform. The French have improved the leisure which our military commander had allowed them; and before Lord Hood commenced his operations, he had the mortification of seeing that the enemy were every day erecting new works, strengthening old ones, and rendering the attempt more difficult. La Combe St. Michel, the Commissioner from the National Convention, who was in the city, replied in these terms to the summons of the British admiral; " I have hot shot for your ships, and bayonets for your troops. When two-thirds of our men are killed, I will then trust to the generosity of the English." The siege, however, was not sustained with the firmness which such a reply seemed to augur. On the 19th of May a treaty of capitulation was begun : that same evening the troops from St. Fiorenzo made their appearance on the hills, and on the following morning General D'Aubant arrived with the whole army to take possession of Bastia.

The event of the siege had justified the confidence of the sailors ; but they themselves excused the opinion of the generals, when they saw what they had done. " I am all astonishment," said Nelson, "when I reflect on what we have achieved : 1,000 regulars, 1,500 national guards, and a large party of Corsican troops, 4,000 in all, laying down their arms to 1,200 soldiers, marines, and seamen ! I always was of opinion, have ever acted up to it, and never had any reason to repent it, that one Englishman was equal to three Frenchmen. Had this been an English town, I am sure it would not have been taken by them." When it had been resolved to attack the place, the enemy were supposed to be far inferior in number; and it was not till the whole had been arranged, and the siege publicly undertaken, that Nelson received certain information of the great superiority of the garrison.   This intelligence he kept secret, fearing lest, if so fair a pretext were afforded, the attempt would be abandoned.   "My own honour," said he to his wife, "Lord Hood's honour, and the honour of our country, must have been sacrificed, had I mentioned what I knew; therefore you will believe what must have been my feelings during the whole siege, when I had often proposals made to me to write to Lord Hood to raise it." Those very persons who thus advised him were rewarded for their conduct at the siege of Bastia : Nelson, by whom it may truly be affirmed that Bastia was taken, received no reward, Lord Hood's thanks to him, both public and private, were, as he himself said, the handsomest which man could give : but his signal merits were not so mentioned in the despatches as to make them sufficiently known to the nation, nor to obtain for him from Government those honours to which they so amply entitled him.   This could only have arisen from the haste in which the despatches were written; certainly not from any deliberate purpose, for Lord Hood was uniformly his steady and sincere friend.

One of the Cartel's ships, which carried the garrison of Bastia to Toulon, brought back intelligence that the French were about to sail from that port;—such exertions had they made to repair the damage done at the evacuation, and to fit out a fleet.   The intelligence was speedily verified.   Lord Hood sailed in quest of them towards the islands of Hieres.   The *Agamemnon* was with him.   "I pray God," said Nelson, writing to his wife, "that we may meet their fleet.   If any accident should happen to me, I am sure my conduct will be such as will entitle you to the royal favour,—not that I have the least idea but I shall return to you, and full of honour ;—if not, the Lord's will be done. My name shall never be a disgrace to those who may belong to me. The little I have, I have given to you, except a small annuity; I wish it was more, but I have never got a farthing dishonestly, —it descends from clean hands. Whatever fate awaits me, I pray God to bless you, and preserve you for your son's sake." With a mind thus prepared, and thus confident, his hopes and wishes seemed on the point of being gratified, when the enemy were discovered close under the land, near St. Tropez. The wind fell, and prevented Lord Hood from getting between them and the shore, as he designed; boats came out from Antibes and other places to their assistance, and towed them within the shoals in Gourjean roads, where they were protected by the batteries on isles St. Honore and St. Marguerite, and on Cape Garousse. Here the English admiral planned a new mode of attack, meaning to double on five of the nearest ships; but the wind again died away, and it was found that they had anchored in compact order, guarding the only passage for large ships. There was no way of effecting this passage, except by towing or warping the vessels; and this rendered the attempt impracticable. For this time the enemy escaped; but Nelson bore in mind the admirable plan of attack which Lord Hood had devised, and there came a day when they felt its tremendous effects.

The *Agamemnon* was now despatched to co-operate at the siege of Calvi with General Sir Charles Stuart; an officer who, unfortunately for his country, never had an adequate field allotted him for the display of those eminent talents which were, to all who knew him, so conspicuous. Nelson had less responsibility here than at Bastia; and was acting with a man after his own heart, who was never sparing of himself, and slept every night in the advanced battery. But the service was not less hard than that of the former siege. "We will fag ourselves to death," said he to Lord Hood, " before any blame shall lie at our doors. I trust it will not be forgotten that twenty-five pieces of heavy ordnance have been dragged to the different batteries, mounted, and all but three, fought by seamen, except one artilleryman to point the guns." The climate proved more destructive than the service; for this was during the lion sun, as they there call our season of the dog-days. Of 2,000 men above half were sick, and the rest like so many phantoms. Nelson described himself as the reed among the oaks, bowing before the storm when they were laid low by it. "All the prevailing disorders have attacked me," said he, "but I have not strength enough for them to fasten on." The loss from the enemy was not great; but Nelson received a serious injury; a shot struck the ground near him, and drove the sand and small gravel into one of his eyes. He spoke of it slightly at the time: writing the same day to Lord Hood, he only said that he got a little hurt that morning, not much; and the next day, he said he should be able to attend his duty in the evening. In fact, he suffered it to confine him only one day; but the sight was lost.

After the fall of Calvi, his services were, by a strange omission, altogether overlooked; and his name was not even mentioned in the list of wounded. This was no ways imputable to the admiral, for he sent home to Government Nelson's journal of the siege, that they might fully understand the nature of his indefatigable and unequalled exertions. If those exertions were not rewarded in the conspicuous manner which they deserved, the fault was in the administration of the day, not in Lord Hood. Nelson felt himself neglected. "One hundred and ten days," said he, "I have been actually engaged, at sea and on shore, against the enemy; three actions against ships, two against Bastia in my ship, four boat actions, and two villages taken, and twelve sail of vessels burnt. I do not know that any one has done more. I have had the comfort to be always applauded by my commander-in-chief, but never to be rewarded; and, what

is more mortifying, for services in which I have been
wounded, others have been praised, who, at the same
time, were actually in bed, far from the scene of
action. They have not done me justice. But, never
mind, I'll have a gazette of my own." How amply
was this second-sight of glory realised!

The health of his ship's company had now, in his
own words, been miserably torn to pieces by as hard
service as a ship's crew ever performed : 150 were in
their beds when he left Calvi; of them he lost 50, and
believed that the constitutions of the rest were entirely
destroyed. He was now sent with despatches to Mr.
Drake, at Genoa, and had his first interview with the
Doge. The French had, at this time, taken possession of Vado Bay, in the Genoese territory; and
Nelson foresaw that, if their thoughts were bent on
the invasion of Italy, they would accomplish it the
ensuing spring. "The allied powers," he said,
"were jealous of each other; and none but England
was hearty in the cause." His wish was for peace,
on fair terms, because England, he thought, was
draining herself, to maintain allies who would not fight
for themselves. Lord Hood had now returned to
England; and the command devolved on Admiral
Hotham. The affairs of the Mediterranean wore at
this time a gloomy aspect. The arts, as well as the
arms of the enemy, were gaining the ascendency there.
Tuscany concluded peace, relying upon the faith of
France, which was, in fact, placing itself at her mercy.
Corsica was in danger. We had taken that island
for ourselves, annexed it formally to the Crown of
Great Britain, and given it a constitution as free as
our own. This was done with the consent of the
majority of the inhabitants : and no transaction
between two countries was ever more fairly or legiti-
mately conducted : yet our conduct was unwise;—the
island is large enough to form an independent state,
and such we should have made it, under our protection, as long as protection might be needed; the

Corsicans would then have felt as a nation; but when
one party had given up the country to England, the
natural consequence was that the other looked to
France. The question proposed to the people was, to
which would they belong? Our language and our
religion were against us; our unaccommodating
manners, it is to be feared, still more so. The French
were better politicians. In intrigue they have ever
been unrivalled; and it now became apparent, that, in
spite of old wrongs, which ought never to have been
forgotten or forgiven, their partisans were daily
acquiring strength. It is part of the policy of France,
and a wise policy it is, to impress upon other powers
the opinion of its strength by lofty language, and by
threatening before it strikes; a system which, while it
keeps up the spirit of its allies, and perpetually
stimulates their hopes, tends also to dismay its
enemies. Corsica was now loudly threatened. The
French, who had not yet been taught to feel their
own inferiority upon the seas, braved us, in contempt,
upon that element. They had a superior fleet in the
Mediterranean, and they sent it out with express
orders to seek the English and engage them.
Accordingly, the Toulon fleet, consisting of seventeen
ships of the line and five smaller vessels, put to sea.
Admiral Hotham received this information at Leghorn, and sailed immediately in search of them. He
had with him fourteen sail of the line, and one
Neapolitan 74; but his ships were only half manned,
containing but 7,650 men, whereas the enemy had
16,900. He soon came in sight of them; a general
action was expected; and Nelson, as was his custom
on such occasions, wrote a hasty letter to his wife, as
that which might possibly contain his last farewell.
"The lives of all," said he, "are in the hand of
Him who knows best whether to preserve mine or
not : my character and good name are in my own
keeping."

But however confident the French Government

might be of their naval superiority, the officers had no
such feeling; and after manœuvring for a day, in sight
of the English fleet, they suffered themselves to be
chased. One of their ships, the *Ça Ira*, of 84 guns,
carried away her main and fore top-masts. The
Inconstant frigate fired at the disabled ship, but
received so many shot, that she was obliged to leave
her. Soon afterwards a French frigate took the *Ça
Ira* in tow; and the *Sans Culottes*, 120, and the *Jean
Barris*, 74, kept about gun-shot distance off her
weather bow. The *Agamemnon* stood towards her,
having no ship of the line to support her within several
miles. As she drew near, the *Ça Ira* fired her stern
guns so truly that not a shot missed some part of the
ship, and, latterly, the masts were struck by every
shot. It had been Nelson's intention not to fire before
he touched her stern; but seeing how impossible it
was that he should be supported, and how certainly
the *Agamemnon* must be severely cut up if her masts
were disabled, he altered his plan according to the
occasion. As soon, therefore, as he was within a
hundred yards of her stern, he ordered the helm to be
put a-starboard, and the driver and after-sails to be
brailed up and shivered, and, as the ship fell off, gave
the enemy her whole broadside. They instantly
braced up the after-yards, put the helm a-port, and
stood after her again. This manœuvre he practised
for two hours and a quarter, never allowing the *Ça
Ira* to get a single gun from either side to bear on
him; and when the French fired their after-guns now,
it was no longer with coolness and precision, for every
shot went far ahead. By this time her sails were
hanging in tatters, her mizen-topmast, mizen-topsail,
and cross-jack-yards shot away. But the frigate
which had her in tow hove in stays, and got her
round. Both these French ships now brought their
guns to bear, and opened their fire. The *Agamemnon*
passed them within half pistol-shot; almost every shot
passed over her, for the French had elevated their guns

for the rigging, and for distant firing, and did not
think of altering the elevation.   As soon as the
Agamemnon's after-guns ceased to bear, she hove in
stays, keeping a constant fire as she came round; and
being worked, said Nelson, with as much exactness
as if she had been turning into Spithead.   On getting
round, he saw that the *Sans Culottes,* which had wore,
with many of the enemy's ships, was under his lee
bow, and standing to leeward.   The admiral, at the
same time, made the signal for the van ships to join
him.   Upon this Nelson bore away, and prepared to
set all sail; and the enemy, having saved their ship,
hauled close to the wind, and opened upon him a
distant and ineffectual fire.   Only seven of the
Agamemnon's men were hurt,—a thing which Nelson
himself remarked as wonderful: her sails and rigging
were very much cut, and she had many shots in her
hull, and some between wind and water.   The *Ça Ira*
lost 110 men that day, and was so cut up that she
could not get a top-mast aloft during the night.

At daylight, on the following morning, the English
ships were taken aback with a fine breeze at N.W.,
while the enemy's fleet kept the southerly wind.   The
body of their fleet was about five miles distant; the
Ça Ira, and the *Censeur*, 74, which had her in tow,
about three and a half.   All sail was made to cut
these ships off: and as the French attempted to save
them, a partial action was brought on.   The *Agamemnon* was again engaged with her yesterday's
antagonist; but she had to fight on both sides the ship
at the same time.   The *Ça Ira* and the *Censeur* fought
most gallantly: the first lost nearly 300 men, in addition to her former loss; the last, 350.   Both at last
struck: and Lieutenant Andrews, of the *Agamemnon*,
brother to the lady to whom Nelson had become
attached in France, and, in Nelson's own words, " as
gallant an officer as ever stepped a quarter-deck,"
hoisted English colours on board them both.   The
rest of the enemy's ships behaved very ill.   As soon

as these vessels had struck, Nelson went to Admiral
Hotham and proposed that the two prizes should be
left with the *Illustrious* and *Courageux*, which had
been crippled in the action, and with four frigates, and
that the rest of the fleet should pursue the enemy, and
follow up the advantage to the utmost. But his reply
was—" We must be contented : we have done very
well." " Now," said Nelson, "had we taken ten
sail, and allowed the eleventh to escape, when it had
been possible to have got at her, I could never have
called it well done. Goodall backed me ; I got him to
write to the admiral; but it would not do. We should
have had such a day as, I believe, the annals of England never produced." In this letter the character of
Nelson fully manifests itself. " I wish," said he, " to
be an admiral, and in the command of the English
fleet ; I should very soon either do much, or be ruined :
my disposition cannot bear tame and slow measures.
Sure I am, had I commanded on the 14th, that either
the whole French fleet would have graced my triumph,
or I should have been in a confounded scrape."
What the event would have been, he knew from his
prophetic feelings, and his own consciousness of
power ; and we also know it now, for Aboukir and
Trafalgar have told it us.

The *Ça Ira* and *Censeur* probably defended themselves with more obstinacy in this action, from a
persuasion that, if they struck, no quarter would be
given ; because they had fired red-hot shot, and had
also a preparation, sent, as they said, by the Convention from Paris, which seems to have been of the
nature of the Greek fire ; for it became liquid when it
was discharged, and water would not extinguish its
flame. This combustible was concealed with great
care in the captured ships ; like the red-hot shot, it
had been found useless in battle. Admiral Hotham's
action saved Corsica for the time ; but the victory had
been incomplete, and the arrival at Toulon of six sail
of the line, two frigates, and two cutters from Brest,

gave the French a superiority which, had they known
how to use it, would materially have endangered the
British Mediterranean fleet. That fleet had been
greatly neglected during Lord Chatham's administration at the Admiralty; and it did not, for some time,
feel the beneficial effect of his removal. Lord Hood
had gone home to represent the real state of affairs,
and solicit reinforcements adequate to the exigencies
of the time, and the importance of the scene of action.
But that fatal error of under-proportioning the force
to the service, that ruinous economy, which, by
sparing a little, renders all that is spent useless,
infected the British councils; and Lord Hood, not
being able to obtain such reinforcements as he knew
were necessary, resigned the command. "Surely,"
said Nelson, "the people at home have forgotten us."
Another Neapolitan 74 joined Admiral Hotham; and
Nelson observed with sorrow that this was matter of
exultation to an English fleet. When the store-ships
and victuallers from Gibraltar arrived, their escape
from the enemy was thought wonderful; and yet, had
they not escaped, "the game," said Nelson, "was
up here. At this moment our operations are at a
stand for want of ships to support the Austrians in
getting possession of the sea-coast of the King of
Sardinia; and, behold, our admiral does not feel himself equal to show himself, much less to give assistance in their operations." It was reported that the
French were again out with eighteen or twenty sail.
The combined British and Neapolitan were but sixteen; should the enemy be only eighteen, Nelson made
no doubt of a complete victory; but if they were
twenty, he said, it was not to be expected : and a battle
without complete victory would have been destruction,
because another mast was not to be got on that side
Gibraltar. At length Admiral Man arrived with a
squadron from England. "What they can mean by
sending him with only five sail of the line," said
Nelson, "is truly astonishing : but all men are alike,

and we in this country do not find any amendment or alteration from the old Board of Admiralty. They should know that half the ships in the fleet require to go to England; and that long ago they ought to have reinforced us.''

About this time Nelson was made colonel of marines,—a mark of approbation which he had long wished for rather than expected. It came in good season, for his spirits were oppressed by the thought that his services had not been acknowledged as they deserved; and it abated the resentful feeling which would else have been excited by the answer to an application to the War Office. During his four months' land service in Corsica, he had lost all his ship-furniture, owing to the movements of a camp. Upon this he wrote to the Secretary at War, briefly stating what his services on shore had been, and saying, he trusted it was not asking an improper thing to request that the same allowance might be made to him which would be made to a land officer of his rank, which, situated as he was, would be that of a brigadier-general : if this could not be accorded, he hoped that his additional expenses would be paid him. The answer which he received was, that " no pay had ever been issued under the direction of the War Office to officers of the navy serving with the army on shore.''

He now entered upon a new line of service. The Austrian and Sardinian armies, under General de Vins, required a British squadron to co-operate with them in driving the French from the Riviera di Genoa ; and as Nelson had been so much in the habit of soldiering, it was immediately fixed that the bri-gadier should go. He sailed from St. Fiorenzo on this destination; but fell in, off Cape del Mele, with the enemy's fleet, who immediately gave his squadron chase. The chase lasted four-and-twenty hours ; and, owing to the fickleness of the wind, the British ships were sometimes hard pressed ; but the want of skill on

the part of the French gave them many advantages.
Nelson bent his way back to St. Fiorenzo, where the
fleet, which was in the midst of watering and refitting,
had, for seven hours, the mortification of seeing him
almost in possession of the enemy, before the wind
would allow them to put out to his assistance.   The
French, however, at evening, went off, not choosing
to approach nearer the shore.   During the night
Admiral Hotham, by great exertions, got under
weigh; and, having sought the enemy four days,
came in sight of them on the 5th.   Baffling winds, and
vexatious calms, so common in the Mediterranean,
rendered it impossible to close with them; only a
partial action could be brought on : and then the
firing made a perfect calm.   The French being to
windward, drew in shore; and the English fleet was
becalmed six or seven miles to the westward.
L'Alcide, of 74 guns, struck; but, before she could be
taken possession of, a box of combustibles in her foretop took fire, and the unhappy crew experienced how
far more perilous their inventions were to themselves
than to their enemies.   So rapid was the conflagration,
that the French, in their official account, say, the hull,
the masts, and sails, all seemed to take fire at the
same moment; and though the English boats were put
out to the assistance of the poor wretches on board,
not more than 200 could be saved.   The Agamemnon,
and Captain Rowley, in the Cumberland, were just
getting into close action a second time, when the
admiral called them off, the wind now being directly
into the Gulf of Frejus, where the enemy anchored
after the evening closed.

Nelson now proceeded to his station with eight sail
of frigates under his command.   Arriving at Genoa,
he had a conference with Mr. Drake, the British envoy
to that state; the result of which was, that the object
of the British must be to put an entire stop to all
trade between Genoa, France, and the places occupied
by the French troops; for, unless this trade were

stopped, it would be scarcely possible for the allied armies to hold their situation, and impossible for them to make any progress in driving the enemy out of the Riviera di Genoa. Mr. Drake was of opinion that even Nice might fall for want of supplies, if the trade with Genoa were cut off. This sort of blockade Nelson could not carry on without great risk to himself. A captain in the navy, as he represented to the envoy, is liable to prosecution for detention and damages. This danger was increased by an order which had then lately been issued; by which, when a neutral ship was detained, a complete specification of her cargo was directed to be sent to the Secretary of the Admiralty, and no legal process instituted against her till the pleasure of that board should be communicated. This was requiring an impossibility. The cargoes of ships detained upon this station, consisting chiefly of corn, would be spoiled long before the orders of the Admiralty could be known; and then, if they should happen to release the vessel, the owners would look to the captain for damages. Even the only precaution which could be taken against this danger, involved another danger not less to be apprehended; for if the captain should direct the cargo to be taken out, the freight paid for, and the vessel released, the agent employed might prove fraudulent and become bankrupt; and in that case the captain became responsible. Such things had happened: Nelson therefore required, as the only means for carrying on that service which was judged essential to the common cause, without exposing the officers to ruin, that the British envoy should appoint agents to pay the freight, release the vessels, sell the cargo, and hold the amount till process was had upon it: Government thus securing its officers. "I am acting," said Nelson, "not only without the orders of my commander-in-chief, but, in some measure, contrary to him. However, I have not only the support of His

Majesty's ministers, both at Turin and Genoa, but a consciousness that I am doing what is right and proper for the service of our king and country. Political courage, in an officer abroad, is as highly necessary as military courage."

This quality, which is as much rarer than military courage, as it is more valuable, and without which the soldier's bravery is often of little avail, Nelson possessed in an eminent degree. His representations were attended to as they deserved. Admiral Hotham commended him for what he had done; and the attention of Government was awakened to the injury which the cause of the allies continually suffered from the frauds of neutral vessels. "What changes in my life of activity!" said this indefatigable man. "Here I am; having commenced a co-operation with an old Austrian general, almost fancying myself charging at the head of a troop of horse!—I do not write less than from ten to twenty letters everv day; which, with the Austrian general and aides-de-camp, and my own little squadron, fully employ my time. This I like—active service, or none." It was Nelson's mind which supported his feeble body through these exertions. He was at this time almost blind, and wrote with very great pain. "Poor *Agamemnon*," he sometimes said, "was as nearly worn out as her captain; and both must soon be laid up to repair."

When Nelson first saw General de Vins, he thought him an able man, who was willing to act with vigour. The general charged his inactivity upon the Piedmontese and Neapolitans, whom, he said, nothing could induce to act; and he concerted a plan with Nelson for embarking a part of the Austrian army, and landing it in the rear of the French. But the English commodore soon began to suspect that the Austrian general was little disposed to any active operations. In the hope of spurring him on, he wrote to him, telling him that he had surveyed the coast to the westward as far as Nice, and would undertake to embark 4,000 or 5,000 men, with their arms and a few days' provisions, on board the squadron, and land them within two miles of St. Remo, with their field-pieces. Respecting further provisions for the Austrian army, he would provide convoys, that they should arrive in safety; and if a re-embarkation should be found necessary, he would cover it with a squadron. The possession of St. Remo, as headquarters for magazines of every kind, would enable the Austrian general to turn his army to the eastward or westward. The enemy at Oneglia would be cut off from provisions, and men could be landed to attack that place whenever it was judged necessary. St. Remo was the only place between Vado and Ville Franche where the squadron could lie in safety, and anchor in almost all winds. The bay was not as good as Vado for large ships; but it had a mole, which Vado had not, where all small vessels could lie, and load and unload their cargoes. This bay being in possession of the allies, Nice could be completely blockaded by sea. General De Vins affecting, in his reply, to consider that Nelson's proposal had no other end than that of obtaining the Bay of St. Remo as a station for the ships, told him, what he well knew, and had expressed before, that Vado Bay was a better anchorage; nevertheless, if *Monsieur le Commandant Nelson* was well assured that part of the fleet could winter there, there was no risk to which he would not expose himself with pleasure, for the sake of procuring a safe station for the vessels of His Britannic Majesty. Nelson soon assured the Austrian commander that this was not the object of his memorial. He now began to suspect that both the Austrian courts and their general had other ends in view than the cause of the allies. "This army," said he, " is slow beyond all description; and I begin to think that the Emperor is anxious to touch another four millions of English

F 52

money. As for the German generals, war is their
trade, and peace is ruin to them ; therefore we cannot
expect that they should have any wish to finish the
war. The politics of courts are so mean, that private
people would be ashamed to act in the same way :
all is trick and finesse, to which the common cause
is sacrificed. The general wants a loophole : it has
for some time appeared to me that he means to go
no farther than his present position, and to lay the
miscarriage of the enterprise against Nice, which
has always been held out as the great object of his
army, to the non-co-operation of the British fleet,
and of the Sardinians.''

To prevent this plea Nelson again addressed De
Vins, requesting only to know the time, and the
number of troops ready to embark ; then he would,
he said, despatch a ship to Admiral Hotham, requesting transports, having no doubt of obtaining them,
and trusting that the plan would be successful to its
fullest extent. Nelson thought at the time, that if
the whole fleet were offered him for transports, he
would find some other excuse : and Mr. Drake, who
was now appointed to reside at the Austrian headquarters, entertained the same idea of the general's
sincerity. It was not, however, put so clearly to
the proof as it ought to have been. He replied, that
as soon as Nelson could declare himself ready with
the vessels necessary for conveying 10,000 men, with
their artillery and baggage, he would put the army
in motion. But Nelson was not enabled to do this :
Admiral Hotham, who was highly meritorious in
leaving such a man so much at his own discretion,
pursued a cautious system, ill-according with the
bold and comprehensive views of Nelson, who continually regretted Lord Hood, saying, that the nation
had suffered much by his resignation of the Mediterranean command. The plan which had been concerted, he said, would astonish the French, and
perhaps the English.

There was no unity in the views of the allied powers, no cordiality in their co-operation, no energy in their councils. The neutral powers assisted France more effectually than the allies assisted each other. The Genoese ports were at this time filled with French privateers, which swarmed out every night, and covered the gulf; and French vessels were allowed to tow out of the port of Genoa itself, board vessels which were coming in, and then return into the mole. This was allowed without a remonstrance; while, though Nelson abstained most carefully from offering any offence to the Genoese territory or flag, complaints were so repeatedly made against his squadron, that, he says, it seemed a trial who should be tired first—they of complaining or he of answering their complaints. But the question of neutrality was soon at an end. An Austrian commissary was travelling from Genoa towards Vado; it was known that he was to sleep at Voltri, and that he had £10,000 with him; a booty which the French minister in that city, and the captain of a French frigate in that port, considered as far more important than the word of honour of the one, the duties of the other, and the laws of neutrality. The boats of the frigate went out with some privateers, landed, robbed the commissary, and brought back the money to Genoa. The next day men were publicly enlisted in that city for the French army: 700 men were embarked, with 7,000 stand of arms, on board the frigates and other vessels, who were to land between Voltri and Savona:—there a detachment from the French army was to join them, and the Genoese peasantry were to be invited to insurrection,—a measure for which everything had been prepared. The night of the 13th was fixed for the sailing of this expedition: the Austrians called loudly for Nelson to prevent it; and he, on the evening of the 13th, arrived at Genoa. His presence checked the plan: the frigate, knowing her deserts, got within the merchant-ships, in the inner mole;

and the Genoese Government did not now even demand of Nelson respect to the neutral port, knowing that they had allowed, if not connived at, a flagrant breach of neutrality, and expecting the answer which he was prepared to return, that it was useless and impossible for him to respect it longer.

But though this movement produced the immediate effect which was designed, it led to ill consequences, which Nelson foresaw, but, for want of sufficient force, was unable to prevent. His squadron was too small for the service which it had to perform. He required two seventy-fours, and eight or ten frigates and sloops; but when he demanded this reinforcement, Admiral Hotham had left the command; Sir Hyde Parker succeeded, till the new commander should arrive; and he immediately reduced it almost to nothing, leaving him only one frigate and a brig. This was a fatal error. While the Austrian and Sardinian troops, whether from the imbecility or the treachery of their leaders, remained inactive, the French were preparing for the invasion of Italy. Not many days before Nelson was thus summoned to Genoa, he chased a large convoy into Alassio. Twelve vessels he had formerly destroyed in that port, though 2,000 French troops occupied the town: this former attack had made them take new measures of defence; and there were now above 100 sail of victuallers, gun-boats, and ships of war. Nelson represented to the admiral how important it was to destroy these vessels; and offered, with his squadron of frigates, and the *Culloden* and *Courageux*, to lead himself in the *Agamemnon*, and take or destroy the whole. The attempt was not permitted; but it was Nelson's belief that, if it had been made, it would have prevented the attack upon the Austrian army, which took place almost immediately afterwards.

General de Vins demanded satisfaction of the Genoese Government for the seizure of his commissary; and then, not waiting for their reply, took

possession of some empty magazines of the French,
and pushed his sentinels to the very gates of Genoa.
Had he done so at first he would have found the
magazines full; but, timed as the measure was, and
useless as it was to the cause of the allies, it was
in character with the whole of the Austrian general's
conduct; and it is no small proof of the dexterity with
which he served the enemy, that in such circumstances he could so act with Genoa as to contrive to
put himself in the wrong. Nelson was at this time,
according to his own expression, placed in a cleft
stick. Mr. Drake, the Austrian minister, and the
Austrian general, all joined in requiring him not to
leave Genoa; if he left that port unguarded, they
said, not only the imperial troops at St. Pier d'Arena
and Voltri would be lost, but the French plan for
taking post between Voltri and Savona would certainly succeed; if the Austrians should be worsted in
the advanced posts, the retreat by the Bocchetta
would be cut off; and if this happened, the loss of
the army would be imputed to him for having left
Genoa. On the other hand, he knew, that if he were
not at Pietra, the enemy's gun-boats would harass
the left flank of the Austrians, who, if they were
defeated, as was to be expected from the spirit of
all their operations, would, very probably, lay their
defeat to the want of assistance from the *Agamemnon*.
Had the force for which Nelson applied been given
him, he could have attended to both objects : and had
he been permitted to attack the convoy in Alassio,
he would have disconcerted the plans of the French,
in spite of the Austrian general. He had foreseen
the danger, and pointed out how it might be prevented ; but the means of preventing it were withheld.
The attack was made, as he foresaw ; and the gun-
boats brought their fire to bear upon the Austrians.
It so happened, however, that the left flank, which
was exposed to them, was the only part of the army
that behaved well; this division stood its ground till

the centre and the right wing fled, and then retreated in a soldier-like manner. General de Vins gave up the command in the middle of the battle, pleading ill-health. "From that moment," says Nelson, "not a soldier stayed at his post—it was the devil take the hindmost. Many thousands ran away who had never seen the enemy; some of them thirty miles from the advanced posts. Had I not, though, I own, against my inclination, been kept at Genoa, from 8,000 to 10,000 men would have been taken prisoners, and, amongst the number General de Vins himself; but, by this means, the pass of the Bocchetta was kept open. The purser of the ship, who was at Vado, ran with the Austrians eighteen miles without stopping; the men without arms, officers without soldiers, women without assistance. The oldest officer, say they, never heard of so complete a defeat, and certainly without any reason. Thus has ended my campaign. We have established the French Republic, which, but for us, I verily believe, would never have been settled by such a volatile, changeable people. I hate a Frenchman: they are equally objects of my detestation, whether Royalists or Republicans; in some points, I believe the latter are the best." Nelson had a lieutenant and two midshipmen taken at Vado; they told him, in their letter, that few of the French soldiers were more than three- or four-and-twenty years old, a great many not more than fourteen, and all were nearly naked; they were sure, they said, his barge's crew could have beat a hundred of them; and that, had he himself seen them, he would not have thought, if the world had been covered with such people, that they could have beaten the Austrian army.

The defeat of General de Vins gave the enemy possession of the Genoese coast from Savona to Voltri; and it deprived the Austrians of their direct communication with the English fleet. The *Agamemnon*, therefore, could no longer be useful on this station, and Nelson sailed for Leghorn to refit. When his ship went into dock, there was not a mast, yard, sail, or any part of the rigging, but what stood in need of repair, having been cut to pieces with shot. The hull was so damaged that it had for some time been secured by having cables served or thrapped round.

CHAPTER IV

Sir John Jervis had now arrived to take the command of the Mediterranean fleet. The *Agamemnon* having, as her captain said, been made as fit for sea as a rotten ship could be, Nelson sailed from Leghorn, and joined the admiral in Fiorenzo Bay. "I found him," said he, "anxious to know many things, which I was a good deal surprised to find had not been communicated to him by others in the fleet; and it would appear that he was so well satisfied with my opinion of what is likely to happen, and the means of prevention to be taken, that he had no reserve with me respecting his information, and ideas of what is likely to be done." The manner in which Nelson was received is said to have excited some envy. One captain observed to him : " You did just as you pleased in Lord Hood's time, the same in Admiral Hotham's, and now again with Sir John Jervis : it makes no difference to you who is commander-in-chief." A higher compliment could not have been paid to any commander-in-chief, than to say of him, that he understood the merits of Nelson, and left him, as far as possible, to act upon his own judgment.

Sir John Jervis offered him the *St. George*, 90, or the *Zealous*, 74, and asked if he should have any objection to serve under him with his flag. He replied, that if the *Agamemnon* were ordered home, and his flag were not arrived, he should, on many accounts, wish to return to England; still, if the war continued, he should be very proud of hoisting his flag under Sir John's command. "We cannot spare you," said Sir John, "either as captain or admiral." Accordingly, he resumed his station in the Gulf of Genoa. The French had not followed up their successes in that quarter with their usual celerity. Scherer, who commanded there, was one of the few French generals, during the Revolution, who owed their advancement to other causes than merit: he was a favourite of the Directory; but, for the present, through the influence of Barras, he was removed from a command for which his incapacity was afterwards clearly proved, and Buonaparte was appointed to succeed him. Buonaparte had given indications of his military talents at Toulon, and of his remorseless nature at Paris; but the extent either of his ability or his wickedness was at this time known to none, and perhaps not even suspected by himself.

Nelson supposed, from the information which he had obtained, that one column of the French army would take possession of Port Especia, either penetrating through the Genoese territory, or proceeding coastways in light vessels—our ships of war not being able to approach the coast because of the shallowness of the water. To prevent this, he said, two things were necessary;—the possession of Vado Bay, and the taking of Port Especia. If either of these points were secured, Italy would be safe from any attack of the French by sea. General Beaulieu, who had now superseded De Vins in the command of the allied Austrian and Sardinian army, sent his nephew and aide-de-camp to communicate with Nelson, and inquire whether he could anchor in any other place than Vado Bay. Nelson replied, that Vado was the only place where the British fleet could lie in safety; but all places would suit his squadron; and wherever the general came down to the sea-coast,

there he should find it. The Austrian repeatedly
asked, if there was not a risk of losing the squadron?
and was constantly answered, that if these ships
should be lost, the admiral would find others. But
all plans of co-operation with the Austrians were
soon frustrated by the battle of Montenotte. Beaulieu
ordered an attack to be made upon the post of Voltri :
—it was made twelve hours before the time which he
had fixed, and before he arrived to direct it. In
consequence, the French were enabled to effect their
retreat, and fall back to Montenotte; thus giving the
troops there a decisive superiority in number over the
division which attacked them. This drew on the
defeat of the Austrians. Buonaparte, with a celerity
which had never before been witnessed in modern
war, pursued his advantages; and, in the course of a
fortnight, dictated to the court of Turin terms of
peace, or rather of submission, by which all the
strongest places of Piedmont were put into his hands.

On one occasion, and only on one, Nelson was able
to impede the progress of this new conqueror. Six
vessels, laden with cannon and ordnance-stores for the
siege of Mantua, sailed from Toulon for St. Pier
d'Arena. Assisted by Captain Cockburn, in the
Meleager, he drove them under a battery, pursued
them, silenced the batteries, and captured the whole.
Military books, plans, and maps of Italy, with the
different points marked upon them where former
battles had been fought, sent by the Directory for
Buonaparte's use, were found in the convoy. The
loss of this artillery was one of the chief causes which
compelled the French to raise the siege of Mantua;
but there was too much treachery, and too much imbecility, both in the councils and armies of the allied
powers, for Austria to improve this momentary
success. Buonaparte perceived that the conquest of
all Italy was within his reach : treaties, and the rights
of neutral or of friendly powers, were as little regarded by him as by the Government for which he

acted : in open contempt of both he entered Tuscany,
and took possession of Leghorn. In consequence of
this movement, Nelson blockaded that port, and landed
a British force in the isle of Elba to secure Porto
Ferrajo. Soon afterwards he took the island of
Capraja, which had formerly belonged to Corsica,
being less than forty miles distant from it : a distance,
however, short as it was, which enabled the Genoese
to retain it, after their infamous sale of Corsica to
France. Genoa had now taken part with France; its
Government had long covertly assisted the French,
and now willingly yielded to the first compulsory
menace which required them to exclude the English
from their ports. Capraja was seized, in consequence; but this act of vigour was not followed up as
it ought to have been. England at that time depended
too much upon the rotten governments of the Continent, and too little upon itself. It was determined
by the British Cabinet to evacuate Corsica, as soon
as Spain should form an offensive alliance with
France. This event, which, from the moment that
Spain had been compelled to make peace, was clearly
foreseen, had now taken place; and orders for the
evacuation of the island were immediately sent out.
It was impolitic to annex this island to the British
dominions; but, having done so, it was disgraceful
thus to abandon it. The disgrace would have been
spared, and every advantage which could have been
derived from the possession of the island secured, if
the people had at first been left to form a government
for themselves, and protected by us in the enjoyment
of their independence.

The viceroy, Sir Gilbert Elliot, deeply felt the impolicy and ignominy of this evacuation. The fleet
also was ordered to leave the Mediterranean. This
resolution was so contrary to the last instructions
which had been received, that Nelson exclaimed :—
" Do his Majesty's ministers know their own minds?
They at home," said he, " do not know what this fleet

is capable of performing—anything and everything. Much as I shall rejoice to see England, I lament our present orders in sackcloth and ashes, so dishonourable to the dignity of England, whose fleets are equal to meet the world in arms : and of all the fleets I ever saw, I never beheld one in point of officers and men, equal to Sir John Jervis's, who is a commander-in-chief able to lead them to glory.'' Sir Gilbert Elliot believed that the great body of the Corsicans were perfectly satisfied, as they had good reason to be, with the British government, sensible of its advantages, and attached to it. However this may have been, when they found that the English intended to evacuate the island, they naturally and necessarily sent to make peace with the French. The partisans of France found none to oppose them. A committee of thirty took upon them the government of Bastia, and sequestered all the British property; armed Corsicans mounted guard at every place, and a plan was laid for seizing the viceroy. Nelson, who was appointed to superintend the evacuation, frustrated these projects. At a time when every one else despaired of saving stores, cannon, provisions, or property of any kind, and a privateer was moored across the mole-head to prevent all boats from passing, he sent word to the committee, that if the slightest opposition were made to the embarkment and removal of British property, he would batter the town down. The privateer pointed her guns at the officer, who carried this message, and muskets were levelled against his boats from the mole-head. Upon this, Captain Sutton, of the *Egmont*, pulling out his watch, gave them a quarter of an hour to deliberate upon their answer. In five minutes after the expiration of that time, the ships, he said, would open their fire. Upon this the very sentinels scampered off, and every vessel came out of the mole. A ship-owner complained to the commodore that the municipality refused to let him take his goods out of the custom-house. Nelson directed him to say, that unless they were instantly delivered, he would open his fire. The committee turned pale, and without answering a word gave him the keys. Their last attempt was to levy a duty upon the things that were re-embarked. He sent them word that he would pay them a disagreeable visit if there were any more complaints. The committee then finding that they had to deal with a man who knew his own power, and was determined to make the British name respected, desisted from the insolent conduct which they had assumed : and it was acknowledged that Bastia never had been so quiet and orderly since the English were in possession of it. This was on the 14th of October : during the five following days the work of embarkation was carried on, the private property was saved, and public stores to the amount of £200,000. The French, favoured by the Spanish fleet, which was at that time within twelve leagues of Bastia, pushed over troops from Leghorn, who landed near Cape Corse on the 18th, and on the 20th, at one in the morning, entered the citadel, an hour only after the British had spiked the guns and evacuated it. Nelson embarked at daybreak, being the last person who left the shore; having thus, as he said, seen the first and the last of Corsica. Provoked at the conduct of the municipality, and the disposition which the populace had shown to profit by the confusion, he turned toward the shore, as he stepped into his boat, and exclaimed : " Now, John Corse, follow the natural bent of your detestable character—plunder and revenge." This, however, was not Nelson's deliberate opinion of the people of Corsica; he knew that their vices were the natural consequences of internal anarchy and foreign oppression, such as the same causes would produce in any people : and when he saw, that of all those who took leave of the viceroy, there was not one who parted from him without tears, he acknowledged that they manifestly acted not from dislike of the English, but from fear of the French. England then might, with more reason, reproach her own rulers for pusillanimity, than the Corsicans for ingratitude.

Having thus ably effected this humiliating service, Nelson was ordered to hoist his broad pendant on board the *Minerve* frigate, Captain George Cockburn, and, with the *Blanche* under his command, proceed to Porto Ferrajo and superintend the evacuation of that place also. On his way he fell in with two Spanish frigates, the *Sabina* and the *Ceres*. The *Minerve* engaged the former, which was commanded by D. Jacobo Stuart, a descendant of the Duke of Berwick. After an action of three hours, during which the Spaniards lost 164 men, the *Sabina* struck. The Spanish captain, who was the only surviving officer, had hardly been conveyed on board the *Minerve*, when another enemy's frigate came up, compelled her to cast off the prize, and brought her a second time to action. After half an hour's trial of strength this new antagonist wore and hauled off; but a Spanish squadron of two ships of the line and two frigates came in sight. The *Blanche*, from which the *Ceres* had got off, was far to windward, and the *Minerve* escaped only by the anxiety of the enemy to recover their own ship. As soon as Nelson reached Porto Ferrajo, he sent his prisoner in a flag of truce to Carthagena, having returned him his sword; this he did in honour of the gallantry which D. Jacobo had displayed, and not without some feeling of respect for his ancestry. "I felt it," said he, "consonant to the dignity of my country, and I always act as I feel right, without regard to custom: he was reputed the best officer in Spain, and his men were worthy of such a commander." By the same flag of truce he sent back all the Spanish prisoners at Porto Ferrajo; in exchange for whom he received his own men who had been taken in the prize.

General de Burgh, who commanded at the isle of

Elba, did not think himself authorised to abandon the place, till he had received specific instructions from England to that effect, professing that he was unable to decide between the contradictory orders of Government, or to guess at what their present intentions might be; but he said his only motive for urging delay in this measure arose from a desire that his own conduct might be properly sanctioned—not from any opinion that Porto Ferrajo ought to be retained. But Naples having made peace, Sir J. Jervis considered his business with Italy as concluded; and the protection of Portugal was the point to which he was now instructed to attend. Nelson, therefore, whose orders were perfectly clear and explicit, withdrew the whole naval establishment from that station, leaving the transports victualled, and so arranged that all the troops and stores could be embarked in three days. He was now about to leave the Mediterranean. Mr. Drake, who had been our minister at Genoa, expressed to him, on this occasion, the very high opinion which the allies entertained of his conspicuous merit; adding, that it was impossible for any one, who had the honour of co-operating with him, not to admire the activity, talents, and zeal which he had so eminently and constantly displayed. In fact, during this long course of services in the Mediterranean, the whole of his conduct had exhibited the same zeal, the same indefatigable energy, the same intuitive judgment, the same prompt and unerring decision, which characterised his after-career of glory. His name was as yet hardly known to the English public; but it was feared and respected throughout Italy. A letter came to him, directed " Horatio Nelson, Genoa "; and the writer, when he was asked how he could direct it so vaguely, replied, " Sir, there is but one Horatio Nelson in the world." At Genoa, in particular, where he had so long been stationed, and where the nature of his duty first led him to continual disputes with the Government, and afterwards compelled him to stop the trade of the port, he was equally respected by the Doge and by the people; for, while he maintained the rights and interests of Great Britain with becoming firmness, he tempered the exercise of power with courtesy and humanity, wherever duty would permit. "Had all my actions," said he, writing at this time to his wife, "been gazetted, not one fortnight would have passed, during the whole war, without a letter from me. One day or other I will have a long gazette to myself. I feel that such an opportunity will be given me. I cannot, if I am in the field of glory, be kept out of sight: wherever there is anything to be done, there Providence is sure to direct my steps."

These hopes and anticipations were soon to be fulfilled. Nelson's mind had long been irritated and depressed by the fear that a general action would take place before he could join the fleet. At length he sailed from Porto Ferrajo with a convoy for Gibraltar; and having reached that place, proceeded to the westward in search of the admiral. Off the mouth of the Straits he fell in with the Spanish fleet; and on the 13th of February, reaching the station off Cape St. Vincent's, communicated this intelligence to Sir John Jervis. He was now directed to shift his broad pendant on board the *Captain*, 74, Captain R. W. Miller; and, before sunset, the signal was made to prepare for action, and to keep, during the night, in close order. At daybreak the enemy were in sight. The British force consisted of two ships of 100 guns, two of 98, two of 90, eight of 74, and one 64—fifteen of the line in all, with four frigates, a sloop, and a cutter. The Spaniards had one four-decker, of 136 guns; six three-deckers, of 112; two 84s; eighteen 74s—in all, twenty-seven ships of the line, with ten frigates and a brig. Their admiral, D. Joseph de Cordova, had learnt from an American, on the 5th, that the English had only nine ships, which was indeed the case when his informer had seen them; for a reinforcement of five ships from England, under Admiral Parker, had not then joined, and the *Culloden* had parted company. Upon this information, the Spanish commander, instead of going into Cadiz, as was his intention when he sailed from Carthagena, determined to seek an enemy so inferior in force; and relying, with fatal confidence, upon the American account, he suffered his ships to remain too far dispersed, and in some disorder. When the morning of the 14th broke, and discovered the English fleet, a fog for some time concealed their number. The look-out ship of the Spaniards, fancying that her signal was disregarded, because so little notice seemed to be taken of it, made another signal, that the English force consisted of forty sail of the line. The captain afterwards said he did this to rouse the admiral: it had the effect of perplexing him, and alarming the whole fleet. The absurdity of such an act shows what was the state of the Spanish navy under that miserable government by which Spain was so long oppressed and degraded, and finally betrayed. In reality, the general incapacity of the naval officers was so well known, that in a pasquinade, which about this time appeared at Madrid, wherein the different orders of the state were advertised for sale, the greater part of the sea-officers, with all their equipments, were offered as a gift; and it was added that any person who would please to take them should receive a handsome gratuity.

Before the enemy could form a regular order of battle, Sir J. Jervis, by carrying a press of sail, came up with them, passed through their fleet, then tacked, and thus cut off nine of their ships from the main body. These ships attempted to form on the larboard tack, either with a design of passing through the British line, or to leeward of it, and thus rejoining their friends. Only one of them succeeded in this attempt; and that only because she was so covered with smoke that her intention was not discovered

till she had reached the rear : the others were so
warmly received that they put about, took to flight,
and did not appear again in the action till its close.
The admiral was now able to direct his attention to
the enemy's main body, which was still superior in
number to his whole fleet, and more so in weight of
metal. He made signal to tack in succession. Nelson, whose station was in the rear of the British
line, perceived that the Spaniards were bearing up
before the wind, with an intention of forming their
line, going large, and joining their separated ships ;
or else, of getting off without an engagement. To
prevent either of these schemes, he disobeyed the
signal without a moment's hesitation, and ordered
his ship to be wore. This at once brought him into
action with the *Santissima Trinidad*, 136, the *San
Joseph*, 112, the *Salvador del Mundo*, 112, the *San
Nicolas*, 80, the *San Isidro*, 74, another 74, and
another first-rate. Trowbridge, in the *Culloden*,
immediately joined, and most nobly supported him ;
and for nearly an hour did the *Culloden* and *Captain*
maintain what Nelson called " this apparently, but
not really, unequal contest ";—such was the advantage of skill and discipline, and the confidence which
brave men derive from them. The *Blenheim*, then
passing between them and the enemy, gave them a
respite, and poured in her fire upon the Spaniards.
The *Salvador del Mundo* and *S. Isidro* dropped
astern, and were fired into, in a masterly style, by the
Excellent, Captain Collingwood. The *S. Isidro*
struck ; and Nelson thought that the *Salvador* struck
also : " But Collingwood," says he, " disdaining the
parade of taking possession of beaten enemies, most
gallantly pushed up, with every sail set, to save his
old friend and messmate, who was, to appearance,
in a critical situation "; for the *Captain* was at this
time actually fired upon by three first-rates, by the
S. Nicolas, and by a 74, within about pistol-shot of
that vessel. The *Blenheim* was ahead, the *Culloden*

G 52

crippled and astern. Collingwood ranged up, and hauling up his mainsail just astern, passed within ten feet of the *S. Nicolas*, giving her a most tremendous fire, then passed on for the *Santissima Trinidad*. The *S. Nicolas* luffing up, the *S. Joseph* fell on board her, and Nelson resumed his station abreast of them, and close alongside. The *Captain* was now incapable of farther service, either in the line or in chase : she had lost her fore-topmast; not a sail, shroud, or rope was left, and her wheel was shot away. Nelson, therefore, directed Captain Miller to put the helm a-starboard, and, calling for the boarders, ordered them to board.

Captain Berry, who had lately been Nelson's first lieutenant, was the first man who leaped into the enemy's mizen-chains. Miller, when in the very act of going, was ordered by Nelson to remain. Berry was supported from the sprit-sailyard, which locked in the *S. Nicolas*'s main rigging. A soldier of the 69th broke the upper quarter-gallery window, and jumped in, followed by the Commodore himself, and by others as fast as possible. The cabin doors were fastened, and the Spanish officers fired their pistols at them through the window : the doors were soon forced, and the Spanish brigadier fell while retreating to the quarter-deck. Nelson pushed on, and found Berry in possession of the poop, and the Spanish ensign hauling down. He passed on to the fore-castle, where he met two or three Spanish officers, and received their swords. The English were now in full possession of every part of the ship ; and a fire of pistols and musketry opened upon them from the admiral's stern gallery of the *San Joseph*. Nelson having placed sentinels at the different ladders, and ordered Captain Miller to send more men into the prize, gave orders for boarding that ship from the *San Nicolas*. It was done in an instant, he himself leading the way, and exclaiming—" Westminster Abbey, or victory ! " Berry assisted him into the main-chains; and at that moment a Spanish officer looked over the quarter-deckrail, and said they surrendered. It was not long before he was on the quarter-deck, where the Spanish captain presented to him his sword, and told him the admiral was below, dying of his wounds. There, on the quarter-deck of an enemy's first-rate, he received the swords of the officers; giving them, as they were delivered, one by one, to William Fearney, one of his old *Agamemnon's* who, with the utmost coolness, put them under his arm. One of his sailors came up, and, with an Englishman's feeling, took him by the hand, saying, he might not soon have such another place to do it in, and he was heartily glad to see him there. Twenty-four of the *Captain's* men were killed, and fifty-six wounded; a fourth part of the loss sustained by the whole squadron falling upon this ship. Nelson received only a few bruises.

The Spaniards had still eighteen or nineteen ships, which had suffered little or no injury: that part of the fleet which had been separated from the main body in the morning was now coming up, and Sir John Jervis made signal to bring to. His ships could not have formed without abandoning those which they had captured, and running to leeward: the *Captain* was lying a perfect wreck on board her two prizes, and many of the other vessels were so shattered in their masts and rigging as to be wholly unmanageable. The Spanish admiral, meantime, according to his official account, being altogether undecided in his own opinion respecting the state of the fleet, inquired of his captains whether it was proper to renew the action: nine of them answered explicitly that it was not; others replied, that it was expedient to delay the business. The *Pelayo* and the *Principe Conquistador* were the only ships that were for fighting.

As soon as the action was discontinued, Nelson went on board the admiral's ship. Sir John Jervis received him on the quarter-deck, took him in his

arms, and said he could not sufficiently thank him.
For this victory the commander-in-chief was rewarded
with the title of Earl St. Vincent. Nelson, who, before the action was known in England, had been
advanced to the rank of rear-admiral, had the Order
of the Bath given him. The sword of the Spanish
rear-admiral, which Sir John Jervis insisted upon his
keeping, he presented to the mayor and corporation
of Norwich, saying that he knew no place where it
could give him or his family more pleasure to have it
kept than in the capital city of the county where he
was born. The freedom of that city was voted him
on this occasion. But of all the numerous congratulations which he received, none could have affected
him with deeper delight than that which came from
his venerable father. " I thank my God," said this
excellent man, " with all the power of a grateful soul,
for the mercies He has most graciously bestowed on
me in preserving you. Not only my few acquaint-
ances here, but the people in general, met me at every
corner with such handsome words, that I was obliged
to retire from the public eye. The height of glory to
which your professional judgment, united with a
proper degree of bravery, guarded by Providence,
has raised you, few sons, my dear child, attain to,
and fewer fathers live to see. Tears of joy have in-
voluntarily trickled down my furrowed cheeks : who
could stand the force of such general congratulation ?
The name and services of Nelson have sounded
throughout this city of Bath—from the common
ballad-singer to the public theatre." The good old
man concluded by telling him that the field of glory,
in which he had so long been conspicuous, was still
open, and by giving him his blessing.

Sir Horatio, who had now hoisted his flag as rear-
admiral of the blue, was sent to bring away the troops
from Porto Ferrajo : having performed this, he shifted
his flag to the *Theseus*. That ship had taken part in
the mutiny in England, and being just arrived from

home, some danger was apprehended from the temper of the men. This was one reason why Nelson was removed to her. He had not been on board many weeks before a paper, signed in the name of all the ship's company, was dropped on the quarter-deck, containing these words : " Success attend Admiral Nelson ! God bless Captain Miller ! We thank them for the officers they have placed over us. We are happy and comfortable, and will shed every drop of blood in our veins to support them ;—and the name of the *Theseus* shall be immortalised as high as her captain's. " Wherever Nelson commanded, the men soon became attached to him ;—in ten days' time he would have restored the most mutinous ship in the navy to order. Whenever an officer fails to win the affections of those who are under his command, he may be assured that the fault is chiefly in himself.

While Sir Horatio was in the *Theseus* he was employed in the command of the inner squadron at the blockade of Cadiz. During this service the most perilous action occurred in which he was ever engaged. Making a night attack upon the Spanish gunboats, his barge was attacked by an armed launch, under their commander, D. Miguel Tregoyen, carrying twenty-six men. Nelson had with him only his ten bargemen, Captain Freemantle, and his coxswain, John Sykes, an old and faithful follower, who twice saved the life of his admiral by parrying the blows that were aimed at him, and at last actually interposed his own head to receive the blow of a Spanish sabre, which he could not by any other means avert ;—thus dearly was Nelson beloved. This was a desperate service—hand to hand with swords : and Nelson always considered that his personal courage was more conspicuous on this occasion than on any other during his whole life. Notwithstanding the great disproportion of numbers, eighteen of the enemy were killed, all the rest wounded, and their launch taken. Nelson would have asked for a lieutenancy for Sykes, if he

had served long enough : his manner and conduct, he
observed, were so entirely above his situation, that
Nature certainly intended him for a gentleman : but
though he recovered from the dangerous wound which
he received in this act of heroic attachment, he did
not live to profit by the gratitude and friendship of
his commander.

Twelve days after this rencontre, Nelson sailed at
the head of an expedition against Teneriffe. A report
had prevailed a few months before, that the viceroy of
Mexico, with the treasure-ships, had put into that
island. This had led Nelson to meditate the plan of
an attack upon it, which he communicated to Earl
St. Vincent. He was perfectly aware of the difficulties of the attempt. "I do not," said he, " reckon
myself equal to Blake; but, if I recollect right, he was
more obliged to the wind coming off the land than to
any exertions of his own. The approach by sea to the
anchoring-place is under very high land, passing three
valleys; therefore the wind is either in from the sea,
or squally with calms from the mountains " : and he
perceived, that if the Spanish ships were won, the
object would still be frustrated if the wind did not
come off shore. The land force, he thought, would
render success certain; and there were the troops from
Elba, with all necessary stores and artillery, already
embarked. " But here," said he, " soldiers must be
consulted; and I know, from experience, they have
not the same boldness in undertaking a political
measure that we have : we look to the benefit of our
country, and risk our own fame every day to serve
her ;—a soldier obeys his orders, and no more."
Nelson's experience at Corsica justified him in this
harsh opinion ;—he did not live to see the glorious
days of the British army under Wellington. The
army from Elba, consisting of 3,700 men, would do
the business, he said, in three days, probably in much
less time; and he would undertake, with a very small
squadron, to perform the naval part; for though the

shore was not easy of access, the transports might run in and land the troops in one day.

The report concerning the viceroy was unfounded; but a homeward-bound Manilla ship put into Santa Cruz at this time, and the expedition was determined upon. It was not fitted out upon the scale which Nelson had proposed. Four ships of the line, three frigates, and the *Fox* cutter, formed the squadron; and he was allowed to choose such ships and officers as he thought proper. No troops were embarked, the seamen and marines of the squadron being thought sufficient. His orders were to make a vigorous attack, but on no account to land in person, unless his presence should be absolutely necessary. The plan was, that the boats should land in the night, between the fort on the N.E. side of Santa Cruz bay and the town, make themselves masters of that fort, and then send a summons to the governor. By midnight, the three frigates, having the force on board which was intended for this debarkation, approached within three miles of the place; but, owing to a strong gale of wind in the offing, and a strong current against them in-shore, they were not able to get within a mile of the landing-place before daybreak; and then they were seen, and their intention discovered. Trowbridge and Bowen, with Captain Oldfield, of the marines, went upon this to consult with the admiral what was to be done; and it was resolved that they should attempt to get possession of the heights above the fort. The frigates accordingly landed their men; and Nelson stood in with the line-of-battle ships, meaning to batter the fort, for the purpose of distracting the attention of the garrison. A calm and contrary currents hindered him from getting within a league of the shore; and the heights were by this time so secured, and manned with such a force, as to be judged impracticable. Thus foiled in his plans by circumstances of wind and tide, he still considered it a point of honour that some attempt should be made.

This was on the 22nd of July : he re-embarked his men that night, got the ships, on the 24th, to anchor about two miles north of the town, and made show as if he intended to attack the heights. At six in the evening signal was made for the boats to prepare to proceed on service as previously ordered.

When this was done, Nelson addressed a letter to the commander-in-chief—the last which was ever written with his right hand. " I shall not," said he, " enter on the subject, why we are not in possession of Santa Cruz. Your partiality will give credit that all has hitherto been done which was possible; but without effect. This night I, humble as I am, command the whole, destined to land under the batteries of the town ; and to-morrow my head will probably be crowned either with laurel or cypress. I have only to recommend Josiah Nisbet to you and my country. The Duke of Clarence, should I fall, will, I am confident, take a lively interest for my step-son, on his name being mentioned." Perfectly aware how desperate a service this was likely to prove, before he left the *Theseus* he called Lieutenant Nisbet, who had the watch on deck, into the cabin, that he might assist in arranging and burning his mother's lett s. Perceiving that the young man was armed, he earnestly begged him to remain behind. " Should we both fall, Josiah," said he, " what would become of your poor mother? The care of the *Theseus* falls to you : stay, therefore, and take charge of her." Nisbet replied : " Sir, the ship must take care of herself ; I will go with you to-night, if I never go again."

He met his captains at supper on board the *Seahorse*, Captain Freemantle, whose wife, whom he had lately married in the Mediterranean, presided at table. At eleven o'clock the boats, containing between 600 and 700 men, with 180 on board the *Fox* cutter, and from 70 to 80 in a boat which had been taken the day before, proceeded in six divisions toward the town, conducted by all the captains of the squadron, except

Freemantle and Bowen, who attended with Nelson to regulate and lead the way to the attack. They were to land on the mole, and thence hasten, as fast as possible, into the great square; then form, and proceed as should be found expedient. They were not discovered till about half-past one o'clock, when, being within half gun-shot of the landing-place, Nelson directed the boats to cast off from each other, give a huzza, and push for the shore. But the Spaniards were excellently well prepared: the alarm-bells answered the huzza, and a fire of thirty or forty pieces of cannon, with musketry from one end of the town to the other, opened upon the invaders. Nothing, however, could check the intrepidity with which they advanced. The night was exceedingly dark; most of the boats missed the mole, and went on shore through a raging surf, which stove all to the left of it. The Admiral, Freemantle, Thompson, Bowen, and four or five other boats, found the mole: they stormed it instantly, and carried it, though it was defended, as they imagined, by four or five hundred men. Its guns, which were six-and-twenty pounders, were spiked; but such a heavy fire of musketry and grape was kept up from the citadel, and the houses at the head of the mole, that the assailants could not advance, and nearly all of them were killed or wounded.

In the act of stepping out of the boat, Nelson received a shot through the right elbow, and fell; but, as he fell, he caught the sword, which he had just drawn, in his left hand, determined never to part with it while he lived, for it had belonged to his uncle, Captain Suckling, and he valued it like a relic. Nisbet, who was close to him, placed him at the bottom of the boat, and laid his hat over the shattered arm, lest the sight of the blood, which gushed out in great abundance, should increase his faintness. He then examined the wound, and taking some silk handkerchiefs from his neck, bound them round tight above the lacerated vessels. Had it not been for this presence of mind in his step-son, Nelson must have perished. One of his bargemen, by name Lovel, tore his shirt into shreds, and made a sling with them for the broken limb. They then collected five other seamen, by whose assistance they succeeded at length in getting the boat afloat; for it had grounded with the falling tide. Nisbet took one of the oars, and ordered the steersman to go close under the guns of the battery, that they might be safe from its tremendous fire. Hearing his voice Nelson roused himself, and desired to be lifted up in the boat, that he might look about him. Nisbet raised him up; but nothing could be seen except the firing of the guns on shore, and what could be discerned by their flashes upon the stormy sea. In a few minutes a general shriek was heard from the crew of the *Fox*, which had received a shot under water, and went down. Ninety-seven men were lost in her; eighty-three were saved, many by Nelson himself, whose exertions on this occasion greatly increased the pain and danger of his wound. The first ship which the boat could reach happened to be the *Seahorse*; but nothing could induce him to go on board, though he was assured that if they attempted to row to another ship it might be at the risk of his life. "I had rather suffer death," he replied, "than alarm Mrs. Freemantle, by letting her see me in this state, when I can give her no tidings whatever of her husband." They pushed on for the *Theseus*. When they came alongside, he peremptorily refused all assistance in getting on board, so impatient was he that the boat should return, in hopes that it might save a few more from the *Fox*. He desired to have only a single rope thrown over the side, which he twisted round his left hand, saying, "Let me alone: I have yet my legs left, and one arm. Tell the surgeon to make haste, and get his instruments. I know I must lose my right arm; so the sooner it is off the better." The spirit which he displayed in jumping up the ship's side astonished everybody.

Freemantle had been severely wounded in the right arm, soon after the admiral. He was fortunate enough to find a boat at the beach, and got instantly to his ship. Thompson was wounded; Bowen killed, to the great regret of Nelson; as was also one of his own officers, Lieutenant Weatherhead, who had followed him from the *Agamemnon*; and whom he greatly and deservedly esteemed. Trowbridge, meantime, fortunately for his party, missed the mole in the darkness, but pushed on shore under the batteries, close to the south end of the citadel. Captain Waller, of the *Emerald*, and two or three other boats, landed at the same time. The surf was so high that many others put back. The boats were instantly filled with water, and stove against the rocks; and most of the ammunition in the men's pouches was wetted. Having collected a few men, they pushed on to the great square, hoping there to find the admiral and the rest of the force. The ladders were all lost, so that they could make no immediate attempt on the citadel; but they sent a sergeant, with two of the town's people, to summon it; this messenger never returned; and Trowbridge having waited about an hour, in painful expectation of his friends, marched to join Captains Hood and Miller, who had effected their landing to the south-west. They then endeavoured to procure some intelligence of the admiral and the rest of the officers, but without success. By daybreak they had gathered together about 80 marines, 80 pikemen, and 180 small-arm seamen; all the survivors of those who had made good their landing. They obtained some ammunition from the prisoners whom they had taken, and marched on, to try what could be done at the citadel without ladders. They found all the streets commanded by field-pieces, and several thousand Spaniards, with about a hundred French, under arms, approaching by every avenue. Finding himself without provisions, their powder wet, and no possibility of obtaining either stores or reinforcements from the ships, the boats being lost, Trowbridge, with great presence of mind, sent Captain Samuel Hood with a flag of truce to the governor, to say he was prepared to burn the town, and would instantly set fire to it if the Spaniards approached one inch nearer. This, however, if he were compelled to do it, he should do with regret, for he had no wish to injure the inhabitants; and he was ready to treat upon these terms,—that the British troops should re-embark, with all their arms of every kind, and take their own boats, if they were saved, or be provided with such others as might be wanting : they, on their part, engaging that the squadron should not molest the town, nor any of the Canary Islands; all prisoners on both sides to be given up. When these terms were proposed, the governor made answer that the English ought to surrender as prisoners of war; but Captain Hood replied, he was instructed to say that if the terms were not accepted in five minutes, Captain Trowbridge would set the town on fire, and attack the Spaniards at the point of the bayonet. Satisfied with his success, which was indeed sufficiently complete, and respecting, like a brave and honourable man, the gallantry of his enemy, the Spaniard acceded to the proposal. " And here," says Nelson in his journal, " it is right we should notice the noble and generous conduct of Don Juan Antonio Gutierrez, the Spanish governor. The moment the terms were agreed to, he directed our wounded men to be received into the hospitals, and all our people to be supplied with the best provisions that could be procured; and made it known that the ships were at liberty to send on shore, and purchase whatever refreshments they were in want of, during the time they might be off the island." A youth, by name Don Bernardo Collagon, stripped himself of his shirt to make bandages for one of those Englishmen against whom, not an hour before, he had been engaged in battle. Nelson wrote to thank the governor for the humanity which he had displayed. Presents were interchanged between them. Sir Horatio offered to take charge of his despatches for the Spanish Government; and thus actually became the first messenger to Spain of his own defeat.

The total loss of the English, in killed, wounded, and drowned, amounted to 250. Nelson made no mention of his own wound in his official despatches: but in a private letter to Lord St. Vincent—the first which he wrote with his left hand—he shows himself to have been deeply affected by the failure of this enterprise. "I am become," he said, "a burthen to my friends, and useless to my country: but by my last letter you will perceive my anxiety for the promotion of my son-in-law, Josiah Nisbet. When I leave your command, I become dead to the world:—'I go hence, and am no more seen.' If from poor Bowen's loss you think it proper to oblige me, I rest confident you will do it. The boy is under obligations to me; but he repaid me by bringing me from the mole of Santa Cruz. I hope you will be able to give me a frigate, to convey the remains of my carcass to England."—"A left-handed admiral," he said in a subsequent letter, "will never again be considered as useful; therefore the sooner I get to a very humble cottage the better; and make room for a sounder man to serve the state." His first letter to Lady Nelson was written under the same opinion, but in a more cheerful strain. "It was the chance of war," said he, "and I have great reason to be thankful: and I know it will add much to your pleasure to find that Josiah, under God's providence, was principally instrumental in saving my life. I shall not be surprised if I am neglected and forgotten: probably I shall no longer be considered as useful; however, I shall feel rich if I continue to enjoy your affection. I beg neither you nor my father will think much of this mishap—my mind has long been made up to such an event.''

His step-son, according to his wish, was immediately promoted; and honours enough to heal his wounded spirit awaited him in England. Letters were addressed to him by the First Lord of the Admiralty, and by his steady friend, the Duke of Clarence, to congratulate him on his return, covered as he was with glory. He assured the Duke, in his reply, that not a scrap of that ardour with which he had hitherto served his king had been shot away. The freedom of the cities of Bristol and London were transmitted to him; he was invested with the Order of the Bath, and received a pension of £1,000 a year. The memorial which, as a matter of form, he was called upon to present on this occasion, exhibited an extraordinary catalogue of services performed during the war. It stated that he had been in four actions with the fleets of the enemy, and in three actions with boats employed in cutting out of harbour, in destroying vessels, and in taking three towns : he had served on shore with the army four months, and commanded the batteries at the sieges of Bastia and Calvi; he had assisted at the capture of seven sail of the line, six frigates, four corvettes, and eleven privateers : taken and destroyed near fifty sail of merchant vessels; and actually been engaged against the enemy upwards of an hundred and twenty times; in which service he had lost his right eye and right arm, and been severely wounded and bruised in his body.

His sufferings from the lost limb were long and painful. A nerve had been taken up in one of the ligatures at the time of the operation; and the ligature, according to the practice of the French surgeons, was of silk, instead of waxed thread; this produced a constant irritation and discharge; and the ends of the ligature being pulled every day, in hopes of bringing it away, occasioned fresh agony. He had scarcely any intermission of pain, day or night, for three months after his return to England. Lady Nelson, at his earnest request, attended the dressing his arm till she had acquired sufficient resolution and skill to dress it herself. One night, during this state of suffering, after a day of constant pain, Nelson retired early to bed, in hope of enjoying some respite by means of laudanum. He was at that time lodging in Bond Street; and the family was soon disturbed by a mob knocking loudly and violently at the door. The news of Duncan's victory had been made public, and the house was not illuminated. But when the mob were told that Admiral Nelson lay there in bed, badly wounded, the foremost of them made answer, "You shall hear no more from us to-night": and, in fact, the feeling of respect and sympathy was communicated from one to another with such effect, that, under the confusion of such a night, the house was not molested again.

About the end of November, after a night of sound sleep, he found the arm nearly free from pain: the surgeon was immediately sent for to examine it, and the ligature came away with the slightest touch. From that time it began to heal. As soon as he thought his health established, he sent the following form of thanksgiving to the minister of St. George's, Hanover Square:—"An officer desires to return thanks to Almighty God for his perfect recovery from a severe wound, and also for the many mercies bestowed on him."

Not having been in England till now since he lost his eye, he went to receive a year's pay, as smart money; but could not obtain payment, because he had neglected to bring a certificate from a surgeon that the sight was actually destroyed. A little irritated that this form should be insisted upon, because, though the fact was not apparent, he thought it was sufficiently notorious, he procured a certificate at the same time for the loss of his arm, saying, they might just as well doubt the one as the other. This put him in good humour with himself, and with the clerk who had offended him. On his return to the office, the clerk finding it was only the annual pay of a captain, observed, he thought it had been more. " Oh ! " replied Nelson, " this is only for an eye. In a few days I shall come for an arm; and in a little time longer, God knows, most probably for a leg." Accordingly, he soon afterwards went, and with perfect good humour exhibited the certificate of the loss of his arm.

CHAPTER V

EARLY in the year 1798 Sir Horatio Nelson hoisted his flag in the *Vanguard*, and was ordered to rejoin Earl St. Vincent. Upon his departure his father addressed him with that affectionate solemnity by which all his letters were distinguished. " I trust in the Lord," said he, " that He will prosper your going out and your coming in. I earnestly desired once more to see you, and that wish has been heard. If I should presume to say, I hope to see you again, the question would be readily asked, How old art thou? *Vale! vale! Domine vale!* " It is said that a gloomy foreboding—hung on the spirits of Lady Nelson at their parting. This could have arisen only from the dread of losing him by the chance of war. Any apprehension of losing his affections could hardly have existed; for all his correspondence to this time shows that he thought himself happy in his marriage; and his private character had hitherto been as spotless as his public conduct. One of the last things he said to her was that his own ambition was satisfied, but that he went to raise her to that rank in which he had long wished to see her.

Immediately on his rejoining the fleet, he was despatched to the Mediterranean, with a small squadron, in order to ascertain, if possible, the object of the great expedition which at that time was fitting out, under Buonaparte, at Toulon. The defeat of this armament, whatever might be its destination, was deemed by the British Government an object paramount to every other; and Earl St. Vincent was directed, if he thought it necessary, to take his whole force into the Mediterranean, to relinquish, for that purpose, the blockade of the Spanish fleet, as a thing of inferior moment: but, if he should deem a detachment sufficient, "I think it almost unnecessary," said the First Lord of the Admiralty, in his secret instructions, "to suggest to you the propriety of putting it under Sir Horatio Nelson." It is to the honour of Earl St. Vincent that he had already made the same choice. The British Government at this time, with a becoming spirit, gave orders that any port in the Mediterranean should be considered as hostile, where the governor, or chief magistrate, should refuse to let our ships of war procure supplies of provisions, or of any article which they might require.

The armament at Toulon consisted of 13 ships of the line, 7 forty-gun frigates, with 24 smaller vessels of war, and nearly 200 transports. Mr. Udney, our consul at Leghorn, was the first person who procured certain intelligence of the enemy's design against Malta; and, from his own sagacity, foresaw that Egypt must be their after object. Nelson sailed from Gibraltar on the 9th of May, with the *Vanguard*, *Orion*, and *Alexander*, 74s; the *Caroline*, *Flora*, *Emerald*, and *Terpsichore* frigates; and the *Bonne Citoyenne* sloop of war; to watch this formidable armament. On the 19th, when they were in the Gulf of Lyons, a gale came on from the N.W. It moderated so much on the 20th as to enable them to get their top-gallant masts and yards aloft. After dark it again began to blow strong, but the ships had been prepared for a gale, and therefore Nelson's mind was easy. Shortly before midnight, however, his main-

H 52

topmast went over the side, and the mizen-topmast soon afterward. The night was so tempestuous that it was impossible for any signal either to be seen or heard, and Nelson determined, as soon as it should be daybreak, to wear, and scud before the gale; but at half-past three the foremast went in three pieces, and the bowsprit was found to be sprung in three places. When day broke, they succeeded in wearing the ship with a remnant of the spritsail: this was hardly to have been expected: the *Vanguard* was at that time twenty-five leagues south of the islands of Hieres, with her head lying to the N.E.; and if she had not wore, the ship must have drifted to Corsica. Captain Ball, in the *Alexander*, took her in tow, to carry her into the Sardinian harbour of St. Pietro. Nelson, apprehensive that this attempt might endanger both vessels, ordered him to cast off; but that excellent officer, with a spirit like his commander's, replied, he was confident he could save the *Vanguard*, and, by God's help, he would do it. There had been a previous coolness between these great men; but from this time Nelson became fully sensible of the extraordinary talents of Captain Ball, and a sincere friendship subsisted between them during the remainder of their lives. "I ought not," said the admiral, writing to his wife,—"I ought not to call what has happened to the *Vanguard* by the cold name of accident: I believe firmly it was the Almighty's goodness, to check my consummate vanity. I hope it has made me a better officer, as I feel confident it has made me a better man. Figure to yourself, on Sunday evening, at sunset, a vain man walking in his cabin, with a squadron around him, who looked up to their chief to lead them to glory, and in whom their chief placed the firmest reliance that the proudest ships of equal numbers belonging to France would have lowered their flags; figure to yourself, on Monday morning, when the sun rose, this proud man, his ship dismasted, his fleet dispersed, and himself in such distress that the meanest frigate out of France would have been an unwelcome guest." Nelson had, indeed, more reason to refuse the cold name of accident to this tempest than he was then aware of; for on that very day the French fleet sailed from Toulon, and must have passed within a few leagues of his little squadron, which was thus preserved by the thick weather that came on.

In the orders of the British Government to consider all ports as hostile where the British ships should be refused supplies, the ports of Sardinia were excepted. The continental possessions of the King of Sardinia were at this time completely at the mercy of the French, and that prince was now discovering, when too late, that the terms to which he had consented, for the purpose of escaping immediate danger, necessarily involved, at last, the loss of the dominions which they were intended to preserve. The citadel of Turin was now occupied by French troops; and his wretched court feared to afford the common rights of humanity to British ships, lest it should give the French occasion to seize on the remainder of his dominions—a measure for which, it was certain, they would soon make a pretext, if they did not find one. Nelson was informed that he could not be permitted to enter the port of St. Pietro. Regardless of this interdict, which, under his circumstances, it would have been an act of suicidal folly to have regarded, he anchored in the harbour; and by the exertions of Sir James Saumarez, Captain Ball, and Captain Berry, the *Vanguard* was refitted in four days; months would have been employed in refitting her in England. Nelson, with that proper sense of merit wherever it was found, which proved at once the goodness and the greatness of his character, especially recommended to Earl St. Vincent the carpenter of the *Alexander*, under whose directions the ship had been repaired, stating that he was an old and faithful servant of the crown, who had been nearly thirty

years a warranted carpenter, and begging most
earnestly that the commander-in-chief would recommend him to the particular notice of the Board of
Admiralty. He did not leave the harbour without
expressing his sense of the treatment which he had
received there, in a letter to the Viceroy of Sardinia.
" Sir," it said, "having, by a gale of wind, sustained
some trifling damages, I anchored a small part of
His Majesty's fleet under my orders off this island,
and was surprised to hear, by an officer sent by the
governor, that admittance was to be refused to the
flag of His Britannic Majesty into this port. When
I reflect that my most gracious Sovereign is the
oldest, I believe, and certainly the most faithful ally,
which the King of Sardinia ever had, I could feel the
sorrow which it must have been to His Majesty to
have given such an order; and also for your Excellency, who had to direct its execution. I cannot but
look at the African shore, where the followers of
Mahomet are performing the part of the good Samari-
tan, which I look for in vain at St. Peter's, where
it is said the Christian religion is professed."

The delay which was thus occasioned was useful
to him in many respects : it enabled him to complete
his supply of water, and to receive a reinforcement,
which Earl St. Vincent, being himself reinforced
from England, was enabled to send him. It consisted
of the best ships of his fleet—the *Culloden*, 74, Captain T. Trowbridge; *Goliath*, 74, Captain T. Foley;
Minotaur, 74, Captain T. Louis; *Defence*, 74, Captain
John Peyton; *Bellerophon*, 74, Captain H. D. E.
Darby; *Majestic*, 74, Captain G. B. Westcott;
Zealous, 74, Captain S. Hood; *Swiftsure*, 74, Captain
B. Hallowell; *Theseus*, 74, Captain R. W. Miller;
Audacious, 74, Captain Davidge Gould. The *Leander*,
50, Captain T. B. Thompson, was afterwards added.
These ships were made ready for the service as soon
as Earl St. Vincent received advice from England
that he was to be reinforced. As soon as the rein-

forcement was seen from the mast-head of the
admiral's ship, off Cadiz Bay, signal was immediately
made to Captain Trowbridge to put to sea; and he
was out of sight before the ships from home cast
anchor in the British station.   Trowbridge took with
him no instructions to Nelson as to the course he was
to steer, nor any certain account of the enemy's
destination : everything was left to his own judgment.   Unfortunately, the frigates had been separated
from him in the tempest, and had not been able to
rejoin : they sought him unsuccessfully in the Bay
of Naples, where they obtained no tidings of his
course; and he sailed without them.

The first news of the enemy's armament was, that
it had surprised Malta.   Nelson formed a plan for
attacking it while at anchor at Gozo; but on the
22nd of June intelligence reached him that the French
had left that island on the 16th, the day after their
arrival.   It was clear that their destination was
eastward—he thought for Egypt,—and for Egypt,
therefore, he made all sail.   Had the frigates been
with him he could scarcely have failed to gain information of the enemy : for want of them, he only
spoke three vessels on the way ; two came from Alexandria, one from the Archipelago ; and neither of them
had seen anything of the French.   He arrived off
Alexandria on the 28th, and the enemy were not
there, neither was there any account of them ; but
the governor was endeavouring to put the city in a
state of defence, having received advice from Leghorn
that the French expedition was intended against
Egypt, after it had taken Malta.   Nelson then shaped
his course to the northward for Caramania, and
steered from thence along the southern side of Candia,
carrying a press of sail both night and day, with a contrary wind.   It would have been his delight, he said,
to have tried Buonaparte on a wind.   It would have
been the delight of Europe too, and the blessing of
the world, if that fleet had been overtaken with its

general on board. But of the myriads and millions of human beings who would have been preserved by that day's victory, there is not one to whom such essential benefit would have resulted as to Buonaparte himself. It would have spared him his defeat at Acre —his only disgrace; for to have been defeated by Nelson upon the seas would not have been disgraceful: it would have spared him all his after enormities. Hitherto his career had been glorious; the baneful principles of his heart had never yet passed his lips: history would have represented him as a soldier of fortune, who had faithfully served the cause in which he engaged; and whose career had been distinguished by a series of successes unexampled in modern times. A romantic obscurity would have hung over the expedition to Egypt, and he would have escaped the perpetration of those crimes which have incarnadined his soul with a deeper dye than that of the purple for which he committed them;—those acts of perfidy, midnight murder, usurpation, and remorseless tyranny, which have consigned his name to universal execration, now and for ever.

Conceiving that when an officer is not successful in his plans it is absolutely necessary that he should explain the motives upon which they were founded, Nelson wrote at this time an account and vindication of his conduct for having carried the fleet to Egypt. The objection which he anticipated was, that he ought not to have made so long a voyage without more certain information. "My answer," said he, "is ready—Who was I to get it from? The Governments of Naples and Sicily either knew not, or chose to keep me in ignorance. Was I to wait patiently until I heard certain accounts? If Egypt were their object, before I could hear of them they would have been in India. To do nothing was disgraceful; therefore I made use of my understanding. I am before your lordships' judgment; and if, under all circumstances, it is decided that I am wrong, I ought, for the sake

of our country, to be superseded; for at this moment,
when I know the French are not in Alexandria, I hold
the same opinion as off Cape Passaro,—that, under
all circumstances, I was right in steering for Alexandria : and by that opinion I must stand or fall."
Captain Ball, to whom he showed this paper, told
him he should recommend a friend never to begin a
defence of his conduct before he was accused of
error : he might give the fullest reasons for what he
had done, expressed in such terms as would evince
that he had acted from the strongest conviction of
being right; and of course he must expect that the
public would view it in the same light. Captain Ball
judged rightly of the public, whose first impulses,
though from want of sufficient information they must
frequently be erroneous, are generally founded upon
just feelings. But the public are easily misled, and
there are always persons ready to mislead them.
Nelson had not yet attained that fame which compels
envy to be silent; and when it was known in England
that he had returned after an unsuccessful pursuit,
it was said that he deserved impeachment; and Earl
St. Vincent was severely censured for having sent
so young an officer upon so important a service.

Baffled in his pursuit, he returned to Sicily. The
Neapolitan ministry had determined to give his
squadron no assistance, being resolved to do nothing
which could possibly endanger their peace with the
French Directory. By means, however, of Lady
Hamilton's influence at court, he procured secret
orders to the Sicilian governors; and, under those
orders, obtained everything which he wanted at
Syracuse—a timely supply, without which, he always
said, he could not have recommenced his pursuit with
any hope of success. "It is an old saying," said he
in his letter, "that 'the devil's children have the
devil's luck.' I cannot to this moment learn, beyond
vague conjecture, where the French fleet are gone to;
and having gone a round of six hundred leagues at

this season of the year, with an expedition incredible, here I am, as ignorant of the situation of the enemy as I was twenty-seven days ago. Every moment I have to regret the frigates having left me; had one-half of them been with me, I could not have wanted information. Should the French be so strongly secured in port that I cannot get at them, I shall immediately shift my flag into some other ship, and send the *Vanguard* to Naples to be refitted, for hardly any person but myself would have continued on service so long in such a wretched state." Vexed, however, and disappointed as he was, Nelson, with the true spirit of a hero, was still full of hope. "Thanks to your exertions," said he, writing to Sir W. and Lady Hamilton, "we have victualled and watered; and surely watering at the fountain of Arethusa, we must have victory. We shall sail with the first breeze; and be assured I will return either crowned with laurel or covered with cypress." Earl St. Vincent he assured, that if the French were above water he would find them out—he still held his opinion that they were bound for Egypt; "but," said he to the First Lord of the Admiralty, "be they bound to the Antipodes, your lordship may rely that I will not lose a moment in bringing them to action."

On the 25th of July he sailed from Syracuse for the Morea. Anxious beyond measure, and irritated that the enemy should so long have eluded him, the tediousness of the nights made him impatient; and the officer of the watch was repeatedly called on to let him know the hour, and convince him, who measured time by his own eagerness, that it was not yet day-break. The squadron made the Gulf of Coron on the 28th. Trowbridge entered the port, and returned with intelligence that the French had been seen about four weeks before steering to the S.E., from Candia. Nelson then determined immediately to return to Alexandria; and the British fleet accordingly, with every sail set, stood once more for the coast of

Egypt. On the 1st of August they came in sight of
Alexandria; and at four in the afternoon, Captain
Hood, in the *Zealous*, made the signal for the French
fleet. For many preceding days Nelson had hardly
taken either sleep or food; he now ordered his dinner
to be served, while preparations were making for
battle; and when his officers rose from the table, and
went to their separate stations, he said to them:
"Before this time to-morrow I shall have gained a
peerage, or Westminster Abbey."

The French, steering direct for Candia, had made
an angular passage for Alexandria; whereas Nelson,
in pursuit of them, made straight for that place, and
thus materially shortened the distance. The comparative smallness of his force made it necessary to
sail in close order, and it covered a less space than it
would have done if the frigates had been with him:
the weather also was constantly hazy. These circumstances prevented the English from falling in
with the enemy on the way to Egypt, and during the
return to Syracuse there was still less probability of
discovering them.

Why Buonaparte, having effected his landing,
should not have suffered the fleet to return, has
never yet been explained. Thus much is certain, that
it was detained by his command; though, with his
accustomed falsehood, he accused Admiral Brueys,
after that officer's death, of having lingered on the
coast, contrary to orders. The French fleet arrived
at Alexandria on the 1st of July; and Brueys, not
being able to enter the port, which time and neglect
had ruined, moored his ships in Aboukir Bay, in a
strong and compact line of battle; the headmost
vessel, according to his own account, being as close
as possible to a shoal on the N.W., and the rest of
the fleet forming a kind of curve along the line of
deep water, so as not to be turned by any means in
the S.W. By Buonaparte's desire he had offered a
reward of 10,000 livres to any pilot of the country

who would carry the squadron in; but none could be found who would venture to take charge of a single vessel drawing more than twenty feet. He had therefore made the best of his situation, and chosen the strongest position which he could possibly take in an open road. The commissary of the fleet said they were moored in such a manner as to bid defiance to a force more than double their own. This presumption could not then be thought unreasonable. Admiral Barrington, when moored in a similar manner off St. Lucia, in the year 1778, beat off the Comte d'Estaign in three several attacks, though his force was inferior by almost one-third to that which assailed it. Here, the advantage of numbers, both in ships, guns, and men, was in favour of the French. They had thirteen ships of the line and four frigates, carrying 1,196 guns and 11,230 men. The English had the same number of ships of the line, and one 50-gun ship, carrying 1,012 guns and 8,068 men. The English ships were all 74s : the French had three 80 gun ships, and one three-decker of 120.

During the whole pursuit, it had been Nelson's practice, whenever circumstances would permit, to have his captains on board the *Vanguard*, and explain to them his own ideas of the different and best modes of attack, and such plans as he proposed to execute on falling in with the enemy, whatever their situation might be. There is no possible position, it is said, which he did not take into calculation. His officers were thus fully acquainted with his principles of tactics : and such was his confidence in their abilities, that the only thing determined upon, in case they should find the French at anchor, was for the ships to form as most convenient for their mutual support, and to anchor by the stern. " First gain the victory," he said, " and then make the best use of it you can." The moment he perceived the position of the French, that intuitive genius with which Nelson was endowed displayed itself; and it in-

stantly struck him, that where there was room for an
enemy's ship to swing, there was room for one of
ours to anchor. The plan which he intended to pursue, therefore, was to keep entirely on the outer side
of the French line, and station his ships, as far as he
was able, one on the outer bow, and another on the
outer quarter, of each of the enemy's. This plan of
doubling on the enemy's ships was projected by Lord
Hood, when he designed to attack the French fleet at
their anchorage in Gourjean Road. Lord Hood
found it impossible to make the attempt; but the
thought was not lost upon Nelson, who acknowledged himself on this occasion indebted for it to his
old and excellent commander. Captain Berry, when
he comprehended the scope of the design, exclaimed
with transport, " If we succeed, what will the world
say?" " There is no *if* in the case," replied the
admiral : " that we shall succeed is certain : who may
live to tell the story is a very different question."

As the squadron advanced, the enemy opened a
steady fire from the starboard side of their whole line,
full into the bows of our van ships. It was received
in silence : the men on board of every ship were employed aloft in furling sails, and below in tending the
braces, and making ready for anchoring. A miserable sight for the French; who with all their skill,
and all their courage, and all their advantages of
numbers and situation, were upon that element, on
which, when the hour of trial comes, a Frenchman
has no hope. Admiral Brueys was a brave and able
man; yet the indelible character of his country broke
out in one of his letters, wherein he delivered it as his
private opinion that the English had missed him,
because, not being superior in force, they did not
think it prudent to try their strength with him. The
moment was now come in which he was to be undeceived.

A French brig was instructed to decoy the English,
by manœuvring so as to tempt them toward a shoal

lying off the island of Bequieres; but Nelson either
knew the danger, or suspected some deceit, and
the lure was unsuccessful.   Captain Foley led the
way in the *Goliath*, outsailing the *Zealous*, which for
some minutes disputed this post of honour with him.
He had long conceived, that if the enemy were
moored in line of battle in with the land, the best
plan of attack would be to lead between them and the
shore, because the French guns on that side were not
likely to be manned, nor even ready for action.   In-
tending, therefore to fix himself on the inner bow of
the *Guerrier*, he kept as near the edge of the bank as
the depth of water would admit; but his anchor hung,
and having opened his fire, he drifted to the second
ship, the *Conquérant*, before it was clear; then
anchored by the stern, inside of her, and in ten
minutes shot away her masts.   Hood, in the *Zealous*,
perceiving this, took the station which the *Goliath*
intended to have occupied, and he totally disabled
the *Guerrier* in twelve minutes.   The third ship which
doubled the enemy's van was the *Orion*, Sir J.
Saumarez; she passed to windward of the *Zealous*,
and opened her larboard guns as long as they bore
on the *Guerrier*; then passing inside the *Goliath*,
sunk a frigate which annoyed her, hauled round
toward the French line, and anchoring inside,
between the fifth and sixth ships from the *Guerrier*,
took her station on the larboard bow of the *Franklin*,
and the quarter of the *Peuple Souverain*, receiving
and returning the fire of both.   The sun was now
nearly down.   The *Audacious*, Captain Gould, pour-
ing a heavy fire into the *Guerrier* and the *Conquérant*,
fixed herself on the larboard bow of the latter; and
when that ship struck, passed on to the *Peuple
Souverain*.   The *Theseus*, Captain Miller, followed,
brought down the *Guerrier's* remaining main and
mizen masts, then anchored inside of the *Spartiate*,
the third in the French line.

While these advanced ships doubled the French

line, the *Vanguard* was the first that anchored on the outer side of the enemy, within half-pistol-shot of their third ship, the *Spartiate*. Nelson had six colours flying in different parts of his rigging, lest they should be shot away;—that they should be struck, no British admiral considers as a possibility. He veered half a cable, and instantly opened a tremendous fire; under cover of which the other four ships of his division, the *Minotaur*, *Bellerophon*, *Defence*, and *Majestic*, sailed on ahead of the admiral. In a few minutes every man stationed at the first six guns in the fore part of the *Vanguard's* deck was killed or wounded:—these guns were three times cleared. Captain Louis, in the *Minotaur*, anchored next ahead, and took off the fire of the *Aquilon*, the fourth in the enemy's line. The *Bellerophon*, Captain Darby, passed ahead, and dropped her stern anchor on the starboard bow of the *Orient*, seventh in the line, Brueys' own ship, of 120 guns, whose difference of force was in proportion of more than seven to three, and whose weight of ball, from the lower deck alone, exceeded that from the whole broadside of the *Bellerophon*. Captain Peyton, in the *Defence*, took his station ahead of the *Minotaur*, and engaged the *Franklin*, the sixth in the line, by which judicious movement the British line remained unbroken. The *Majestic*, Captain Westcott, got entangled with the main rigging of one of the French ships astern of the *Orient*, and suffered dreadfully from that three-decker's fire: but she swung clear, and closely engaging the *Heureux*, the ninth ship on the starboard bow, received also the fire of the *Tonnant*, which was the eighth in the line. The other four ships of the British squadron, having been detached previous to the discovery of the French, were at a considerable distance when the action began. It commenced at half after six; about seven, night closed, and there was no other light than that from the fire of the contending fleets.

Trowbridge, in the *Culloden*, the foremost of the
remaining ships, was two leagues astern. He came
on sounding, as the others had done; as he advanced,
the increasing darkness increased the difficulty of the
navigation; and suddenly, after having found eleven
fathoms' water, before the lead could be hove again,
he was fast aground; nor could all his own exertions,
joined to those of the *Leander* and the *Mutiné* brig,
which came to his assistance, get him off in time to
bear a part in the action. His ship, however, served
as a beacon to the *Alexander* and *Swiftsure*, which
would else, from the course which they were holding,
have gone considerably farther on the reef, and must
inevitably have been lost. These ships entered the
bay, and took their stations, in the darkness, in a
manner still spoken of with admiration by all who
remember it. Captain Hallowell, in the *Swiftsure*,
as he was bearing down, fell in with what seemed to
be a strange sail; Nelson had directed his ships to
hoist four lights horizontally at the mizen-peak, as
soon as it became dark; and this vessel had no such
distinction. Hallowell, however, with great judgment, ordered his men not to fire; if she was an
enemy, he said, she was in too disabled a state to
escape; but, from her sails being loose, and the way
in which her head was, it was probable she might be
an English ship. It was the *Bellerophon*, overpowered
by the huge *Orient*; her lights had gone overboard,
nearly 200 of her crew were killed or wounded, all her
masts and cables had been shot away, and she was
drifting out of the line, toward the lee side of the bay.
Her station, at this important time, was occupied by
the *Swiftsure*, which opened a steady fire on the
quarter of the *Franklin* and the bows of the French
admiral. At the same instant, Captain Ball, with the
Alexander, passed under his stern, and anchored
within side on his larboard quarter, raking him, and
keeping up a severe fire of musketry upon his decks.
The last ship which arrived to complete the destruc-

tion of the enemy was the *Leander*. Captain Thompson, finding that nothing could be done that night to get off the *Culloden*, advanced with the intention of anchoring athwart hawse of the *Orient*. The *Franklin* was so near her ahead, that there was not room for him to pass clear of the two; he therefore took his station athwart hawse of the latter, in such a position as to rake both.

The two first ships of the French line had been dismasted within a quarter of an hour after the commencement of the action; and the others had in that time suffered so severely that victory was already certain. The third, fourth, and fifth were taken possession of at half-past eight. Meantime, Nelson received a severe wound on the head from a piece of langridge shot. Captain Berry caught him in his arms as he was falling. The great effusion of blood occasioned an apprehension that the wound was mortal; Nelson himself thought so; a large flap of the skin of the forehead, cut from the bone, had fallen over one eye, and the other being blind, he was in total darkness. When he was carried down, the surgeon—in the midst of a scene scarcely to be conceived by those who have never seen a cock-pit in time of action, and the heroism which is displayed amid its horrors,—with a natural and pardonable eagerness, quitted the poor fellow then under his hands, that he might instantly attend the admiral. "No!" said Nelson, "I will take my turn with my brave fellows." Nor would he suffer his own wound to be examined till every man who had been previously wounded was properly attended to. Fully believing that the wound was mortal, and that he was about to die, as he had ever desired, in battle and in victory, he called the chaplain, and desired him to deliver what he supposed to be his dying remembrance to Lady Nelson; he then sent for Captain Louis on board from the *Minotaur*, that he might thank him personally for the great assistance which he had rendered to the *Vanguard*; and, ever mindful of those who deserved to be his friends, appointed Captain Hardy from the brig to the command of his own ship, Captain Berry having to go home with the news of the victory.   When the surgeon came in due time to examine his wound (for it was in vain to entreat him to let it be examined sooner), the most anxious silence prevailed; and the joy of the wounded men, and of the whole crew, when they heard that the hurt was merely superficial, gave Nelson deeper pleasure than the unexpected assurance that his life was in no danger.   The surgeon requested, and, as far as he could, ordered him to remain quiet, but Nelson could not rest.   He called for his secretary, Mr. Campbell, to write the despatches.   Campbell had himself been wounded, and was so affected at the blind and suffering state of the admiral, that he was unable to write.   The chaplain was then sent for; but before he came, Nelson, with his characteristic eagerness, took the pen, and contrived to trace a few words, marking his devout sense of the success which had already been obtained.   He was now left alone; when suddenly a cry was heard on the deck, that the *Orient* was on fire.   In the confusion he found his way up, unassisted and unnoticed; and, to the astonishment of every one, appeared on the quarter-deck, where he immediately gave order that boats should be sent to the relief of the enemy.

It was soon after nine that the fire on board the *Orient* broke out.   Brueys was dead: he had received three wounds, yet would not leave his post: a fourth cut him almost in two.   He desired not to be carried below, but to be left to die upon deck.   The flames soon mastered his ship.   Her sides had just been painted, and the oil-jars and paint-buckets were lying on the poop.   By the prodigious light of this con-flagration, the situation of the two fleets could now be perceived, the colours of both being clearly dis-tinguishable.   About ten o'clock the ship blew up.

This tremendous explosion was followed by a silence not less awful : the firing immediately ceased on both sides ; and the first sound which broke the silence was the dash of her shattered masts and yards falling into the water from the vast height to which they had been exploded. It is upon record that a battle between two armies was once broken off by an earthquake :— such an event would be felt like a miracle ; but no incident in war, produced by human means, has ever equalled the sublimity of this co-instantaneous pause, and all its circumstances.

About seventy of the *Orient's* crew were saved by the English boats. Among the many hundreds who perished were the commodore, Casa-Bianca, and his son, a brave boy only ten years old. They were seen floating on the wreck of a mast when the ship blew up. She had money on board to the amount of £600,000 sterling. A port fire from her fell into the main-royal of the *Alexander*; the fire which it occasioned was speedily extinguished. Captain Ball had provided, as far as human foresight could provide, against any such danger. All the shrouds and sails of his ship which were not absolutely necessary for its immediate management were thoroughly wetted, and so rolled up, that they were as hard and as little inflammable as so many solid cylinders.

The firing recommenced with the ships to leeward of the centre, and continued till about three. At day-break the *Guillaume Tell* and the *Genereux*, the two rear ships of the enemy, were the only French ships of the line which had their colours flying : they cut their cables in the forenoon, not having been engaged, and stood out to sea, and two frigates with them. The *Zealous* pursued ; but as there was no other ship in a condition to support Captain Hood, he was recalled. It was generally believed by the officers, that if Nelson had not been wounded, not one of these ships could have escaped : the four certainly could not, if the *Culloden* had got into action : and if the frigates belonging to the squadron had been present, not one of the enemy's fleet would have left Aboukir Bay. These four vessels, however, were all that escaped; and the victory was the most complete and glorious in the annals of naval history. "Victory," said Nelson, "is not a name strong enough for such a scene"; he called it a conquest. Of thirteen sail of the line, nine were taken and two burnt: of the four frigates, one burnt, another sunk. The British loss in killed and wounded amounted to 895. Westcott was the only captain who fell. 3,105 of the French, including the wounded, were sent on shore by cartel: and 5,225 perished.

As soon as the conquest was completed, Nelson sent orders through the fleet, to return thanksgiving in every ship for the victory with which Almighty God had blessed His Majesty's arms. The French at Rosetta, who with miserable fear beheld the engagement, were at a loss to understand the stillness of the fleet during the performance of this solemn duty; but it seemed to affect many of the prisoners, officers as well as men: and graceless and godless as the officers were, some of them remarked, that it was no wonder such order was preserved in the British navy, when the minds of our men could be impressed with such sentiments after so great a victory, and at a moment of such confusion. The French at Rosetta seeing their four ships sail out of the bay unmolested, endeavoured persuade themselves that they were in possession of the place of battle. But it was in vain thus to attempt, against their own secret and certain conviction, to deceive themselves: and even if they could have succeeded in this, the bonfires which the Arabs kindled along the whole coast, and over the country, for three following nights, would soon have undeceived them. Thousands of Arabs and Egyptians lined the shore, and covered the house-tops during the action, rejoicing in the destruction which had overtaken their invaders. Long after the battle, innumerable bodies were seen floating about the bay, in spite of all the exertions which were made to sink them, as well from fear of pestilence as from the loathing and horror which the sight occasioned. The shore, for an extent of four leagues, was covered with wreck; and the Arabs found employment for many days in burning on the beach the fragments which were cast up, for the sake of the iron. Part of the *Orient's* main-mast was picked up by the *Swiftsure*. Captain Hallowell ordered his carpenter to make a coffin of it; the iron as well as wood was taken from the wreck of the same ship : it was finished as well and handsomely as the workman's skill and materials would permit; and Hallowell then sent it to the admiral with the following letter :—" Sir, I have taken the liberty of presenting you a coffin made from the mainmast of *l'Orient*, that when you have finished your military career in this world you may be buried in one of your trophies. But that that period may be far distant, is the earnest wish of your sincere friend, Benjamin Hallowell." An offering so strange, and yet so suited to the occasion, was received by Nelson in the spirit with which it was sent. As if he felt it good for him, now that he was at the summit of his wishes, to have death before his eyes, he ordered the coffin to be placed upright in his cabin. Such a piece of furni-ture, however, was more suitable to his own feelings than to those of his guests and attendants; and an old favourite servant entreated him so earnestly to let it be removed, that at length he consented to have the coffin carried below; but he gave strict orders that it should be safely stowed, and reserved for the purpose for which its brave and worthy donor had designed it.

The victory was complete; but Nelson could not pursue it as he would have done, for want of means. Had he been provided with small craft, nothing could have prevented the destruction of the storeships and transports in the port of Alexandria—four bomb-vessels would at that time have burnt the whole in a few hours. " Were I to die this moment," said he in his despatches to the Admiralty, " *want of frigates* would be found stamped on my heart ! No words of mine can express what I have suffered, and am suffering, for want of them." He had also to bear up against great bodily suffering : the blow had so shaken his head, that from its constant and violent aching, and the perpetual sickness which accompanied the pain, he could scarcely persuade himself that the skull was not fractured. Had it not been for Trowbridge, Ball, Hood, and Hallowell, he declared that he should have sunk under the fatigue of refitting the squadron. " All," he said, " had done well; but these officers were his supporters." But, amidst his sufferings and exertions, Nelson could yet think of all the consequences of his victory; and, that no advantage from it might be lost, he despatched an officer overland to India, with letters to the governor of Bombay, informing him of the arrival of the French in Egypt, the total destruction of their fleet, and the consequent preservation of India from any attempt against it on the part of this formidable armament. " He knew that Bombay," he said, " was their first object, if they could get there; but he trusted that Almighty God would overthrow in Egypt these pests of the human race. Buonaparte had never yet had to contend with an English officer, and he would endeavour to make him respect us." This despatch he sent upon his own responsibility, with letters of credit upon the East India Company, addressed to the British consuls, vice-consuls, and merchants on his route, Nelson saying, " that if he had done wrong, he hoped the bills would be paid, and he would repay the Company : for, as an Englishman, he should be proud that it had been in his power to put our settlements on their guard." The information which by this means reached India was of great importance. Orders had just been received for defensive preparations, upon a scale proportionate to the apprehended danger; and the extraordinary expenses, which would otherwise have been incurred, were thus prevented.

Nelson was now at the summit of glory : congratulations, rewards, and honours were showered upon him by all the states, and princes, and powers, to whom his victory gave a respite. The first communication of this nature which he received was from the Turkish Sultan, who, as soon as the invasion of Egypt was known, had called upon " all true believers to take arms against those swinish infidels the French, that they might deliver these blessed habitations from their accursed hands "; and who had ordered " his pashas to turn night into day in their efforts to take vengeance." The present of " His Imperial Majesty, the powerful, formidable, and most magnificent Grand Seignior," was a pelisse of sables, with broad sleeves, valued at five thousand dollars ; and a diamond aigrette, valued at eighteen thousand—the most honourable badge among the Turks, and in this instance more especially honourable, because it was taken from one of the royal turbans. " If it were worth a million," said Nelson to his wife, " my pleasure would be to see it in your possession." The Sultan also sent, in a spirit worthy of imitation, a purse of two thousand sequins to be distributed among the wounded. The mother of the Sultan sent him a box, set with diamonds, valued at one thousand pounds. The Czar Paul, in whom the better part of his strangely-compounded nature at this time predominated, presented him with his portrait set in diamonds, in a gold box, accompanied with a letter of congratulation written by his own hand. The King of Sardinia also wrote to him, and sent a gold box set with diamonds. Honours in profusion were awaiting him at Naples. In his own country the king granted these honourable augmentations to his armorial ensign : a chief undulated, *argent* ; thereon waves of the sea ; from which a palm-tree issuant, between a disabled ship on the dexter, and a ruinous battery on the sinister, all proper ; and for his crest, on a naval crown, *or*, the chelengk, or plume, presented to him by the Turk, with the motto, *Palman qui meruit ferat.*   And to his supporters, being a sailor on the dexter, and a lion on the sinister, were given these honourable augmentations : a palm branch in the sailor's hand, and another in the paw of the lion, both proper, with a tri-coloured flag and staff in the lion's mouth.   He was created Baron Nelson of the Nile, and of Burnham Thorpe, with a pension of £2,000 for his own life, and those of his two immediate successors.   When the grant was moved in the House of Commons, General Walpole expressed an opinion that a higher degree of rank ought to be conferred.   Mr. Pitt made answer that he thought it needless to enter into that question.   " Admiral Nelson's fame," he said, " would be co-equal with the British name, and it would be remembered that he had obtained the greatest naval victory on record : when no man would think of asking, Whether he had been created a baron, a viscount, or an earl? " It was strange that, in the very act of conferring a title, the minister should have excused himself for not having conferred a higher one, by representing all titles, on such an occasion, as nugatory and superfluous.   True, indeed, whatever title had been bestowed, whether viscount, earl, marquis, duke, or prince, if our laws had so permitted, he who received it would have been Nelson still.   That name he had ennobled beyond all addition of nobility : it was the name by which England loved him, France feared him, Italy, Egypt, and Turkey celebrated him, and by which he will continue to be known while the present kingdoms and languages of the world endure, and as long as their history after them shall be held in remembrance.   It depended upon the degree of rank what should be the fashion of his coronet, in what page of the red-book his name was to be inserted, and what precedency should be allowed his lady in the drawing-room and at the ball.   That Nelson's

honours were affected thus far, and no farther, might
be conceded to Mr. Pitt and his colleagues in administration : but the degree of rank which they thought
proper to allot was the measure of their gratitude,
though not of his services. This Nelson felt ; and this
he expressed with indignation among his friends.

Whatever may have been the motives of the ministry, and whatever the formalities with which they
excused their conduct to themselves, the importance
and magnitude of the victory were universally acknowledged. A grant of £10,000 was voted to
Nelson by the East India Company ; the Turkish Company presented him with a piece of plate ; the City of
London presented a sword to him, and to each of his
captains. Gold medals were distributed to the captains, and the first lieutenants of all the ships were
promoted, as had been done after Lord Howe's victory. Nelson was exceedingly anxious that the captain and first lieutenant of the *Culloden* should not be
passed over because of their misfortune. To Trowbridge himself he said, " Let us rejoice that the ship
which got on shore was commanded by an officer
whose character is so thoroughly established." To
the Admiralty he stated that Captain Trowbridge's
conduct was as fully entitled to praise as that of any
one officer in the squadron, and as highly deserving
of reward. " It was Trowbridge," said he, " who
equipped the squadron so soon at Syracuse ; it was
Trowbridge who exerted himself for me after the
action ; it was Trowbridge who saved the *Culloden*,
when none that I know in the service would have attempted it." The gold medal, therefore, by the
king's express desire, was given to Captain Trowbridge, " for his services both before and since, and
for the great and wonderful exertions which he made
at the time of the action, in saving and getting off
his ship." The private letter from the Admiralty to
Nelson informed him, that the first lieutenants of all
the ships *engaged* were to be promoted. Nelson in-

stantly wrote to the commander-in-chief. " I sincerely hope," said he, " this is not intended to exclude
the first lieutenant of the *Culloden*. For Heaven's
sake—for my sake—if it be so, get it altered. Our
dear friend Trowbridge has endured enough. His
sufferings were, in every respect, more than any of
us." To the Admiralty he wrote in terms equally
warm : " I hope, and believe, the word *engaged* is not
intended to exclude the *Culloden*. The merit of that
ship, and her gallant captain, are too well known to
benefit by anything I could say. Her misfortune was
great in getting aground, while her more fortunate
companions were in the full tide of happiness. No ;
I am confident that my good Lord Spencer will never
add misery to misfortune. Captain Trowbridge on
shore is superior to captains afloat : in the midst of his
great misfortunes he made those signals which prevented certainly the *Alexander* and *Swiftsure* from
running on the shoals. I beg your pardon for writing
on a subject which, I verily believe, has never entered
your Lordship's head ; but my heart, as it ought to
be, is warm to my gallant friends." Thus feelingly
alive was Nelson to the claims and interests and feelings of others. The Admiralty replied that the exception was necessary, as the ship had not been in action ;
but they desired the commander-in-chief to promote
the lieutenant upon the first vacancy which should
occur.

Nelson, in remembrance of an old and uninterrupted
friendship, appointed Alexander Davison sole prize
agent for the captured ships : upon which Davison
ordered medals to be struck in gold, for the captains ;
in silver, for the lieutenants and warrant officers ;
in gilt metal, for the petty officers ; and in copper,
for the seamen and marines. The cost of this act of
liberality amounted to nearly £2,000. It is worthy of
record on another account ;—for some of the gallant
men, who received no other honorary badge of their
conduct on that memorable day than this copper medal

from a private individual, years afterwards, when
they died upon a foreign station, made it their last
request that the medals might carefully be sent home
to their respective friends,—so sensible are brave men
of honour, in whatever rank they may be placed.

Three of the frigates, whose presence would have
been so essential a few weeks sooner, joined the
squadron on the twelfth day after the action. The
fourth joined a few days after them. Nelson thus received despatches which rendered it necessary for him
to return to Naples. Before he left Egypt he burnt
three of the prizes : they could not have been fitted
for a passage to Gibraltar in less than a month, and
that at a great expense, and with the loss of the service of at least two sail of the line. " I rest assured,"
he said to the Admiralty, " that they will be paid for,
and have held out that assurance to the squadron.
For if an admiral, after a victory, is to look after the
captured ships, and not to the distressing of the
enemy, very dearly, indeed, must the nation pay for
the prizes. I trust that £60,000 will be deemed a
very moderate sum for them; and when the services,
time, and men, with the expense of fitting the three
ships for a voyage to England, are considered,
Government will save nearly as much as they are
valued at. Paying for prizes," he continued, " is no
new idea of mine, and would often prove an amazing
saving to the state, even without taking into calculation what the nation loses by the attention of admirals
to the property of the captors,—an attention absolutely necessary, as a recompense for the exertions of
the officers and men. An admiral may be amply rewarded by his own feelings, and by the approbation
of his superiors; but what reward have the inferior
officers and men but the value of the prizes? If an
admiral takes that from them, on any consideration,
he cannot expect to be well supported." To Earl
St. Vincent he said, " If he could have been sure
that Government would have paid a reasonable value

for them, he would have ordered two of the other prizes to be burnt : for they would cost more in re-fitting, and by the loss of ships attending them, than they were worth."

Having sent the six remaining prizes forward under Sir James Saumarez, Nelson left Captain Hood, in the *Zealous*, off Alexandria, with the *Swiftsure*, *Goliath*, *Alcmene*, *Zealous*, and *Emerald*, and stood out to sea himself on the seventeenth day after the battle.

CHAPTER VI

NELSON'S health had suffered greatly while he was in the *Agamemnon*. "My complaint," he said, "is as if a girth were buckled taut over my breast; and my endeavour in the night is to get it loose." After the battle of Cape St. Vincent he felt a little rest to be so essential to his recovery, that he declared he could not continue to serve longer than the ensuing sum-mer, unless it should be absolutely necessary; for, in his own strong language, he had then been four years and nine months without one moment's repose for body or mind. A few months' intermission of labour he had obtained—not of rest, for it was purchased with the loss of a limb, and the greater part of the time had been a season of constant pain. As soon as his shattered frame had sufficiently recovered for him to resume his duties, he was called to services of greater importance than any on which he had hitherto been employed, and they brought with them com-mensurate fatigue and care. The anxiety which he endured, during his long pursuit of the enemy, was rather changed in its direction than abated by their defeat; and this constant wakefulness of thought, added to the effect of his wound, and the exertions from which it was not possible for one of so ardent and wide-reaching a mind to spare himself, nearly proved fatal. On his way back to Italy he was seized with fever. For eighteen hours his life was despaired of; and even when the disorder took a favourable turn, and he was so far recovered as again to appear on deck, he himself thought that his end was approaching,—such was the weakness to which the fever and cough had reduced him. Writing to Earl St. Vincent on the passage, he said to him, "I never expect, my dear lord, to see your face again. It may please God that this will be the finish to that fever of anxiety which I have endured from the middle of June; but be that as it pleases His goodness, I am resigned to His will."

The kindest attentions of the warmest friendship were awaiting him at Naples. "Come here," said Sir William Hamilton, "for God's sake, my dear friend, as soon as the service will permit you. A pleasant apartment is ready for you in my house, and Emma is looking out for the softest pillows to repose the few wearied limbs you have left." Happy would it have been for Nelson if warm and careful friendship had been all that awaited him there! He himself saw at that time the character of the Neapolitan court, as it first struck an Englishman, in its true light; and when he was on the way, he declared that he detested the voyage to Naples, and that nothing but necessity could have forced him to it. But never was any hero, on his return from victory, welcomed with more heartfelt joy. Before the battle of Aboukir the court of Naples had been trembling for its existence. The language which the Directory held towards it was well described by Sir William Hamilton, as being exactly the language of a highwayman. The Neapolitans were told that Benevento might be added to their dominions, provided they would pay a large sum, sufficient to satisfy the Directory; and they were warned, that if the proposal were refused, or even if there were any delay in accepting it, the French would

revolutionise all Italy. The joy, therefore, of the
court at Nelson's success, was in proportion to the
dismay from which that success relieved them. The
queen was a daughter of Maria Theresa, and sister of
Marie Antoinette. Had she been the wisest and
gentlest of her sex, it would not have been possible for
her to have regarded the French without hatred and
horror; and the progress of revolutionary opinions,
while it perpetually reminded her of her sister's fate,
excited no unreasonable apprehensions for her own.
Her feelings, naturally ardent, and little accustomed
to restraint, were excited to the highest pitch when
the news of the victory arrived. Lady Hamilton, her
constant friend and favourite, who was present, says,
" It is not possible to describe her transports; she
wept, she kissed her husband, her children, walked
frantically about the room, burst into tears again,
and again kissed and embraced every person near her,
exclaiming, ' O brave Nelson ! O God ! bless and protect our brave deliverer ! O Nelson ! Nelson ! what do
we not owe you ! O conqueror—saviour of Italy ! O
that my swollen heart could now tell him personally
what we owe to him ! ' '' She herself wrote to the
Neapolitan ambassador at London upon the occasion,
in terms which show the fulness of her joy, and the
height of the hopes which it had excited. " I wish
I could give wings," said she, " to the bearer of the
news, and, at the same time, to our most sincere
gratitude. The whole of the sea-coast of Italy is
saved ; and this is owing alone to the generous English. This battle, or, to speak more correctly, this
total defeat of the regicide squadron, was obtained by
the valour of this brave admiral, seconded by a navy
which is the terror of its enemies. The victory is so
complete that I can still scarcely believe it ; and if it
were not the brave English nation, which is accustomed to perform prodigies by sea, I could not persuade myself that it had happened. It would have
moved you to have seen all my children, boys and

girls, hanging on my neck, and crying for joy at the
happy news. Recommend the hero to his master; he
has filled the whole of Italy with admiration of the
English. Great hopes were entertained of some advantages being gained by his bravery, but no one
could look for so total a destruction. All here are
drunk with joy.''

Such being the feelings of the royal family, it may
well be supposed with what delight, and with what
honours, Nelson would be welcomed. Early on the
22nd of September, the poor wretched *Vanguard*, as
he called his shattered vessel, appeared in sight of
Naples. The *Culloden* and *Alexander* had preceded
her by some days, and given notice of her approach.
Many hundred boats and barges were ready to go
forth and meet him, with music and streamers and
every demonstration of joy and triumph. Sir William
and Lady Hamilton led the way in their state barge.
They had seen Nelson only for a few days four years
ago, but they then perceived in him that heroic spirit
which was now so fully and gloriously manifested to
the world. Emma, Lady Hamilton, who from this
time so greatly influenced his future life, was a woman
whose personal accomplishments have seldom been
equalled, and whose powers of mind were not less fascinating than her person. She was passionately attached to the queen; and by her influence the British
fleet had obtained those supplies at Syracuse, without
which, Nelson always asserted, the battle of Aboukir
could not have been fought. During the long interval
which passed before any tidings were received, her
anxiety had been hardly less than that of Nelson himself while pursuing an enemy of whom he could obtain
no information; and when the tidings were brought
her by a joyful bearer open-mouthed, its effect was
such that she fell like one who had been shot. She
and Sir William had literally been made ill by their
hopes and fears and joy at a catastrophe so far exceeding all that they had dared to hope for. Their

admiration for the hero necessarily produced a degree
of proportionate gratitude and affection; and when
their barge came alongside the *Vanguard*, at the sight
of Nelson, Lady Hamilton sprang up the ship's side,
and exclaiming " O God ! is it possible ! " fell into his
arms,—more, he says, like one dead than alive.   He
described the meeting as " terribly affecting." These
friends had scarcely recovered from their tears, when
the king, who went out to meet him three leagues in
the royal barge, came on board and took him by the
hand, calling him his deliverer and preserver; from
all the boats around he was saluted with the same
appellations; the multitude who surrounded him when
he landed repeated the same enthusiastic cries; and
the lazzaroni displayed their joy by holding up birds
in cages, and giving them their liberty as he passed.

His birthday, which occurred a week after his arrival, was celebrated with one of the most splendid
fêtes ever beheld at Naples.   But, notwithstanding
the splendour with which he was encircled, and the
flattering honours with which all ranks welcomed him,
Nelson was fully sensible of the depravity, as well as
weakness, of those by whom he was surrounded.
" What precious moments," said he, " the courts of
Naples and Vienna are losing !   Three months would
liberate Italy; but this court is so enervated that the
happy moment will be lost.   I am very unwell; and
their miserable conduct is not likely to cool my irritable temper.   It is a country of fiddlers and poets,
whores and scoundrels."   This sense of their ruinous
weakness he always retained; nor was he ever blind
to the mingled folly and treachery of the Neapolitan
ministers, and the complication of iniquities under
which the country groaned; but he insensibly, under
the influence of Lady Hamilton, formed an affection
for the court, to whose misgovernment the miserable
condition of the country was so greatly to be imputed.

The state of Naples may be described in few words.
The king was one of the Spanish Bourbons.   As the

Cæsars have shown us to what wickedness the moral
nature of princes may be perverted, so in this family,
the degradation to which their intellectual nature can
be reduced has been not less conspicuously evinced.
Ferdinand, like the rest of his race, was passionately
fond of field-sports, and cared for nothing else. His
queen had all the vices of the house of Austria, with
little to mitigate, and nothing to ennoble them;—provided she could have her pleasures, and the king his
sports, they cared not in what manner the revenue
was raised or administered. Of course a system of
favouritism existed at court, and the vilest and most
impudent corruption prevailed in every department of
state, and in every branch of administration, from the
highest to the lowest. It is only the institutions of
Christianity, and the vicinity of better regulated
states, which prevent kingdoms, under such circumstances of misrule, from sinking into a barbarism
like that of Turkey. A sense of better things was
kept alive in some of the Neapolitans by literature,
and by their intercourse with happier countries. These
persons naturally looked to France, at the commencement of the Revolution; and, during all the horrors of
that Revolution, still cherished a hope that, by the
aid of France, they might be enabled to establish a
new order of things in Naples. They were grievously
mistaken in supposing that the principles of liberty
would ever be supported by France, but they were
not mistaken in believing, that no government could
be worse than their own; and, therefore, they considered any change as desirable. In this opinion men
of the most different characters agreed. Many of the
nobles, who were not in favour, wished for a revolution, that they might obtain the ascendency to which
they thought themselves entitled: men of desperate
fortunes desired it, in the hope of enriching themselves; knaves and intriguers sold themselves to the
French, to promote it; and a few enlightened men,
and true lovers of their country, joined in the same

cause from the purest and noblest motives. All these were confounded under the common name of Jacobins; and the Jacobins of the Continental kingdoms were regarded by the English with more hatred than they deserved. They were classed with Philippe Egalité, Marat, and Hebert; whereas they deserved rather to be ranked, if not with Locke, and Sidney, and Russel, at least with Argyle and Monmouth, and those who, having the same object as the prime movers of our own revolution, failed in their premature, but not unworthy attempt.

No circumstances could be more unfavourable to the best interests of Europe than those which placed England in strict alliance with the superannuated and abominable governments of the Continent. The subjects of those governments who wished for freedom thus became enemies to England, and dupes and agents of France. They looked to their own grinding grievances, and did not see the danger with which the liberties of the world were threatened. England, on the other hand, saw the danger in its true magnitude, but was blind to these grievances, and found herself compelled to support systems which had formerly been equally the object of her abhorrence and her contempt. This was the state of Nelson's mind : he knew that there could be no peace for Europe till the pride of France was humbled and her strength broken; and he regarded all those who were the friends of France as traitors to the common cause, as well as to their own individual sovereigns. There are situations in which the most opposite and hostile parties may mean equally well, and yet act equally wrong. The court of Naples, unconscious of committing any crime by continuing the system of misrule to which they had succeeded, conceived that, in maintaining things as they were, they were maintaining their own rights, and preserving the people from such horrors as had been perpetrated in France. The Neapolitan revolutionists thought that without a

total change of system, any relief from the present
evils was impossible, and they believed themselves
justified in bringing about that change by any means.
Both parties knew that it was the fixed intention of
the French to revolutionise Naples. The revolutionists supposed that it was for the purpose of
establishing a free government: the court, and all
disinterested persons, were perfectly aware that
the enemy had no other object than conquest and
plunder.

The battle of the Nile shook the power of France.
Her most successful general and her finest army were
blocked up in Egypt, hopeless, as it appeared, of
return; and the government was in the hands of men
without talents, without character, and divided among
themselves. Austria, whom Buonaparte had terrified
into a peace at a time when constancy on her part
would probably have led to his destruction, took
advantage of the crisis to renew the war. Russia
also was preparing to enter the field with unbroken
forces; led by a general, whose extraordinary military genius would have entitled him to a high and
honourable rank in history, if it had not been sullied
by all the ferocity of a barbarian. Naples, seeing
its destruction at hand, and thinking that the only
means of averting it was by meeting the danger,
after long vacillations, which were produced by the
fears, and weakness, and treachery, of its council,
agreed at last to join this new coalition with a
numerical force of 80,000 men. Nelson told the king
in plain terms, that he had his choice, either to
advance, trusting to God for His blessing on a just
cause, and prepared to die sword in hand, or to
remain quiet and be kicked out of his kingdom;—
one of these things must happen. The king made
answer he would go on, and trust in God and Nelson;
and Nelson, who would else have returned to Egypt,
for the purpose of destroying the French shipping
in Alexandria, gave up his intention at the desire of

K 52

the Neapolitan court, and resolved to remain on that
station in the hope that he might be useful to the
movements of the army.   He suspected also, with
reason, that the continuance of his fleet was so
earnestly requested, because the royal family thought
their persons would be safer, in case of any mishap,
under the British flag than under their own.

His first object was the recovery of Malta, an
island which the King of Naples pretended to claim.
The Maltese, whom the villainous knights of their
order had betrayed to France, had taken up arms
against their rapacious invaders with a spirit and
unanimity worthy of the highest praise.   They
blockaded the French garrison by land, and a small
squadron, under Captain Ball, began to blockade them
by sea on the 12th of October.   Twelve days afterwards Nelson arrived, and the little island of Gozo,
dependent upon Malta, which had also been seized
and garrisoned by the French, capitulated soon after
his arrival, and was taken possession of by the British
in the name of His Sicilian Majesty,—a power who
had no better claim to it than France.   Having seen
this effected, and reinforced Captain Ball, he left that
able officer to perform a most arduous and important
part, and returned himself to co-operate with the
intended movements of the Neapolitans.

General Mack was at the head of the Neapolitan
troops;—all that is now doubtful concerning this
man is, whether he was a coward or a traitor;—at
that time he was assiduously extolled as a most consummate commander to whom Europe might look for
deliverance; and when he was introduced by the king
and queen to the British admiral, the queen said to
him, "Be to us by land, general, what my hero
Nelson has been by sea."   Mack, on his part, did
not fail to praise the force which he was appointed
to command: "It was," he said, "the finest army in
Europe."   Nelson agreed with him that there could
not be finer men; but when the general, at a review,

so directed the operations of a mock fight, that, by an unhappy blunder, his own troops were surrounded instead of those of the enemy, he turned to his friends and exclaimed, with bitterness, that the fellow did not understand his business. Another circumstance, not less characteristic, confirmed Nelson in this judgment. " General Mack," said he, in one of his letters, " cannot move without five carriages ! I have formed my opinion. I heartily pray I may be mistaken."

While Mack, at the head of 32,000 men, marched into the Roman state, 5,000 Neapolitans were embarked on board the British and Portuguese squadron, to take possession of Leghorn. This was effected without opposition; and the Grand Duke of Tuscany, whose neutrality had been so outrageously violated by the French, was better satisfied with the measure than some of the Neapolitans themselves. Naselli, their general, refused to seize the French vessels at Leghorn, because he, and the Duke di Sangro, who was ambassador at the Tuscan court, maintained that the King of Naples was not at war with France. " What ! " said Nelson, " has not the king received, as a conquest made by him, the republican flag taken at Gozo? Is not his own flag flying there and at Malta, not only by his permission, but by his order? Is not his flag shot at every day by the French, and their shot returned from batteries which bear that flag? Are not two frigates and a corvette placed under my orders, ready to fight the French, meet them where they may? Has not the king sent publicly from Naples guns, mortars, &c., with officers and artillery, against the French in Malta? If these acts are not tantamount to any written paper, I give up all knowledge of what is war." This reasoning was of less avail than an argument addressed to the general's fears. Nelson told him, that if he permitted the many hundred French who were then in the mole to remain neutral, till they had a fair opportunity of being active, they had one sure resource, if all other schemes failed, which was to set one vessel on fire; the mole would be destroyed, probably the town also, and the port ruined for twenty years. This representation made Naselli agree to the half measure of laying an embargo on the vessels. Among them were a great number of French privateers, some of which were of such force as to threaten the greatest mischief to our commerce, and about seventy sail of vessels belonging to the Ligurian Republic, as Genoa was now called, laden with corn, and ready to sail for Genoa and France, where their arrival would have expedited the entrance of more French troops into Italy. "The general," said Nelson, "saw, I believe, the consequence of permitting these vessels to depart, in the same light as myself; but there is this difference between us : he, prudently, and certainly safely, waits the orders of his court, taking no responsibility on himself. I act from the circumstances of the moment, as I feel may be most advantageous for the cause which I serve, taking all responsibility on myself." It was in vain to hope for anything vigorous or manly from such men as Nelson was compelled to act with. The crews of the French ships, and their allies, were ordered to depart in two days. Four days elapsed, and nobody obeyed the order; nor, in spite of the representations of the British minister, Mr. Windham, were any means taken to enforce it. The true Neapolitan shuffle, as Nelson called it, took place on all occasions. After an absence of ten days he returned to Naples, and receiving intelligence there, from Mr. Windham, that the privateers were at last to be disarmed, the corn landed, and the crews sent away, he expressed his satisfaction at the news in characteristic language, saying, "So far I am content. The enemy will be distressed; and, thank God, I shall get no money. The world, I know, think that money is our god; and now they will be undeceived, as far as relates to us. Down, down with the French! is my constant prayer."

Odes, sonnets, and congratulatory poems of every description, were poured in upon Nelson on his arrival at Naples. An Irish Franciscan, who was one of the poets, not being content with panegyric upon this occasion, ventured upon a flight of prophecy, and predicted that Lord Nelson would take Rome with his ships. His lordship reminded Father M'Cormick that ships could not ascend the Tiber; but the father, who had probably forgotten this circumstance, met the objection with a bold front, and declared he saw that it would come to pass notwithstanding. Rejoicings of this kind were of short duration. The King of Naples was with the army which had entered Rome; but the Castle of St. Angelo was held by the French, and 13,000 French were strongly posted in the Roman states at Castallana. Mack had marched against them with 20,000 men. Nelson saw that the event was doubtful, or rather, that there could be very little hope of the result. But the immediate fate of Naples, as he well knew, hung upon the issue. "If Mack is defeated," said he, "in fourteen days this country is lost; for the emperor has not yet moved his army, and Naples has not the power of resisting the enemy. It was not a case of choice, but of necessity, which induced the king to march out of his kingdom, and not wait till the French had collected a force sufficient to drive him out of it in a week." He had no reliance upon the Neapolitan officers, who, as he described them, seemed frightened at a drawn sword or a loaded gun; and he was perfectly aware of the consequences which the sluggish movements and deceitful policy of the Austrians were likely to bring down upon themselves, and all their Continental allies. "A delayed war, on the part of the emperor," said he, writing to the British minister at Vienna, "will be destructive to this monarchy of Naples, and, of course, to the newly

acquired dominions of the emperor in Italy. Had the
war commenced in September or October, all Italy
would, at this moment, have been liberated.   This
month is worse than the last : the next will render
the contest doubtful; and in six months, when the
Neapolitan Republic will be organised, armed, and
with its numerous resources called forth, the emperor
will not only be defeated in Italy, but will totter on
his throne at Vienna. *Down, down with the French !*
ought to be written in the council-room of every
country in the world; and may Almighty God give
right thoughts to every sovereign, is my constant
prayer.''   His perfect foresight of the immediate
event was clearly shown in this letter, when he desired
the ambassador to assure the empress (who was a
daughter of the house of Naples), that notwithstanding the councils which had shaken the throne of her
father and mother, he would remain there, ready to
save their persons, and her brothers and sisters; and
that he had also left ships at Leghorn, to save the
lives of the Grand Duke and her sister : '' For all,''
said he, '' must be a republic, if the emperor does
not act with expedition and vigour.''

His fears were soon verified.   '' The Neapolitan
officers,'' said Nelson, '' did not lose much honour,
for, God knows. they had not much to lose; but they
lost all they had.''   General St. Philip commanded
the right wing, of 19,000 men. He fell in with 3,000
of the enemy; and, as soon as he came near enough,
deserted to them. One of his men had virtue enough
to level a musket at him, and shot him through the
arm ; but the wound was not sufficient to prevent him
from joining with the French in pursuit of his own
countrymen. Cannon, tents, baggage, and military
chest, were all forsaken by the runaways, though they
lost only forty men ; for the French, having put them
to flight, and got possession of everything, did not
pursue an army of more than three times their own
number. The main body of the Neapolitans, under

Mack, did not behave better. The king returned to Naples, where every day brought with it the tidings of some new disgrace from the army, and the discovery of some new treachery at home; till, four days after his return, the general sent him advice that there was no prospect of stopping the progress of the enemy, and that the royal family must look to their own personal safety. The state of the public mind in Naples was such, at this time, that neither the British minister, nor the British admiral, thought it prudent to appear at court. Their motions were watched; and the revolutionists had even formed a plan for seizing and detaining them as hostages, to prevent any attack upon the city after the French should have taken possession of it. A letter which Nelson addressed at this time to the First Lord of the Admiralty shows in what manner he contemplated the possible issue of the storm. It was in these words :—" MY DEAR LORD,—There is an old saying, that when things are at the worst, they must mend. Now the mind of man cannot fancy things worse than they are here. But, thank God ! my health is better, my mind never firmer, and my heart in the right trim to comfort, relieve, and protect those whom it is my duty to afford assistance to. Pray, my lord, assure our gracious sovereign, that, while I live, I will support his glory; and that, if I fall, it shall be in a manner worthy of your lordship's faithful and obliged Nelson. I must not write more. Every word may be a text for a long letter."

Meantime Lady Hamilton arranged everything for the removal of the royal family. This was conducted, on her part, with the greatest address, and without suspicion, because she had been in habits of constant correspondence with the queen. It was known that the removal could not be effected without danger; for the mob, and especially the lazzaroni, were attached to the king; and as, at this time, they felt a natural presumption in their own numbers and strength, they insisted that he should not leave Naples. Several persons fell victims to their fury; among others was a messenger from Vienna, whose body was dragged under the windows of the palace in the king's sight. The king and queen spoke to the mob, and pacified them; but it would not have been safe, while they were in this agitated state, to have embarked the effects of the royal family openly. Lady Hamilton, like a heroine of modern romance, explored, with no little danger, a subterraneous passage, leading from the palace to the seaside; through this passage the royal treasure, the choicest pieces of painting and sculpture, and other property, to the amount of two millions and a half, were conveyed to the shore, and stowed safely on board the English ships. On the night of the 21st, at half-past eight, Nelson landed, brought out the whole royal family, embarked them in three barges, and carried them safely through a tremendous sea, to the *Vanguard*. Notice was then immediately given to the British merchants that they would be received on board any ship in the squadron. Their property had previously been embarked in transports. Two days were passed in the bay, for the purpose of taking such persons on board as required an asylum; and on the night of the 23rd the fleet sailed. The next day a more violent storm arose than Nelson had ever before encountered. On the 25th, the youngest of the princes was taken ill, and died in Lady Hamilton's arms. During this whole trying season Lady Hamilton waited upon the royal family with the zeal of the most devoted servant, at a time when, except one man, no person belonging to the court assisted them.

On the morning of the 26th the royal family were landed at Palermo. It was soon seen that their flight had not been premature. Prince Pignatelli, who had been left as vicar-general and viceroy, with orders to defend the kingdom to the last rock in Calabria, sent plenipotentiaries to the French camp before Capua;

and they, for the sake of saving the capital, signed
an armistice, by which the greater part of the kingdom was given up to the enemy : a cession that
necessarily led to the loss of the whole. This was on
the 10th of January. The French advanced toward
Naples. Mack, under pretext of taking shelter from
the fury of the lazzaroni, fled to the French general
Championet, who sent him under an escort to Milan ;
but as France hoped for further services from this
wretched traitor, it was thought prudent to treat him
apparently as a prisoner of war. The Neapolitan
army disappeared in a few days : of the men, some
following their officers, deserted to the enemy. The
greater part took the opportunity of disbanding themselves. The lazzaroni proved true to their country.
They attacked the enemy's advanced posts, drove
them in, and were not dispirited by the murderous
defeat which they suffered from the main body.
Flying into the city, they continued to defend it, even
after the French had planted their artillery in the
principal streets. Had there been a man of genius to
have directed their enthusiasm, or had there been any
correspondent feeling in the higher ranks, Naples
might have set a glorious example to Europe, and
have proved the grave of every Frenchman who
entered it. But the vices of the Government had
extinguished all other patriotism than that of a
rabble, who had no other virtue than that sort of
loyalty, which was like the fidelity of a dog to its
master. This fidelity the French and their adherents
counteracted by another kind of devotion. The
priests affirmed that St. Januarius had declared in
favour of the Revolution : the miracle of his blood
was performed with the usual success, and more than
usual effect, on the very evening when, after two
days of desperate fighting, the French obtained possession of Naples. A French guard of honour was
stationed at his church. Championet gave " respect
for St. Januarius " as the word for the army ; and the

next day *Te Deum* was sung by the archbishop in the cathedral, and the inhabitants were invited to attend the ceremony, and join in thanksgiving for the glorious entry of the French; who, it was said, being under the peculiar protection of Providence, had regenerated the Neapolitans, and were come to establish and consolidate their happiness.

It seems to have been Nelson's opinion, that the Austrian cabinet regarded the conquest of Naples with complacency, and that its measures were directed so as designedly not to prevent the French from overrunning it. That cabinet was assuredly capable of any folly and of any baseness; and it is not improbable that, at this time, calculating upon the success of the new coalition, it indulged a dream of adding extensively to its former Italian possessions, and therefore left the few remaining powers of Italy to be overthrown, as a means which would facilitate its own ambitious views. The King of Sardinia, finding it impossible longer to endure the exactions of France and the insults of the French commissary, went to Leghorn, embarked on board a Danish frigate, and sailed, under British protection, to Sardinia; that part of his dominions which the maritime supremacy of England rendered a secure asylum. On his arrival he published a protest against the conduct of France; declaring, upon the faith and word of a king, that he had never infringed, even in the slightest degree, the treaties which he had made with the French Republic. Tuscany was soon occupied by French troops,—a fate which bolder policy might, perhaps, have failed to avert, but which its weak and timid neutrality rendered inevitable. Nelson began to fear even for Sicily. " Oh, my dear sir !" said he, writing to Commodore Duckworth, " one thousand English troops would save Messina,—and I fear General Stuart cannot give me men to save this most important island ! " But his representations were not lost upon Sir Charles Stuart. This officer hastened immediately from Minorca, with a thousand men, assisted in the measures of defence which were taken, and did not return before he had satisfied himself that, if the Neapolitans were excluded from the management of affairs, and the spirit of the peasantry properly directed, Sicily was safe. Before his coming, Nelson had offered the king, if no resources should arrive, to defend Messina with the ship's company of an English man-of-war.

Russia had now entered into the war. Corfu surrendered to a Russian and Turkish fleet, acting now, for the first time, in strange confederacy, yet against a power which was certainly the common and worst enemy of both. Trowbridge, having given up the blockade of Alexandria to Sir Sidney Smith, rejoined Nelson, bringing with him a considerable addition of strength; and in himself, what Nelson valued more, a man upon whose sagacity, indefatigable zeal, and inexhaustible resources, he could place full reliance. Trowbridge was intrusted to commence the operations against the French in the Bay of Naples. Meantime Cardinal Ruffo, a man of questionable character, but of a temper fitted for such times, having landed in Calabria, raised what he called a Christian army, composed of the best and the vilest material: loyal peasants, enthusiastic priests and friars, galley slaves, the emptying of the jails, and banditti. The islands in the Bay of Naples were joyfully delivered up by the inhabitants, who were in a state of famine already from the effects of this baleful revolution. Trowbridge distributed among them all his flour; and Nelson pressed the Sicilian court incessantly for supplies, telling them that £100,000 given away in provisions would, at this time, purchase a kingdom. Money, he was told, they had not to give; and the wisdom and integrity which might have supplied its want were not to be found. "There is nothing," said he, "which I propose, that is not, as far as orders go, implicitly complied with; but the execution is dreadful and almost makes me mad. My desire to serve their Majesties faithfully, as is my duty, has been such that I am almost blind and worn-out, and cannot, in my present state, hold much longer."

Before any government can be overthrown by the consent of the people, the government must be intolerably oppressive, or the people thoroughly corrupted. Bad as the misrule at Naples had been, its consequences had been felt far less there than in Sicily; and the peasantry had that attachment to the soil which gives birth to so many of the noblest, as well as of the happiest, feelings. In all the islands the people were perfectly frantic with joy when they saw the Neapolitan colours hoisted. At Procida Trowbridge could not procure even a rag of the tri-coloured flag to lay at the king's feet;—it was rent into ten thousand pieces by the inhabitants, and entirely destroyed. "The horrid treatment of the French," he said, "had made them mad." It exasperated the ferocity of a character which neither the laws nor the religion under which they lived tended to mitigate. Their hatred was especially directed against the Neapolitan revolutionists;—and the fishermen, in concert among themselves, chose each his own victim, whom he would stiletto when the day of vengeance should arrive. The head of one was sent off one morning to Trowbridge, with his basket of grapes for breakfast; and a note from the Italian, who had, what he called, the glory of presenting it, saying he had killed the man as he was running away, and begging his Excellency to accept the head, and consider it as a proof of the writer's attachment to the crown. With the first successes of the court the work of punishment began. The judge at Ischia said it was necessary to have a bishop to degrade the traitorous priests before he could execute them; upon which Trowbridge advised him to hang them first, and send them to him afterwards, if he did not think that degradation sufficient. This was said with the straightforward feeling of a sailor, who cared as little for canon law as he knew about it; but when he discovered that the judge's orders were to go through the business in a summary manner, under his sanction, he told him at once that could not be, for the prisoners were not British subjects; and he declined to have anything to do with it. They were manifestly persons about the court who, while they thirsted for the pleasure of vengeance, were devising how to throw the odium of it upon the English. They wanted to employ an English man-of-war to carry the priests to Palermo, for degradation, and then bring them back for execution;—and they applied to Trowbridge for a hangman, which he indignantly refused. He, meantime, was almost heart-broken by the situation in which he found himself. He had promised relief to the islanders, relying upon the queen's promise to him. He had distributed the whole of his private stock,—there was plenty of grain at Palermo, and in its neighbourhood, and yet none was sent him; —the enemy, he complained, had more interest there than the king; and the distress for bread which he witnessed was such, he said, that it would move even a Frenchman to pity.

Nelson's mind was not in a happier state respecting public affairs. "As to politics," said he, "at this time they are my abomination : the ministers of kings and princes are as great scoundrels as ever lived. The brother of the emperor is just going to marry the great Something of Russia, and it is more than expected that a kingdom is to be found for him in Italy, and that the King of Naples will be sacrificed." Had there been a wise and manly spirit in the Italian states, or had the conduct of Austria been directed by anything like a principle of honour, a more favourable opportunity could not have been desired, for restoring order and prosperity in Europe, than the misconduct of the French Directory at this time afforded. But

Nelson saw selfishness and knavery wherever he looked; and even the pleasure of seeing a cause prosper, in which he was so zealously engaged, was poisoned by his sense of the rascality of those with whom he was compelled to act. At this juncture intelligence arrived that the French fleet had escaped from Brest, under cover of a fog, passed Cadiz, unseen by Lord Keith's squadron, in hazy weather, and entered the Mediterranean. It was said to consist of twenty-four sail of the line, six frigates, and three sloops. The object of the French was to liberate the Spanish fleet, form a junction with them, act against Minorca and Sicily, and overpower our naval force in the Mediterranean, by falling in with detached squadrons, and thus destroying it in detail. When they arrived off Carthagena, they requested the Spanish ships to make sail and join: but the Spaniards replied, they had not men to man them. To this it was answered, that the French had men enough on board for that purpose. But the Spaniards seem to have been apprehensive of delivering up their ships thus entirely into the power of such allies, and refused to come out. The fleet from Cadiz, however, consisting of from seventeen to twenty sail of the line, got out, under Masarredo, a man who then bore an honourable name, which he has since rendered infamous by betraying his country. They met with a violent storm off the coast of Oran, which dismasted many of their ships, and so effectually disabled them as to prevent the junction, and frustrate a well-planned expedition.

Before this occurred, and while the junction was as probable as it would have been formidable, Nelson was in a state of the greatest anxiety. "What a state am I in!" said he to Earl St. Vincent. "If I go, I risk, and more than risk, Sicily; for we know, from experience, that more depends upon opinion than upon acts themselves; and as I stay, my heart is breaking." His first business was to summon Trowbridge to join him with all the ships of the line under his command, and a frigate, if possible. Then hearing that the French had entered the Mediterranean, and expecting them at Palermo, where he had only his own ship—with that single ship he prepared to make all the resistance possible. Trowbridge having joined him, he left Captain E. J. Foote, of the *Seahorse*, to command the smaller vessels in the Bay of Naples, and sailed with six ships—one a Portuguese, and a Portuguese corvette—telling Earl St. Vincent that the squadron should never fall into the hands of the enemy : " And before we are destroyed," said he, " I have little doubt but they will have their wings so completely clipped that they may be easily overtaken." It was just at this time that he received from Captain Hallowell the present of the coffin. Such a present was regarded by the men with natural astonishment; one of his old shipmates in the *Agamemnon* said—" We shall have hot work of it indeed ! You see the admiral intends to fight till he is killed; and there is to be buried." Nelson placed it upright against the bulkhead of his cabin, behind his chair where he sat at dinner. The gift suited him at this time. It is said that he was disappointed in the stepson whom he had loved so dearly from his childhood, and who had saved his life at Teneriffe; and it is certain that he now formed an infatuated attachment for Lady Hamilton which totally weaned his affections from his wife. Farther than this, there is no reason to believe that this most unfortunate attachment was criminal :—but this was criminality enough, and it brought with it its punishment. Nelson was dissatisfied with himself ; and, therefore, weary of the world. This feeling he now frequently expressed. " There is no true happiness in this life," said he, "and in my present state I could quit it with a smile." And in a letter to his old friend Davison he said, " Believe me, my only wish is to sink with honour into the grave ; and when that shall please God, I shall meet death with a smile. Not that I am insensible to the honours and riches my king and country have heaped upon me,—so much more than any officer could deserve; yet am I ready to quit this world of trouble, and envy none but those of the estate six feet by two."

Well had it been for Nelson if he had made no other sacrifices to this unhappy attachment than his peace of mind; but it led to the only blot upon his public character. While he sailed from Palermo, with the intention of collecting his whole force, and keeping off Maretimo, either to receive reinforcements there, if the French were bound upwards, or to hasten to Minorca, if that should be their destination, Captain Foote, in the *Seahorse*, with the Neapolitan frigates and some small vessels, under his command, was left to act with a land force, consisting of a few regular troops, of four different nations, and with the armed rabble which Cardinal Ruffo called the Christian army. His directions were to co-operate to the utmost of his power with the royalists, at whose head Ruffo had been placed, and he had no other instructions whatever. Ruffo advancing, without any plan, but relying upon the enemy's want of numbers, which prevented them from attempting to act upon the offensive, and ready to take advantage of any accident which might occur, approached Naples. Fort St. Elmo, which commands the town, was wholly garrisoned by French troops; the castles of Uovo and Nuovo, which commanded the anchorage, were chiefly defended by Neapolitan revolutionists, the powerful men among them having taken shelter there. If these castles were taken, the reduction of Fort St. Elmo would be greatly expedited. They were strong places, and there was reason to apprehend that the French fleet might arrive to relieve them. Ruffo proposed to the garrison to capitulate, on condition that their persons and property should be guaranteed, and that they should, at their own option, either be sent to Toulon, or remain at Naples, without being molested either in their persons or families. This capitulation was accepted : it was signed by the cardinal, and the Russian and Turkish commanders, and lastly, by Captain Foote, as commander of the British force. About six-and-thirty hours afterwards Nelson arrived in the bay, with a force, which had joined him during his cruise, consisting of seventeen sail of the line, with 1,700 troops on board, and the Prince Royal of Naples in the admiral's ship. A flag of truce was flying on the castles, and on board the *Seahorse*. Nelson made a signal to annul the treaty; declaring that he would grant rebels no other terms than those of unconditional submission. The cardinal objected to this : nor could all the arguments of Nelson, Sir W. Hamilton, and Lady Hamilton, who took an active part in the conference, convince him that a treaty of such a nature, solemnly concluded, could honourably be set aside. He retired at last, silenced by Nelson's authority, but not convinced. Captain Foote was sent out of the bay; and the garrisons, taken out of the castles, under pretence of carrying the treaty into effect, were delivered over as rebels to the vengeance of the Sicilian court.—A deplorable transaction ! A stain upon the memory of Nelson, and the honour of England ! To palliate it would be in vain ; to justify it would be wicked : there is no alternative, for one who will not make himself a participator in guilt, but to record the disgraceful story with sorrow and with shame.

Prince Francesco Caraccioli, a younger branch of one of the noblest Neapolitan families, escaped from one of these castles before it capitulated. He was at the head of the marine, and was nearly seventy years of age, bearing a high character, both for professional and personal merit. He had accompanied the Court to Sicily ; but when the revolutionary government, or Parthenopæan Republic, as it was called, issued an edict, ordering all absent Neapolitans to return, on pain of confiscation of their property, he solicited and obtained permission of the king to return, his estates being very great. It is said that the king, when he granted him this permission, warned him not to take any part in politics; expressing, at the same time, his own persuasion that he should recover his kingdom. But neither the king, nor he himself, ought to have imagined that, in such times, a man of such reputation would be permitted to remain inactive; and it soon appeared that Caraccioli was again in command of the navy, and serving under the republic against his late sovereign. The sailors reported that he was forced to act thus : and this was believed, till it was seen that he directed ably the offensive operations of the revolutionists, and did not avail himself of opportunities for escaping when they offered. When the recovery of Naples was evidently near, he applied to Cardinal Ruffo, and to the Duke of Calvirrano, for protection; expressing his hope that the few days during which he had been forced to obey the French, would not outweigh forty years of faithful services:—but, perhaps not receiving such assurances as he wished, and knowing too well the temper of the Sicilian court, he endeavoured to secrete himself, and a price was set upon his head. More unfortunately for others than for himself, he was brought in alive, having been discovered in the disguise of a peasant, and carried one morning on board Lord Nelson's ship, with his hands tied behind him.

Caraccioli was well known to the British officers, and had been ever highly esteemed by all who knew him. Captain Hardy ordered him immediately to be unbound, and to be treated with all those attentions which he felt due to a man who, when last on board the *Foudroyant*, had been received as an admiral and a prince. Sir William and Lady Hamilton were in the ship; but Nelson, it is affirmed, saw no one, except his own officers, during the tragedy which ensued. His own determination was made; and he issued an order to the Neapolitan commodore, Count Thurn, to

assemble a court-martial of Neapolitan officers, on
board the British flag-ship, proceed immediately to try
the prisoner, and report to him, if the charges were
proved, what punishment he ought to suffer. These
proceedings were as rapid as possible : Caraccioli was
brought on board at nine in the forenoon, and the
trial began at ten. It lasted two hours : he averred
in his defence that he had acted under compulsion,
having been compelled to serve as a common soldier,
till he consented to take command of the fleet. This,
the apologists of Lord Nelson say, he failed in proving. They forget that the possibility of proving it was
not allowed him ; for he was brought to trial within an
hour after he was legally in arrest ; and how, in that
time, was he to collect his witnesses? He was found
guilty, and sentenced to death ; and Nelson gave
orders that the sentence should be carried into effect
that evening, at five o'clock, on board the Sicilian
frigate, *La Minerva*, by hanging him at the fore-yard-
arm till sunset ; when the body was to be cut down
and thrown into the sea. Caraccioli requested Lieutenant Parkinson, under whose custody he was placed,
to intercede with Lord Nelson for a second trial,—for
this, among other reasons, that Count Thurn, who
presided at the court-martial, was notoriously his personal enemy. Nelson made answer, that the prisoner
had been fairly tried by the officers of his own country,
and he could not interfere : forgetting that, if he felt
himself justified in ordering the trial and the execution, no human being could ever have questioned the
propriety of his interfering on the side of mercy.
Caraccioli then entreated that he might be shot. " I
am an old man, sir," said he ; " I leave no family
to lament me, and therefore cannot be supposed to be
very anxious about prolonging my life ; but the disgrace of being hanged is dreadful to me." When this
was repeated to Nelson, he only told the lieutenant,
with much agitation, to go and attend his duty. As a
last hope, Caraccioli asked the lieutenant if he thought

an application to Lady Hamilton would be beneficial;
Parkinson went to seek her : she was not to be seen
on this occasion,—but she was present at the execution. She had the most devoted attachment to the
Neapolitan court; and the hatred which she felt
against those whom she regarded as its enemies
made her, at this time, forget what was due to the
character of her sex, as well as of her country. Here,
also, a faithful historian is called upon to pronounce
a severe and unqualified condemnation of Nelson's
conduct. Had he the authority of His Sicilian
Majesty for proceeding as he did? If so, why was
not that authority produced? If not, why were the
proceedings hurried on without it? Why was the
trial precipitated, so that it was impossible for the
prisoner, if he had been innocent, to provide the witnesses who might have proved him so? Why was a
second trial refused, when the known animosity of the
president of the court against the prisoner was considered? Why was the execution hastened so as to
preclude any appeal for mercy, and render the pre-
rogative of mercy useless?—Doubtless the British admiral seemed to himself to be acting under a rigid
sense of justice; but to all other persons it was
obvious that he was influenced by an infatuated attachment,—a baneful passion, which destroyed his
domestic happiness, and now, in a second instance,
stained ineffaceably his public character.

The body was carried out to a considerable distance, and sunk in the bay, with three double-headed
shot, weighing 250 pounds, tied to its legs. Between
two and three weeks afterwards, when the king was
on board the *Foudroyant*, a Neapolitan fisherman
came to the ship and solemnly declared that Caraccioli
had risen from the bottom of the sea, and was coming
as fast as he could to Naples, swimming half out of
the water. Such an account was listened to like a
tale of idle credulity. The day being fair, Nelson, to
please the king, stood out to sea; but the ship had

not proceeded far before a body was distinctly seen, upright in the water, and approaching them. It was soon recognised to be, indeed, the corpse of Caraccioli, which had risen, and floated, while the great weights attached to the legs kept the body in a position like that of a living man. A fact so extraordinary astonished the king, and perhaps excited some feelings of superstitious fear, akin to regret. He gave permission for the body to be taken on shore, and receive Christian burial. It produced no better effect. Naples exhibited more dreadful scenes than it had witnessed in the days of Massaniello. After the mob had had their fill of blood and plunder, the reins were given to justice;—if that can be called justice which annuls its own stipulations, looks to the naked facts alone, disregarding all motives and all circumstances; and, without considering character, or science, or sex, or youth, sacrifices its victims, not for the public weal, but for the gratification of greedy vengeance.

The Castles of St. Elmo, Gaieta, and Capua, remained to be subdued. On the land side there was no danger that the French in these garrisons should be relieved, for Suvorof was now beginning to drive the enemy before him; but Nelson thought his presence necessary in the Bay of Naples: and when Lord Keith, having received intelligence that the French and Spanish fleets had formed a junction, and sailed for Carthagena, ordered him to repair to Minorca, with the whole, or the greater part, of his force, he sent Admiral Duckworth with a small part only. This was a dilemma which he had foreseen. "Should such an order come at this moment," he said, in a letter previously written to the Admiralty, "it would be a case for some consideration, whether Minorca is to be risked, or the two kingdoms of Naples and Sicily. I rather think my decision would be to risk the former." And, after he had acted upon this opinion, he wrote in these terms to the Duke of

Clarence, with whose high notions of obedience he was well acquainted : "I am well aware of the consequences of disobeying my orders; but as I have often before risked my life for the good cause, so I, with cheerfulness, did my commission; for, although a military tribunal may think me criminal, the world will approve of my conduct : and I regard not my own safety when the honour of my king is at stake."

Nelson was right in his judgment; no attempt was made upon Minorca; and the expulsion of the French from Naples may rather be said to have been effected, than accelerated, by the English and Portuguese of the allied fleet, acting upon shore, under Trowbridge. The French commandant at St. Elmo, relying upon the strength of the place, and the nature of the force which attacked it, had insulted Captain Foote in the grossest terms; but *citoyen* Mejan was soon taught better manners, when Trowbridge, in spite of every obstacle, opened five batteries upon the fort. He was informed that none of his letters, with the insolent printed words at the top, *Liberté, Egalité, Guerre aux Tyrans,* &c., would be received; but that, if he wrote like a soldier and a gentleman, he should be answered in the same style. The Frenchman then began to flatter his antagonist upon the *bienfaisance* and *humanité*, which were the least of the many virtues which distinguished Monsieur Trowbridge. Monsieur Trowbridge's *bienfaisance* was, at this time, thinking of mining the fort. " If we can accomplish that," said he, " I am a strong advocate to send them, hostages and all, to Old Nick, and surprise him with a group of nobility and republicans. Meantime," he added, "it was some satisfaction to perceive that the shells fell well, and broke some of their shins." Finally, to complete his character, Mejan offered to surrender for 150,000 ducats. Great Britain, perhaps, has made too little use of this kind of artillery, which France has found so effectual towards subjugating the Continent : but Trowbridge had the prey within

his reach; and, in the course of a few days, his last
battery, " after much trouble and palaver," as he
said, " brought the vagabonds to their senses."

Trowbridge had more difficulties to overcome in
this siege, from the character of the Neapolitans who
pretended to assist him, and whom he made useful,
than even from the strength of the place and the skill
of the French. " Such damned cowards and
villains," he declared, " he had never seen before."
The men at the advanced posts carried on, what he
called, " a diabolical good understanding " with the
enemy, and the workmen would sometimes take fright
and run away. " I make the best I can," said he,
" of the degenerate race I have to deal with : the
whole means of guns, ammunition, pioneers, &c.,
with all materials, rest with them. With fair
promises to the men, and threats of instant death if
I find any one erring, a little spur has been given."
Nelson said of him, with truth, upon this occasion,
that he was a first-rate general. " I find, sir," said
he afterwards, in a letter to the Duke of Clarence,
" that General Koehler does not approve of such
irregular proceedings as naval officers attacking and
defending fortifications. We have but one idea,—to
get close alongside. None but a sailor would have
placed a battery only 180 yards from the Castle of St.
Elmo : a soldier must have gone according to art,
and the ～～～ way. My brave Trowbridge went
straight on, for we had no time to spare."

Trowbridge then proceeded to Capua, and took the
command of the motley besieging force. One
thousand of the best men in the fleet were sent to
assist in the siege. Just at this time Nelson received
a peremptory order from Lord Keith to sail with the
whole of his force for the protection of Minorca; or,
at least, to retain no more than was absolutely necessary at Sicily. " You will easily conceive my feelings," said he, in communicating this to Earl St.
Vincent : " but my mind, as your lordship knows,

was perfectly prepared for this order; and it is now, more than ever, made up. At this moment I will not part with a single ship; as I cannot do that without drawing a hundred and twenty men from each ship, now at the siege of Capua. I am fully aware of the act I have committed; but I am prepared for any fate which may await my disobedience. Capua and Gaieta will soon fall; and the moment the scoundrels of French are out of this kingdom I shall send eight or nine ships of the line to Minorca. I have done what I thought right: others may think differently: but it will be my consolation that I have gained a kingdom, seated a faithful ally of His Majesty firmly on his throne, and restored happiness to millions."

At Capua Trowbridge had the same difficulties as at St. Elmo; and being farther from Naples, and from the fleet, was less able to overcome them. The powder was so bad that he suspected treachery; and when he asked Nelson to spare him forty casks from the ships, he told him it would be necessary that some Englishmen should accompany it, or they would steal one half, and change the other. "Every man you see," said he, "gentle and simple, are such notorious villains, that it is misery to be with them." Capua, however, soon fell. Gaieta immediately afterwards surrendered to Captain Louis, of the *Minotaur.* Here the commanding officer acted more unlike a Frenchman, Captain Louis said, than any one he had ever met; meaning, that he acted like a man of honour. He required, however, that the garrison should carry away their horses and other pillaged property, to which Nelson replied, "that no property which they did not bring with them into the country could be theirs, and that the greatest care should be taken to prevent them from carrying it away." "I am sorry," said he to Captain Louis, "that you have entered into any altercation. There is no way of dealing with a Frenchman but to knock him down—to be civil to them is only to be laughed at, when they are enemies."

The whole kingdom of Naples was thus delivered by Nelson from the French. The Admiralty, however, thought it expedient to censure him for disobeying Lord Keith's orders, and thus hazarding Minorca, without, as it appeared to them, any sufficient reason; and also for having landed seamen for the siege of Capua, to form part of an army employed in operations at a distance from the coast, where, in case of defeat, they might have been prevented from returning to their ships; and they enjoined him "not to employ the seamen in like manner in future." This reprimand was issued before the event was known: though, indeed, the event would not affect the principle upon which it proceeded. When Nelson communicated the tidings of his complete success, he said, in his public letter, "that it would not be the less acceptable for having been principally brought about by British sailors." His judgment in thus employing them had been justified by the result; and his joy was evidently heightened by the gratification of a professional and becoming pride. To the First Lord he said, at the same time, "I certainly, from having only a left hand, cannot enter into details which may explain the motives that actuated my conduct. My principle is, to assist in driving the French to the devil, and in restoring peace and happiness to mankind. I feel that I am fitter to do the action than to describe it." He then added, that he would take care of Minorca.

In expelling the French from Naples, Nelson had, with characteristic zeal and ability, discharged his duty; but he deceived himself when he imagined that he had seated Ferdinand firmly on his throne, and that he had restored happiness to millions. These objects might have been accomplished if it had been possible to inspire virtue and wisdom into a vicious and infatuated court; and if Nelson's eyes had not

been, as it were, spellbound by that unhappy attachment which had now completely mastered him, he
would have seen things as they were; and might,
perhaps, have awakened the Sicilian court to a sense
of their interest, if not of their duty.   That court
employed itself in a miserable round of folly and
festivity, while the prisons of Naples were filled with
groans, and the scaffolds streamed with blood.   St.
Januarius was solemnly removed from his rank as
patron saint of the kingdom, having been convicted
of Jacobinism, and St. Antonio as solemnly installed
in his place.   The king, instead of re-establishing
order at Naples by his presence, speedily returned to
Palermo to indulge in his favourite amusements.
Nelson and the ambassador's family accompanied the
court, and Trowbridge remained, groaning over the
villainy and frivolity of those with whom he was compelled to deal.   A party of officers applied to him for
a passage to Palermo, to see the procession of St.
Rosalia :—he recommended them to exercise their
troops, and not behave like children.   It was grief
enough for him that the court should be busied in
these follies, and Nelson involved in them.   " I dread,
my lord," said he, " all the feasting, &c., at Palermo.
I am sure your health will be hurt.   If so, all their
saints will be damned by the navy.   The king would
be better employed digesting a good government.
Everything gives way to their pleasures.   The money
spent at Palermo gives discontent here : fifty thousand
people are unemployed, trade discouraged, manu-
factures at a stand.   It is the interest of many here
to keep the king away;—they all dread reform :—
their villainies are so deeply rooted, that, if some
method is not taken to dig them out, this Government cannot hold together.   Out of twenty millions
of ducats collected as the revenue, only thirteen
millions reach the treasury, and the king pays four
ducats where he should pay one.   He is surrounded
by thieves ; and none of them have honour or honesty

enough to tell him the real and true state of things."
In another letter he expressed his sense of the miserable state of Naples. "There are upwards of forty
thousand families," said he, "who have relations
confined. If some act of oblivion is not passed, there
will be no end of persecution; for the people of this
country have no idea of anything but revenge; and
to gain a point, would swear ten thousand false
oaths. Constant efforts are made to get a man taken
up in order to rob him. The confiscated property
does not reach the king's treasury.—All thieves! It
is selling for nothing. His own people, whom he
employs, are buying it up, and the vagabonds pocket
the whole. I should not be surprised to hear that
they brought a bill of expenses against him for the
sale."

The Sicilian court, however, were at this time duly
sensible of the services which had been rendered
them by the British fleet, and their gratitude to Nelson was shown with proper and princely munificence.
They gave him the dukedom and domain of Bronté,
worth about £3,000 a year. It was some days before
he could be persuaded to accept it: the argument
which finally prevailed is said to have been suggested
by the queen, and urged, at her request, by Lady
Hamilton upon her knees. "He considered his own
honour too much," she said, "if he persisted in
refusing what the king and queen felt to be absolutely necessary for the preservation of theirs." The
king himself also is said to have addressed him in
words which show that the sense of rank will sometimes confer a virtue upon those who seem to be most
unworthy of the lot to which they have been born:—
"Lord Nelson, do you wish that your name alone
should pass with honour to posterity; and that I,
Ferdinand Bourbon, should appear ungrateful?" He
gave him also, when the dukedom was accepted, a
diamond-hilted sword, which his father, Charles III.
of Spain, had given him on his accession to the throne

of the Two Sicilies. Nelson said, "The reward was magnificent, and worthy of a king, and he was determined that the inhabitants on the domain should be the happiest in all His Sicilian Majesty's dominions. Yet," said he, speaking of these, and the other remunerations which were made him for his services, "these presents, rich as they are, do not elevate me. My pride is, that at Constantinople, from the Grand Seignior to the lowest Turk, the name of Nelson is familiar in their mouths; and in this country I am everything which a grateful monarch and people can call me." Nelson, however, had a pardonable pride in the outward and visible signs of honour which he had so fairly won; he was fond of his Sicilian title; the signification, perhaps, pleased him. Duke of Thunder was what in Dahomey would be called a *strong name*; it was to a sailor's taste; and certainly, to no man could it ever be more applicable. But a simple offering, which he received, not long afterwards, from the island of Zante, affected him with a deeper and finer feeling. The Greeks of that little community sent him a golden-headed sword, and a truncheon, set round with all the diamonds that the island could furnish, in a single row. They thanked him "for having, by his victory, preserved that part of Greece from the horrors of anarchy; and prayed that his exploits might accelerate the day, in which, amidst the glory and peace of thrones, the miseries of the human race would cease." This unexpected tribute touched Nelson to the heart. "No officer," he said, "had ever received from any country a higher acknowledgment of his services."

The French still occupied the Roman states; from which, according to their own admission, they had extorted, in jewels, plate, specie, and requisitions of every kind, to the enormous amount of eight millions sterling : yet they affected to appear as deliverers among the people whom they were thus cruelly plundering; and they distributed portraits of Buonaparte, with the blasphemous inscription—" This is the true likeness of the holy saviour of the world! " The people, detesting the impiety, and groaning beneath the exactions of these perfidious robbers, were ready to join any regular force that should come to their assistance; but they dreaded Cardinal Ruffo's rabble, and declared they would resist them as banditti, who came only for the purpose of pillage. Nelson perceived that no object was now so essential for the tranquillity of Naples as the recovery of Rome, which, in the present state of things, when Suvorof was driving the French before him, would complete the deliverance of Italy. He applied, therefore, to Sir James St. Clair Erskine, who, in the absence of General Fox, commanded at Minorca, to assist in this great object with 1,200 men. " The field of glory," said he, " is a large one, and was never more open to any one, than at this moment to you. Rome would throw open her gates, and receive you as her deliverer; and the Pope would owe his restoration to a heretic." But Sir James Erskine looked only at the difficulties of the undertaking. " Twelve hundred men, he thought, would be too small a force to be committed in such an enterprise; for Civita Vecchia was a regular fortress;—the local situation and climate also were such, that, even if this force were adequate, it would be proper to delay the expedition till October. General Fox, too, was soon expected; and during his absence, and under existing circumstances, he did not feel justified in sending away such a detachment."

What this general thought it imprudent to attempt, Nelson and Trowbridge effected without his assistance by a small detachment from the fleet. Trowbridge first sent Captain Hallowell to Civita Vecchia, to offer the garrison there, and at Castle St. Angelo, the same terms which had been granted to Gaieta. Hallowell perceived, by the overstrained civility of the officers who came off to him, and the compliments which they paid to the English nation, that they were sensible of their own weakness, and their inability to offer any effectual resistance; but the French know, that while they are in a condition to serve their Government, they can rely upon it for every possible exertion in their support; and this reliance gives them hope and confidence to the last. Upon Hallowell's report, Trowbridge, who had now been made Sir Thomas for his services, sent Captain Louis with a squadron, to enforce the terms which he had offered; and, as soon as he could leave Naples, he himself followed. The French, who had no longer any hope from the fate of arms, relied upon their skill in negotiation, and proposed terms to Trowbridge with that effrontery which characterises their public proceedings, but which is often as successful as it is impudent. They had a man of the right stamp to deal with. Their ambassador at Rome began by saying that the Roman territory was the property of the French by right of conquest. The British commodore settled that point by replying, " It is mine by reconquest." A capitulation was soon concluded for all the Roman states, and Captain Louis rowed up the Tiber in his barge, hoisted English colours on the Capitol, and acted, for the time, as governor of Rome. The prophecy of the Irish poet was thus accomplished, and the friar reaped the fruits : for Nelson, who was struck with the oddity of the circumstance, and not a little pleased with it, obtained preferment for him from the King of Sicily, and recommended him to the Pope.

Having thus completed his work upon the continent of Italy, Nelson's whole attention was directed towards Malta, where Captain Ball, with most inadequate means, was besieging the French garrison. Never was any officer engaged in a more anxious and painful service : the smallest reinforcements from France would, at any moment, have turned the scale against him : and had it not been for his consummate ability, and the love and veneration with which the Maltese regarded him, Malta must have remained in the hands of the enemy. Men, money, food,—all things were wanting. The garrison consisted of five thousand troops—the besieging force of five hundred English and Portuguese marines, and about fifteen hundred armed peasants. Long and repeatedly did Nelson solicit troops to effect the reduction of this important place. " It has been no fault of the navy," said he, " that Malta has not been attacked by land; but we have neither the means ourselves nor influence with those who have." The same causes of demurral existed which prevented British troops from assisting in the expulsion of the French from Rome. Sir James Erskine was expecting General Fox, he could not act without orders; and not having, like Nelson, that lively spring of hope within him, which partakes enough of the nature of faith to work miracles in war, he thought it " evident, that unless a respectable land force, in numbers sufficient to undertake the siege of such a garrison in one of the strongest places of Europe, and supplied with proportionate artillery and stores, were sent against it, no reasonable hope could be entertained of its surrender." Nelson groaned over the spirit of over-reasoning caution, and unreasoning obedience. " My heart," said he, " is almost broken. If the enemy get supplies in, we may bid adieu to Malta :—all the force we can collect would then be of little use against the strongest place in Europe. To say that an officer is never, for any object, to alter his orders, is what I cannot comprehend. The circumstances of this war so often vary, that an officer has almost every moment to consider, what would my superiors direct did they know what is passing under my nose? But, sir," said he, writing to the Duke of Clarence, " I find few think as I do. To obey orders is all perfection. To serve my king and destroy the French, I consider as the great order of all, from which little ones spring ;

and if one of these militate against it (for who can tell
exactly at a distance?), I go back, and obey the great
order and object, to down—down with the damned
French villains !   My blood boils at the name of a
Frenchman ! "

At length General Fox arrived at Minorca,—and,
at length, permitted Colonel Graham to go to Malta,
but with means miserably limited.   In fact, the expedition was at a stand for want of money; when
Trowbridge, arriving at Messina to co-operate in it,
and finding this fresh delay, immediately offered all
that he could command of his own.   " I procured
him, my lord," said he to Nelson, " fifteen thousand
of my cobs :—every farthing, and every atom of me,
shall be devoted to the cause."   " What can this
mean? " said Nelson, when he learnt that Colonel
Graham was ordered not to incur any expense for
stores, or any articles except provisions :—" the cause
cannot stand still for want of a little money.   If nobody will pay it, I will sell Bronté, and the Emperor
of Russia's box."   And he actually pledged Bronté
for £6,600, if there should be any difficulty about
paying the bills.   The long-delayed expedition was
thus, at last, sent forth—but Trowbridge little
imagined in what scenes of misery he was to bear his
part.   He looked to Sicily for supplies; it was the
interest, as well as the duty, of the Sicilian Government to use every exertion for furnishing them; and
Nelson and the British ambassador were on the spot
to press upon them the necessity of exertion.   But,
though Nelson saw with what a knavish crew the
Sicilian court was surrounded, he was blind to the
vices of the court itself; and resigning himself wholly
to Lady Hamilton's influence, never even suspected
the crooked policy which it was remorselessly pursuing.   The Maltese, and the British in Malta,
severely felt it.   Trowbridge, who had the truest
affection for Nelson, knew his infatuation, and feared
that it might prove injurious to his character, as

well as fatal to an enterprise which had been begun so well, and carried on so patiently. " My lord," said he, writing to him from the siege, " we are dying off fast for want. I learn that Sir William Hamilton says Prince Luzzi refused corn some time ago, and Sir William does not think it worth while making another application. If that be the case, I wish he commanded at this distressing scene, instead of me. Puglia had an immense harvest : near thirty sail left Messina, before I did, to load corn. Will they let us have any? If not, a short time will decide the business. The German interest prevails. I wish I was at your lordship's elbow for an hour. *All, all*, will be thrown on you ! I will parry the blow as much as in my power : I foresee much mischief brewing. God bless your lordship ! I am miserable, I cannot assist your operations more. Many happy returns of this day to you—(it was the first of the new year)—I never spent so miserable a one. I am not very tender-hearted; but really the distress here would even move a Neapolitan." Soon afterwards he wrote : " I have this day saved thirty thousand people from starving; but with this day my ability ceases. As the Government are bent on starving us, I see no alternative but to leave these poor unhappy people to perish, without our being witnesses to their distress. I curse the day I ever served the Neapolitan Government. We have characters, my lord, to lose : these people have none. Do not suffer their infamous conduct to fall on us. Our country is just, but severe. Such is the fever of my brain this minute, that I assure you, on my honour, if the Palermo traitors were here, I would shoot them first, and then myself. Girgenti is full of corn; the money is ready to pay for it; we do not ask it as a gift. Oh ! could you see the horrid distress I daily experience, something would be done. Some engine is at work against us in Naples; and I believe I hit on the proper person. If you complain, he will be immediately promoted—agreeably to the Neapolitan custom. All I write to you is known at the queen's. For my own part, I look upon the Neapolitans as the worst of intriguing enemies; every hour shows me their infamy and duplicity. I pray your lordship be cautious; your honest, open manner of acting will be made a handle of. When I see you, and tell of their infamous tricks, you will be as much surprised as I am. The whole will fall on you."

Nelson was not, and could not, be insensible to the distress which his friend so earnestly represented. He begged, almost on his knees, he said, small supplies of money and corn, to keep the Maltese from starving. And when the court granted a small supply, protesting their poverty, he believed their protestations, and was satisfied with their professions, instead of insisting that the restrictions upon the exportation of corn should be withdrawn. The anxiety, however, which he endured, affected him so deeply, that he said it had broken his spirit for ever. Happily all that Trowbridge, with so much reason, foreboded, did not come to pass. For Captain Ball, with more decision than Nelson himself would have shown at that time, and upon that occasion, ventured upon a resolute measure, for which his name would deserve always to be held in veneration by the Maltese, even if it had no other claims to the love and reverence of a grateful people. Finding it hopeless longer to look for succour, or common humanity, from the deceitful and infatuated court of Sicily, which persisted in prohibiting, by sanguinary edicts, the exportation of supplies, at his own risk he sent his first lieutenant to the port of Messina, with orders to seize, and bring with him to Malta, the ships which were there lying laden with corn, of the number of which he had received accurate information. These orders were executed, to the great delight and advantage of the shipowners and proprietors; the necessity of raising the siege was removed, and Captain

Ball waited, in calmness, for the consequences to himself. "But," says Mr. Coleridge (who, it is to be hoped, will do that full justice to the memory of this great man which he is so fully capable of doing), "not a complaint, not a murmur, proceeded from the court of Naples. The sole result was that the governor of Malta became an especial object of its hatred, its fear, and its respect."

Nelson himself, at the beginning of February, sailed for that island. On the way he fell in with a French squadron bound for its relief, and consisting of the *Genereux*, 74, three frigates, and a corvette. One of the frigates, and the line-of-battle ship, were taken; the others escaped, but failed in their purpose of reaching La Valette. This success was peculiarly gratifying to Nelson, for many reasons. During some months he had acted as commander-in-chief in the Mediterranean, while Lord Keith was in England. Lord Keith was now returned, and Nelson had, upon his own plan, and at his own risk, left him, to sail for Malta,—"for which," said he, "if I had not succeeded, I might have been broke;—and, if I had not acted thus, the *Genereux* never would have been taken." This ship was one of those which had ascaped from Aboukir. Two frigates, and the *Guillaume Tell*, 86, were all that now remained of the fleet which Buonaparte had conducted to Egypt. The *Guillaume Tell* was at this time closely watched in the harbour of La Valette; and shortly afterwards, attempting to make her escape from thence, was taken, after an action in which greater skill was never displayed by British ships, nor greater gallantry by an enemy. She was taken by the *Foudroyant*, *Lion*, and *Penelope* frigate. Nelson, rejoicing at what he called this glorious finish to the whole French Mediterranean fleet, rejoiced also that he was not present, to have taken a sprig of these brave men's laurels. "They are," said he, "and I glory in them, my children : they served in

my school; and all of us caught our professional zeal
and fire from the great and good Earl St. Vincent.
What a pleasure, what happiness, to have the Nile
fleet all taken, under my orders and regulations!"
The two frigates still remained in La Valette; before
its surrender they stole out: one was taken in the
attempt; the other was the only ship of the whole
fleet which escaped capture or destruction.

Letters were found on board the *Guillaume Tell*,
showing that the French were now become hopeless
of preserving the conquest which they had so foully
acquired.   Trowbridge, and his brother officers, were
anxious that Nelson should have the honour of signing the capitulation.   They told him that they absolutely, as far as they dared, insisted on his staying to
do this; but their earnest and affectionate entreaties
were vain.   Sir William Hamilton had just been
superseded; Nelson had no feeling of cordiality towards Lord Keith; and thinking that, after Earl St.
Vincent, no man had so good a claim to the command in the Mediterranean as himself, he applied for
permission to return to England, telling the First
Lord of the Admiralty that his spirit could not submit
patiently, and that he was a broken-hearted man.
From the time of his return from Egypt, amid all
the honours which were showered upon him, he had
suffered many mortifications.   Sir Sidney Smith had
been sent to Egypt, with orders to take under his
command the squadron which Nelson had left there.
Sir Sidney appears to have thought that this command was to be independent of Nelson; and Nelson
himself thinking so, determined to return, saying to
Earl St. Vincent, " I do feel, for I am man, that it
is impossible for me to serve in these seas with a
squadron under a junior officer." Earl St. Vincent
seems to have dissuaded him from this resolution;
some heartburnings, however, still remained, and
some incautious expressions of Sir Sidney's were
noticed by him in terms of evident displeasure.   But

this did not continue long; and no man bore more willing testimony than Nelson to the admirable defence of Acre.

He differed from Sir Sidney as to the policy which ought to be pursued toward the French in Egypt; and strictly commanded him, in the strongest language, not, on any pretence, to permit a single Frenchman to leave the country; saying, that he considered it nothing short of madness to permit that band of thieves to return to Europe. "No," said he; "to Egypt they went with their own consent, and there they shall remain while Nelson commands this squadron :—for never, never, will he consent to the return of one ship or Frenchman. I wish them to perish in Egypt, and give an awful lesson to the world of the justice of the Almighty." If Nelson had not thoroughly understood the character of the enemy against whom he was engaged, their conduct in Egypt would have disclosed it. After the battle of the Nile he had landed all his prisoners, upon a solemn engagement, made between Trowbridge on one side, and Captain Barré on the other, that none of them should serve till regularly exchanged. They were no sooner on shore than part of them were drafted into the different regiments, and the remainder formed into a corps, called the Nautic Legion. This occasioned Captain Hallowell to say, that the French had forfeited all claim to respect from us. "The army of Buonaparte," said he, "are entirely destitute of every principle of honour; they have always acted like licentious thieves." Buonaparte's escape was the more regretted by Nelson, because, if he had had sufficient force, he thought it would certainly have been prevented. He wished to keep ships upon the watch, to intercept anything coming from Egypt; but the Admiralty calculated upon the assistance of the Russian fleet, which failed when it was most wanted. The ships which should have been thus employed were then required for more pressing services; and

the bloody Corsican was thus enabled to reach Europe
in safety—there to become the guilty instrument of a
wider-spreading destruction than any with which the
world had ever before been visited.

Nelson had other causes of chagrin.   Earl St. Vincent, for whom he felt such high respect, and whom
Sir John Orde had challenged for having nominated
Nelson, instead of himself, to the command of the
Nile squadron, laid claim to prize-money, as commander-in-chief, after he had quitted the station.   The
point was contested, and decided against him.   Nelson, perhaps, felt this the more, because his own
feelings, with regard to money, were so different.
An opinion had been given by Dr. Lawrence, which
would have excluded the junior flag-officers from
prize-money.   When this was made known to him,
his reply was in these words : " Notwithstanding Dr.
Lawrence's opinion, I do not believe I have any right
to exclude the junior flag-officers ; and if I have, I
desire that no such claim may be made ;—no, not if
it were sixty times the sum, and, poor as I am, I
were never to see prize-money."

A ship could not be spared to convey him to England ; he therefore travelled through Germany to
Hamburgh, in company with his inseparable friends,
Sir William and Lady Hamilton.   The Queen of
Naples went with them to Vienna.   While they were
at Leghorn, upon a report that the French were approaching (for, through the folly of weak courts, and
the treachery of venal cabinets, they had now recovered their ascendency in Italy), the people rose
tumultuously, and would fain have persuaded Nelson
to lead them against the enemy.   Public honours, and
yet more gratifying testimonials of public admiration, awaited Nelson wherever he went.   The Prince
of Esterhazy entertained him in a style of Hungarian
magnificence, a hundred grenadiers, each six feet in
height, constantly waiting at table.   At Magdeburg,
the master of the hotel where he was entertained con-

trived to show him for money; admitting the curious to mount a ladder, and peep at him through a small window. A wine-merchant at Hamburgh, who was above seventy years of age, requested to speak with Lady Hamilton; and told her he had some Rhenish wine, of the vintage of 1625, which had been in his own possession more than half a century; he had preserved it for some extraordinary occasion; and that which had now arrived was far beyond any that he could ever have expected. His request was, that her ladyship would prevail upon Lord Nelson to accept six dozen of this incomparable wine : part of it would then have the honour to flow into the heart's blood of that immortal hero, and this thought would make him happy during the remainder of his life. Nelson, when this singular request was reported to him, went into the room, and taking the worthy old gentleman kindly by the hand, consented to receive six bottles, provided the donor would dine with him next day. Twelve were sent; and Nelson, saying that he hoped yet to win half a dozen more great victories, promised to lay by six bottles of his Hamburgh friend's wine, for the purpose of drinking one after each. A German pastor, between seventy and eighty years of age, travelled forty miles, with the Bible of his parish church, to request that Nelson would write his name on the first leaf of it. He called him the saviour of the Christian world. The old man's hope deceived him. There was no Nelson upon shore, or Europe would have been saved; but, in his foresight of the horrors with which all Germany and all Christendom were threatened by France, the pastor could not possibly have apprehended more than has actually taken place.

CHAPTER VII

NELSON was welcomed in England with every mark of popular honour. At Yarmouth, where he landed, every ship in the harbour hoisted her colours. The mayor and corporation waited upon him with the freedom of the town, and accompanied him in procession to church, with all the naval officers on shore, and the principal inhabitants. Bonfires and illuminations concluded the day; and, on the morrow, the volunteer cavalry drew up and saluted him as he departed, and followed the carriage to the borders of the county. At Ipswich the people came out to meet him, drew him a mile into the town, and three miles out. When he was in the *Agamemnon* he wished to represent this place in Parliament, and some of his friends had consulted the leading men of the corporation: the result was not successful; and Nelson, observing that he would endeavour to find a preferable path into Parliament, said there might come a time when the people of Ipswich would think it an honour to have had him for their representative. In London he was feasted by the City, drawn by the populace from Ludgate Hill to Guildhall, and received the thanks of the Common Council for his great victory, and a golden-hilted sword studded with diamonds. Nelson had every earthly blessing except domestic happiness: he had forfeited that for ever. Before he had been three months in England he separated from Lady Nelson. Some of his last words to her were: "I call God to witness, there is nothing in you, or your conduct, that I wish otherwise." This was the consequence of his infatuated attachment to Lady Hamilton. It had before caused a quarrel with his stepson, and occasioned remonstrances from his truest friends, which produced no other effect than that of making him displeased with them, and more dissatisfied with himself.

The Addington administration was just at this time formed; and Nelson, who had solicited employment, and been made vice-admiral of the blue, was sent to the Baltic, as second in command, under Sir Hyde Parker, by Earl St. Vincent, the new First Lord of the Admiralty. The three northern courts had formed a confederacy for making England resign her naval rights. Of these courts, Russia was guided by the passions of its emperor, Paul; a man not without fits of generosity and some natural goodness, but subject to the wildest humours of caprice, and crazed by the possession of greater power than can ever be safely, or, perhaps, innocently, possessed by weak humanity. Denmark was French at heart; ready to co-operate in all the views of France, to recognise all her usurpations, and obey all her injunctions. Sweden, under a king whose principles were right and whose feelings were generous, but who had a taint of hereditary insanity, acted in acquiescence to the dictates of two powers, whom it feared to offend. The Danish navy, at this time, consisted of twenty-three ships of the line, with about thirty-one frigates, and smaller vessels, exclusive of guard-ships. The Swedes had eighteen ships of the line, fourteen frigates and sloops, seventy-four galleys and smaller vessels, besides gun-boats: and this force was in a far better state of equipment than the Danish. The Russians had eighty-two sail of the line and forty frigates. Of these, there were forty-seven sail of the line at Cronstadt, Revel, Petersburgh, and Archangel: but the Russian fleet was ill-manned, ill-officered, and ill-equipped. Such a combination, under the influence of France, would soon have become formidable; and never did the British Cabinet display more decision than in instantly preparing to crush it. They erred, however, in permitting any petty consideration to prevent them from appointing Nelson to the command. The public properly murmured at seeing it intrusted to another: and he himself said to Earl St. Vincent, that, circumstanced as he was, this expedition would probably be the last service that he should ever perform. The Earl, in reply, besought him, for God's sake, not to suffer himself to be carried away by any sudden impulse.

The season happened to be unusually favourable : so mild a winter had not been known in the Baltic for many years. When Nelson joined the fleet at Yarmouth, he found the admiral " a little nervous about dark nights and fields of ice." " But we must brace up," said he; " these are not times for nervous systems. I hope we shall give our northern enemies that hailstorm of bullets which gives our dear country the dominion of the sea. We have it, and all the devils in the North cannot take it from us if our wooden walls have fair play." Before the fleet left Yarmouth, it was sufficiently known that its destination was against Denmark. Some Danes who belonged to the *Amazon* frigate, went to Captain Riou, and telling him what they had heard, begged that he would get them exchanged into a ship bound on some other destination. " They had no wish," they said, " to quit the British service; but they entreated that they might not be forced to fight against their own country." There was not in our whole navy a man who had a higher and more chivalrous sense of duty than Riou. Tears came into his eyes while the men were speaking : without making any reply, he instantly ordered his boat, and did not return to the *Amazon* till he could tell them that their wish was effected.

The fleet sailed on the 12th of March. Mr. Vansittart sailed in it, the British Cabinet still hoping to obtain its end by negotiation. It was well for England that Sir Hyde Parker placed a fuller confidence in Nelson than the Government seems to have done at this most important crisis. Her enemies might well have been astonished at learning that any other man should, for a moment, have been thought of for the command. But so little deference was paid, even at this time, to his intuitive and all-commanding genius, that when the fleet had reached its first rendezvous, at the entrance of the Cattegat, he had received no official communication whatever of the intended operations. His own mind had been made up upon them with its accustomed decision. "All I have gathered of our first plans," said he, "I disapprove most exceedingly. Honour may arise from them; good cannot. I hear we are likely to anchor outside of Cronenburg Castle, instead of Copenhagen, which would give weight to our negotiation. A Danish minister would think twice before he would put his name to war with England, when the next moment he would probably see his master's fleet in flames, and his capital in ruins. The Dane should see our flag every moment he lifted up his head."

Mr. Vansittart left the fleet at the Scaw, and preceded it in a frigate, with a flag of truce. Precious time was lost by this delay, which was to be purchased by the dearest blood of Britain and of Denmark : according to the Danes themselves, the intelligence that a British fleet was seen off the Sound produced a much more general alarm in Copenhagen than its actual arrival in the roads; for their means of defence were, at that time, in such a state, that they could hardly hope to resist, still less to repel, an enemy. On the 21st Nelson had a long conference with Sir Hyde; and the next day addressed a letter to him, worthy of himself and of the occasion. Mr. Vansittart's report had then been received. It represented the Danish Government as in the highest degree hostile, and their state of preparation as exceeding what our Cabinet had supposed possible : for Denmark had profited, with all activity, of the leisure which had so impoliticly been given her. "The more I have reflected," said Nelson to his commander, "the more I am confirmed in opinion, that not a moment should be lost in attacking the enemy.

They will every day and hour be stronger : we never shall be so good a match for them as at this moment. The only consideration is, how to get at them with the least risk to our ships.   Here you are, with almost the safety—certainly with the honour—of England more intrusted to you than ever yet fell to the lot of any British officer. On your decision depends whether our country shall be degraded in the eyes of Europe, or whether she shall rear her head higher than ever. Again do I repeat, never did our country depend so much on the success of any fleet as on this.   How best to honour her and abate the pride of her enemies, must be the subject of your deepest consideration.''

Supposing him to force the passage of the Sound, Nelson thought some damage might be done among the masts and yards; though, perhaps, not one of them but would be serviceable again. '' If the wind be fair,'' said he, '' and you determine to attack the ships and Crown Islands, you must expect the natural issue of such a battle—ships crippled, and, perhaps, one or two lost; for the wind which carries you in will, most probably, not bring out a crippled ship. This mode I call taking the bull by the horns. It, however, will not prevent the Revel ships, or the Swedes, from joining the Danes : and to prevent this is, in my humble opinion, a measure absolutely neces-sary; and still to attack Copenhagen.'' For this he proposed two modes. One was to pass Cronenburg, taking the risk of danger; take the deepest and straitest channel along the Middle Grounds ; and then coming down the Garbar, or King's Channel, attack the Danish line of floating batteries and ships, as might be found convenient. This would prevent the junction, and might give an opportunity of bombard-ing Copenhagen.   Or to take the passage of the Belt, which might be accomplished in four or five days ; and then the attack by Draco might be made, and the junction of the Russians prevented. Supposing them through the Belt, he proposed that a detachment

of the fleet should be sent to destroy the Russian
squadron at Revel; and that the business at Copenhagen should be attempted with the remainder. "The
measure," he said, "may be thought bold; but the
boldest measures are the safest."

The pilots, as men who had nothing but safety to
think of, were terrified by the formidable report of
the batteries of Elsineur, and the tremendous preparations which our negotiators, who were now
returned from their fruitless mission, had witnessed.
They, therefore, persuaded Sir Hyde to prefer the
passage of the Belt. "Let it be by the Sound, by
the Belt, or anyhow," cried Nelson. "only lose not
an hour!" On the 26th they sailed for the Belt,
but, after a few hours, this resolution was changed,
and the fleet returned to its former anchorage. The
difficulty of the course is said to have been one
reason; Nelson's advice another. The next day was
more idly expended in despatching a flag of truce to
the governor of Cronenburg Castle, to ask whether
he had received orders to fire at the British fleet;
as the admiral must consider the first gun to be a
declaration of war on the part of Denmark. A
soldier-like and becoming answer was returned to this
formality. The governor said that the British
minister had not been sent away from Copenhagen,
but had obtained a passport at his own demand. He
himself, as a soldier, could not meddle with politics;
but he was not at liberty to suffer a fleet, of which
the intention was not yet known, to approach the
guns of the castle which he had the honour to command; and he requested, if the British admiral should
think proper to make any proposals to the King of
Denmark, that he might be apprised of it before the
fleet approached nearer. During this intercourse, a
Dane, who came on board the commander's ship,
having occasion to express his business in writing,
found the pen blunt; and, holding it up, sarcastically
said: "If your guns are not better pointed than your

pens, you will make little impression on Copenhagen!''

On that day intelligence reached the admiral of the loss of one of his fleet, the *Invincible*, 74, wrecked on a sandbank as she was coming out of Yarmouth, 400 of her men perishing in her. Nelson, who was now appointed to lead the van, shifted his flag to the *Elephant*, Captain Foley, a lighter ship than the *St. George*, and therefore fitter for the expected operations. The two following days were calm. Orders had been given to pass the Sound as soon as the wind would permit; and, on the afternoon of the 29th, the ships were cleared for action, with an alacrity characteristic of British seamen. At daybreak, on the 30th, it blew a top-sail breeze from N.W. The signal was made, and the fleet moved on in order of battle—Nelson's division in the van, Sir Hyde's in the centre, and Admiral Graves' in the rear.

Great actions, whether military or naval, have generally given celebrity to the scenes from whence they are denominated; and thus petty villages, and capes, and bays, known only to the coasting trader, become associated with mighty deeds, and their names are made conspicuous in the history of the world. Here, however, the scene was every way worthy of the drama. The political importance of the Sound is such, that grand objects are not needed there to impress the imagination; yet is the channel full of grand and interesting objects, both of art and nature. This passage, which Denmark had so long considered as the key of the Baltic, is, in its narrowest part, about three miles wide; and here the city of Elsineur is situated; except Copenhagen, the most flourishing of the Danish towns. Every vessel which passes lowers her top-gallant-sails, and pays toll at Elsineur: a toll which is believed to have had its origin in the consent of the traders to that sea, Denmark taking upon itself the charge of construct-

ing lighthouses, and erecting signals, to mark the
shoals and rocks from the Cattegat to the Baltic :
and they, on their part, agreeing that all ships should
pass this way, in order that all might pay their
shares : none from that time using the passage of
the Belt; because it was not fitting that they, who
enjoyed the benefit of the beacons in dark and stormy
weather, should evade contributing to them in fair
seasons and summer nights. Of late years about ten
thousand vessels had annually paid this contribution
in time of peace. Adjoining Elsineur, and at the edge
of a peninsular promontory, upon the nearest point of
land to the Swedish coast, stands Cronenburg Castle,
built after Tycho Brahe's design—a magnificent pile
—at once a palace, and fortress, and state prison,
with its spires and towers, and battlements and batteries. On the left of the strait is the old Swedish
city of Helsingburg, at the foot, and on the side of a
hill. To the north of Helsingburg the shores are
steep and rocky; they lower to the south; and the
distant spires of Landscrona, Lund, and Malmoe are
seen in the flat country. The Danish shores consist
partly of ridges of sand; but more frequently their
slopes are covered with rich wood, and villages and
villas, denoting the vicinity of a great capital. The
isles of Huen, Saltholm, and Amak, appear in the
widening channel; and at the distance of twenty miles
from Elsineur stands Copenhagen, in full view—the
best built city of the North, and one of the finest
capitals of Europe, visible, with its stately spires, far
off. Amid these magnificent objects, there are some
which possess a peculiar interest for the recollections
which they call forth. The isle of Huen, a lovely
domain, about six miles in circumference, had been
the munificent gift of Frederic the Second to Tycho
Brahe. Here most of his discoveries were made;
and here the ruins are to be seen of his observatory,
and of the mansion where he was visited by princes,
and where, with a princely spirit, he received and

entertained all comers from all parts, and promoted
science by his liberality, as well as by his labours.
Elsineur is a name familiar to English ears, being
inseparably associated with *Hamlet*, and one of the
noblest works of human genius.   Cronenburg had
been the scene of deeper tragedy: here Queen
Matilda was confined, the victim of a foul and murderous court intrigue.   Here, amid heart-breaking
griefs, she found consolation in nursing her infant.
Here she took her everlasting leave of that infant,
when, by the interference of England, her own deliverance was obtained; and, as the ship bore her away
from a country, where the venial indiscretions of
youth and unsuspicious gaiety had been so cruelly
punished, upon these towers she fixed her eyes, and
stood upon the deck, obstinately gazing toward them
till the last speck had disappeared.

The Sound being the only frequented entrance to
the Baltic, the great Mediterranean of the North,
few parts of the sea display so frequent a navigation.
In the height of the season, not fewer than an hundred
vessels pass every four-and-twenty hours, for many
weeks in succession; but never had so busy or so
splendid a scene been exhibited there as on this day,
when the British fleet prepared to force that passage,
where, till now, all ships had vailed their top-sails
to the flag of Denmark.   The whole force consisted
of fifty-one sail, of various descriptions, of which
sixteen were of the line.   The greater part of the
bomb and gun vessels took their station off Cronenburg Castle, to cover the fleet; while others, on the
larboard, were ready to engage the Swedish shore.
The Danes, having improved every moment which
ill-timed negotiation and baffling weather gave them,
had lined their shore with batteries; and as soon as
the *Monarch*, which was the leading ship, came
abreast of them, a fire was opened from about a
hundred pieces of cannon and mortars: our light
vessels immediately, in return, opened their fire upon

the castle. Here was all the pompous circumstance
and exciting reality of war, without its effects; for
this ostentatious display was but a bloodless prelude
to the wide and sweeping destruction which was soon
to follow. The enemy's shot fell near enough to
splash the water on board our ships : not relying upon
any forbearance of the Swedes, they meant to have
kept the mid channel : but, when they perceived that
not a shot was fired from Helsingburg, and that no
batteries were to be seen on the Swedish shore, they
inclined to that side, so as completely to get out of
reach of the Danish guns. The uninterrupted blaze
which was kept up from them till the fleet had passed,
served only to exhilarate our sailors, and afford them
matter for jest, as the shot fell in showers a full
cable's length short of its destined aim. A few
rounds were returned from some of our leading ships,
till they perceived its inutility ;—this, however, occasioned the only bloodshed of the day, some of our
men being killed and wounded by the bursting of a
gun. As soon as the main body had passed, the gun
vessels followed, desisting from their bombardment,
which had been as innocent as that of the enemy ;
and, about mid-day, the whole fleet anchored between
the island of Huen and Copenhagen. Sir Hyde, with
Nelson, Admiral Graves, some of the senior captains,
and the commanding officers of the artillery and the
troops, then proceeded in a lugger to reconnoitre the
enemy's means of defence ; a formidable line of ships,
radeaus, pontoons, galleys, fire-ships, and gunboats,
flanked and supported by extensive batteries, and
occupying, from one extreme point to the other, an
extent of nearly four miles.

A council of war was held in the afternoon. It was
apparent that the Danes could not be attacked without great difficulty and risk ; and some of the mem-
bers of the council spoke of the number of the Swedes
and the Russians, whom they should afterwards have
to engage, as a consideration which ought to be

borne in mind. Nelson, who kept pacing the cabin, impatient as he ever was of anything which savoured of irresolution, repeatedly said, " The more numerous the better : I wish they were twice as many,—the easier the victory, depend on it." The plan upon which he had determined, if ever it should be his fortune to bring a Baltic fleet to action, was to attack the head of their line, and confuse their movements. " Close with a Frenchman," he used to say, " but out-manœuvre a Russian." He offered his services for the attack, requiring ten sail of the line, and the whole of the smaller craft. Sir Hyde gave him two more line of battle ships than he asked, and left everything to his judgment.

The enemy's force was not the only, nor the greatest, obstacle with which the British fleet had to contend : there was another to be overcome before they could come in contact with it. The channel was little known, and extremely intricate; all the buoys had been removed; and the Danes considered this difficulty as almost insuperable, thinking the channel impracticable for so large a fleet. Nelson himself saw the soundings made and the buoys laid down, boating it upon this exhausting service, day and night, till it was effected. When this was done, he thanked God for having enabled him to get through this difficult part of his duty. " It had worn him down," he said, " and was infinitely more grievous to him than any resistance which he could experience from the enemy."

At the first council of war, opinions inclined to an attack from the eastward : but the next day, the wind being southerly, after a second examination of the Danish position, it was determined to attack from the south, approaching in the manner which Nelson had suggested in his first thoughts. On the morning of the 1st of April, the whole fleet removed to an anchorage within two leagues of the town, and off the N.W. end of the Middle Ground, a shoal lying exactly before the town, at about three-quarters of a mile distance, and extending along its whole sea-front. The King's Channel, where there is deep water, is between this shoal and the town; and here the Danes had arranged their line of defence, as near the shore as possible;—nineteen ships and floating batteries, flanked, at the end nearest the town, by the Crown Batteries, which were two artificial islands at the mouth of the harbour,—most formidable works; the larger one having, by the Danish account, sixty-six guns; but, as Nelson believed, eighty-eight. The fleet having anchored, Nelson with Riou in the *Amazon* made his last examination of the ground; and, about one o'clock, returning to his own ship, threw out the signal to weigh. It was received with a shout throughout the whole division; they weighed with a light and favourable wind; the narrow channel between the island of Saltholm and the Middle Ground had been accurately buoyed; the small craft pointed out the course distinctly; Riou led the way: the whole division coasted along the outer edge of the shoal, doubled its farther extremity, and anchored there off Draco Point just as the darkness closed, the head-most of the enemy's line not being more than two miles distant. The signal to prepare for action had been made early in the evening; and, as his own anchor dropped, Nelson called out, " I will fight them the moment I have a fair wind." It had been agreed that Sir Hyde, with the remaining ships, should weigh on the following morning, at the same time as Nelson, to menace the Crown Batteries on his side, and the four ships of the line which lay at the entrance of the arsenal; and to cover our own disabled ships as they came out of action.

The Danes, meantime, had not been idle : no sooner did the guns of Cronenburg make it known to the whole city that all negotiation was at an end, that the British fleet was passing the Sound, and that the dispute between the two crowns must now be decided by arms,

than a spirit displayed itself most honourable to the
Danish character.   All ranks offered themselves to
the service of their country ; the university furnished
a corps of twelve hundred youths, the flower of Denmark :—it was one of those emergencies in which
little drilling or discipline is necessary to render
courage available ; they had nothing to learn but how
to manage the guns, and day and night were employed
in practising them.   When the movements of Nelson's squadron were perceived, it was known when
and where the attack was to be expected, and the
line of defence was manned indiscriminately by
soldiers, sailors, and citizens.   Had not the whole
attention of the Danes been directed to strengthen
their own means of defence, they might most
materially have annoyed the invading squadron, and,
perhaps, frustrated the impending attack ; for the
British ships were crowded in an anchoring-ground
of little extent ; it was calm, so that mortar-boats
might have acted against them to the utmost
advantage ; and they were within range of shells from
Amak Island.   A few fell among them ; but the
enemy soon ceased to fire.   It was learnt afterwards,
that, fortunately for the fleet, the bed of the mortar
had given way ; and the Danes either could not get
it replaced, or, in the darkness, lost the direction.

This was an awful night for Copenhagen,—far
more so than for the British fleet, where the men were
accustomed to battle and victory, and had none of
those objects before their eyes which render death
terrible.   Nelson sat down to table with a large party
of his officers ; he was, as he was ever wont to be
when on the eve of action, in high spirits, and drank
to a leading wind, and to the success of the morrow.
After supper they returned to their respective ships,
except Riou, who remained to arrange the order of
battle with Nelson and Foley, and to draw up instructions ; Hardy, meantime, went in a small boat to
examine the channel between them and the enemy ;

approaching so near that he sounded round their
leading ship with a pole, lest the noise of throwing
the lead should discover him. The incessant fatigue
of body, as well as mind, which Nelson had under-
gone during the last three days, had so exhausted
him that he was earnestly urged to go to his cot;
and his old servant, Allen, using that kind of authority
which long and affectionate services entitled and
enabled him to assume on such occasions, insisted
upon his complying. The cot was placed on the floor,
and he continued to dictate from it. About eleven
Hardy returned, and reported the practicability of
the channel, and the depth of water up to the enemy's
line. About one, the orders were completed; and
half a dozen clerks, in the foremost cabin, proceeded
to transcribe them, Nelson frequently calling out to
them from his cot to hasten their work, for the wind
was becoming fair. Instead of attempting to get a
few hours of sleep, he was constantly receiving
reports upon this important point. At daybreak it
was announced as becoming perfectly fair. The
clerks finished their work about six. Nelson, who
was already up, breakfasted, and made signal for all
captains. The land forces, and five hundred seamen,
under Captain Freemantle and the Honourable
Colonel Stewart, were to storm the Crown Battery as
soon as its fire should be silenced; and Riou, whom
Nelson had never seen till this expedition, but whose
worth he had instantly perceived, and appreciated as
it deserved,—had the *Blanche* and *Alcmene* frigates,
the *Dart* and *Arrow* sloops, and the *Zephyr* and *Otter*
fire-ships, given him, with a special command to act
as circumstances might require;—every other ship
had its station appointed.

Between eight and nine the pilots and masters were
ordered on board the admiral's ship. The pilots were
mostly men who had been mates in Baltic traders;
and their hesitation about the bearing of the east end
of the shoal, and the exact line of deep water, gave

ominous warning of how little their knowledge was
to be trusted. The signal for action had been made,
the wind was fair—not a moment to be lost. Nelson
urged them to be steady—to be resolute, and to
decide;—but they wanted the only ground for steadi-
ness and decision in such cases; and Nelson had
reason to regret that he had not trusted to Hardy's
single report. This was one of the most painful
moments of his life, and he always spoke of it with
bitterness. "I experienced in the Sound," said he,
"the misery of having the honour of our country
intrusted to a set of pilots, who have no other thought
than to keep the ships clear of danger, and their own
silly heads clear of shot. Everybody knows what I
must have suffered; and if any merit attaches itself
to me, it was for combating the dangers of the
shallows in defiance of them." At length Mr. Bryerly,
the master of the *Bellona*, declared that he was prepared to lead the fleet: his judgment was acceded to
by the rest: they returned to their ships, and, at
half-past nine, the signal was made to weigh in
succession.

Captain Murray, in the *Edgar*, led the way; the
Agamemnon was next in order; but, on the first
attempt to leave her anchorage, she could not weather
the edge of the shoal, and Nelson had the grief to see
his old ship, in which he had performed so many
years' gallant services, immoveably aground, at a
moment when her help was so greatly required.
Signal was then made for the *Polyphemus*, and this
change in the order of sailing was executed with the
utmost promptitude: yet so much delay had thus
been unavoidably occasioned, that the *Edgar* was for
some time unsupported: and the *Polyphemus*, whose
place should have been at the end of the enemy's
line where their strength was the greatest, could get
no further than the beginning, owing to the difficulty
of the channel: there she occupied, indeed, an efficient
station, but one where her presence was less required.

The *Isis* followed, with better fortune, and took her own berth. The *Bellona*, Sir Thomas Boulden Thompson, kept too close on the starboard shoal, and grounded abreast of the outer ship of the enemy: this was the more vexatious, inasmuch as the wind was fair, the room ample, and three ships had led the way. The *Russell*, following the *Bellona*, grounded in like manner: both were within reach of shot; but their absence from their intended stations was severely felt. Each ship had been ordered to pass her leader on the starboard side, because the water was supposed to shoal on the larboard shore. Nelson, who came next after these two ships, thought they had kept too far on the starboard direction, and made signal for them to close with the enemy, not knowing that they were aground: but, when he perceived that they did not obey the signal, he ordered the *Elephant's* helm to starboard, and went within these ships: thus quitting the appointed order of sailing, and guiding those which were to follow. The greater part of the fleet were probably, by this act of promptitude on his part, saved from going on shore. Each ship, as she arrived nearly opposite to her appointed station, let her anchor go by the stern, and presented her broadside to the Danes. The distance between each was about a half-cable. The action was fought nearly at the distance of a cable's length from the enemy. This, which rendered its continuance so long, was owing to the ignorance and consequent indecision of the pilots. In pursuance of the same error which had led the *Bellona* and the *Russell* aground, they, when the lead was at a quarter less five, refused to approach nearer, in dread of shoaling their water on the larboard shore: a fear altogether erroneous, for the water deepened up to the very side of the enemy's line.

At five minutes after ten the action began. The first half of our fleet was engaged in about half an hour; and by half-past eleven the battle became

general. The plan of the attack had been complete :
but seldom has any plan been more disconcerted by
untoward accidents. Of twelve ships of the line, one
was entirely useless, and two others in a situation
where they could not render half the service which
was required of them. Of the squadron of gun-brigs
only one could get into action : the rest were prevented, by baffling currents, from weathering the
eastern end of the shoal ; and only two of the bomb-
vessels could reach their station on the Middle
Ground, and open their mortars on the arsenal, firing
over both fleets. Riou took the vacant station against
the Crown Battery, with his frigates ; attempting,
with that unequal force, a service in which three sail
of the line had been directed to assist.

Nelson's agitation had been extreme when he saw
himself, before the action began, deprived of a fourth
part of his ships of the line. But no sooner was he
in battle, where his squadron was received with the
fire of more than a thousand guns, than, as if that
artillery, like music, had driven away all care and
painful thoughts, his countenance brightened ; and,
as a bystander describes him, his conversation
became joyous, animated, elevated, and delightful.
The commander-in-chief, meantime near enough to
the scene of action to know the unfavourable accidents which had so materially weakened Nelson, and
yet too distant to know the real state of the contending parties, suffered the most dreadful anxiety. To
get to his assistance was impossible ; both wind and
current were against him. Fear for the event, in such
circumstances, would naturally preponderate in the
bravest mind ; and, at one o'clock, perceiving that,
after three hours' endurance, the enemy's fire was
unslackened, he began to despair of success ; and
thinking it became him to save what he could from
the hopeless contest, he made signal for retreat.
Nelson was now in all the excitement of action, pacing
the quarter-deck. A shot through the mainmast

knocked the splinters about; and he observed to one
of his officers, with a smile : " It is warm work; and
this day may be the last to any of us at a moment " :
—and then stopping short at the gangway, added,
with emotion—" But mark you : I would not be
elsewhere for thousands." About this time the signal
lieutenant called out that No. 39 (the signal for dis-
continuing the action) was thrown out by the commander-in-chief. He continued to walk the deck, and
appeared to take no notice of it. The signal officer
met him at the next turn, and asked if he should
repeat it. "No," he replied; "acknowledge it."
Presently he called after him, to know if the signal
for close action was still hoisted, and being answered
in the affirmative, said, " Mind you keep it so." He
now paced the deck, moving the stump of his lost
arm in a manner which always indicated great emotion. " Do you know," said he to Mr. Ferguson,
" what is shown on board the commander-in-chief?
No. 39 ! " Mr. Ferguson asked what that meant?—
" Why, to leave off action ! " Then shrugging up
his shoulders, he repeated the words—" Leave off
action ! Now damn me if I do ! You know, Foley,"
turning to the captain, " I have only one eye,—I
have a right to be blind sometimes,"—and then
putting the glass to his blind eye, in that mood of
mind which sports with bitterness, he exclaimed, " I
really do not see the signal ! " Presently he exclaimed, " Damn the signal ! Keep mine for closer
battle flying ! That's the way I answer such signals.
Nail mine to the mast ! " Admiral Graves, who was
so situated that he could not discern what was done
on board the *Elephant*, disobeyed Sir Hyde's signal
in like manner : whether by fortunate mistake, or by
a like brave intention, has not been made known.
The other ships of the line, looking only to Nelson,
continued the action. The signal, however, saved
Riou's little squadron, but did not save its heroic
leader. This squadron, which was nearest the com-

mander-in-chief, obeyed, and hauled off. It had
suffered severely in its most unequal contest. For a
long time the *Amazon* had been firing, enveloped in
smoke, when Riou desired his men to stand fast and
let the smoke clear off, that they might see what they
were about. A fatal order; for the Danes then got
clear sight of her from the batteries, and pointed
their guns with such tremendous effect that nothing
but the signal for retreat saved this frigate from
destruction. "What will Nelson think of us!" was
Riou's mournful exclamation when he unwillingly
drew off. He had been wounded in the head by a
splinter, and was sitting on a gun, encouraging his
men, when, just as the *Amazon* showed her stern to
the Trekroner battery, his clerk was killed by his
side, and another shot swept away several marines
who were hauling in the mainbrace. "Come then,
my boys!" cried Riou, "let us die all together!"
The words had scarcely been uttered, before a raking
shot cut him in two. Except it had been Nelson himself, the British navy could not have suffered a
severer loss.

The action continued along the line with unabated
vigour on our side, and with the most determined
resolution on the part of the Danes. They fought
to great advantage, because most of the vessels in
their line of defence were without masts: the few
which had any standing had their topmasts struck,
and the hulls could only be seen at intervals. The
Isis must have been destroyed by the superior weight
of her enemy's fire, if Captain Inman, in the *Desirée*
frigate, had not judiciously taken a situation which
enabled him to rake the Dane, and if the *Polyphemus*
had not also relieved her. Both in the *Bellona* and
the *Isis* many men were lost by the bursting of their
guns. The former ship was about forty years old,
and these guns were believed to be the same which
she had first taken to sea: they were, probably,
originally faulty, for the fragments were full of little

air-holes.   The *Bellona* lost seventy-five men; the *Isis* one hundred and ten; the *Monarch* two hundred and ten.   She was more than any other line of battle ship exposed to the great battery; and supporting at the same time the united fire of the *Holstein* and the *Zealand*, her loss this day exceeded that of any single ship during the whole war.   Amid the tremendous carnage in this vessel, some of the men displayed a singular instance of coolness: the pork and peas happened to be in the kettle; a shot knocked its contents about; they picked up the pieces, and ate and fought at the same time.

The Prince Royal had taken his station upon one of the batteries, from whence he beheld the action and issued his orders.   Denmark had never been engaged in so arduous a contest, and never did the Danes more nobly display their national courage—a courage not more unhappily, than impoliticly, exerted in subserviency to the interest of France. Captain Thura, of the *Indfoedsretten*, fell early in the action; and all his officers, except one lieutenant and one marine officer, were either killed or wounded.   In the confusion, the colours were either struck or shot away; but she was moored athwart one of the batteries in such a situation that the British made no attempt to board her; and a boat was despatched to the prince, to inform him of her situation.   He turned to those about him, and said, " Gentlemen, Thura is killed; which of you will take the command?" Schroedersee, a captain who had lately resigned on account of extreme ill health, answered, in a feeble voice, "I will," and hastened on board. The crew, perceiving a new commander coming alongside, hoisted their colours again, and fired a broadside. Schroedersee, when he came on deck, found himself surrounded by the dead and wounded, and called to those in the boat to get quickly on board: a ball struck him at that moment.   A lieutenant, who had accompanied him, then took the command, and con-

tinued to fight the ship. A youth of seventeen, by
name Villemoes, particularly distinguished himself on
this memorable day. He had volunteered to take
the command of a floating battery, which was a raft,
consisting merely of a number of beams nailed together, with a flooring to support the guns : it was
square, with a breast-work full of portholes and
without masts, carrying twenty-four guns and one
hundred and twenty men. With this he got under
the stern of the *Elephant*, below the reach of the
stern-chasers ; and, under a heavy fire of small arms
from the marines, fought his raft, till the truce
was announced, with such skill, as well as courage, as to
excite Nelson's warmest admiration.

Between one and two the fire of the Danes slack-
ened ; about two it ceased from the greater part of
their line, and some of their lighter ships were adrift.
It was, however, difficult to take possession of those
who struck, because the batteries on Amak Island protected them, and because an irregular fire was kept
up from the ships themselves as the boats approached.
This arose from the nature of the action ; the crews
were continually reinforced from the shore : and fresh
men coming on board, did not inquire whether the
flag had been struck, or, perhaps, did not heed it ;—
many, or most of them, never having been engaged
in war before,—knowing nothing, therefore, of its
laws, and thinking only of defending their country to
the last extremity. The *Danbrog* fired upon the
Elephant's boats in this manner, though her commodore had removed her pendant and deserted her,
though she had struck, and though she was in flames.
After she had been abandoned by the commodore,
Braun fought her till he lost his right hand, and then
Captain Lemming took the command. This unexpected renewal of her fire made the *Elephant* and
Glatton renew theirs, till she was not only silenced,
but nearly every man in the praams, ahead and astern
of her, was killed. When the smoke of their guns

died away, she was seen drifting in flames before the wind; those of her crew who remained alive, and able to exert themselves, throwing themselves out at her portholes.

Captain Rothe commanded the *Nyeborg* praam, and perceiving that she could not much longer be kept afloat, made for the inner road. As he passed the line he found the *Aggershuus* praam in a more miserable condition than his own; her masts had all gone by the board, and she was on the point of sinking. Rothe made fast a cable to her stern, and towed her off; but he could get her no further than a shoal, called Stubben, when she sunk; and soon after he had worked the *Nyeborg* up to the landing-place, that vessel also sunk to her gunwale. Never did any vessel come out of action in a more dreadful plight. The stump of her foremast was the only stick standing; her cabin had been stove in; every gun, except a single one, was dismounted; and her deck was covered with shattered limbs and dead bodies.

By half-past two the action had ceased along that part of the line which was astern of the *Elephant*, but not with the ships ahead and the Crown Batteries. Nelson, seeing the manner in which his boats were fired upon when they went to take possession of the prizes, became angry, and said he must either send on shore to have this irregular proceeding stopped, or send a fire-ship and burn them: and, with a presence of mind peculiar to himself, and never more signally displayed than now, he availed himself of this occasion to secure the advantage which he had gained, and open a negotiation. He retired into the stern gallery, and wrote thus to the Crown Prince: " Vice-Admiral Lord Nelson has been commanded to spare Denmark, when she no longer resists. The line of defence which covered her shores has struck to the British flag, but if the firing is continued on the part of Denmark, he must set on fire all the prizes that he has taken, without having the power of saving the

men who have so nobly defended them. The brave
Danes are the brothers, and should never be the
enemies, of the English." A wafer was given him;
but he ordered a candle to be brought from the cockpit, and sealed the letter with wax, affixing a larger
seal than he ordinarily used. " This," said he, " is
no time to appear hurried and informal." Captain
Sir Frederic Thesiger, who acted as his aide-de-camp,
carried this letter with a flag of truce. Meantime the
fire of the ships ahead, and the approach of the *Ramil-
lies* and *Defence*, from Sir Hyde's division, which
had now worked near enough to alarm the enemy,
though not to injure them, silenced the remainder of
the Danish line to the eastward of the Trekroner. That
battery, however, continued its fire. This formidable
work, owing to the want of the ships which had been
destined to attack it, and the inadequate force of
Riou's little squadron, was comparatively uninjured :
towards the close of the action it had been manned
with nearly fifteen hundred men, and the intention of
storming it, for which every preparation had been
made, was abandoned as impracticable.

During Thesiger's absence, Nelson sent for Freemantle from the *Ganges*, and consulted with him and
Foley, whether it was advisable to advance, with
those ships which had sustained least damage, against
the yet uninjured part of the Danish line. They were
decidedly of opinion that the best thing which could
be done was, while the wind continued fair, to remove
the fleet out of the intricate channel from which it had
to retreat. In somewhat more than half an hour
after Thesiger had been despatched, the Danish adjutant-general Lindholm came, bearing a flag of truce :
upon which the Trekroner ceased to fire, and the
action closed, after four hours' continuance. He
brought an inquiry from the prince, What was the
object of Nelson's note? The British admiral wrote
in reply : " Lord Nelson's object in sending the flag of
truce was humanity : he therefore consents that hos-

tilities shall cease, and that the wounded Danes may
be taken on shore. And Lord Nelson will take his
prisoners out of the vessels, and burn or carry off his
prizes as he shall think fit. Lord Nelson, with
humble duty to His Royal Highness the Prince, will
consider this the greatest victory he has ever gained,
if it may be the cause of a happy reconciliation and
union between his own most gracious Sovereign and
His Majesty the King of Denmark." Sir Frederic
Thesiger was despatched a second time with the
reply; and the Danish adjutant-general was referred
to the commander-in-chief for a conference upon this
overture. Lindholm assenting to this, proceeded to
the *London*, which was riding at anchor full four
miles off; and Nelson, losing not one of the critical
moments which he had thus gained, made signal for his
leading ships to weigh in succession. They had the
shoal to clear; they were much crippled; and
their course was immediately under the guns of the
Trekroner.

The *Monarch* led the way. This ship had received
six-and-twenty shot between wind and water. She
had not a shroud standing : there was a double-headed
shot in the heart of her foremast, and the slightest
wind would have sent every mast over her side. The
imminent danger from which Nelson had extricated
himself soon became apparent; the *Monarch* touched
immediately upon a shoal, over which she was pushed
by the *Ganges* taking her amidships; the *Glatton* went
clear; but the other two, the *Defiance* and the *Elephant*, grounded about a mile from the Trekroner, and
there remained fixed for many hours, in spite of all the
exertions of their wearied crews. The *Desirée* frigate
also, at the other end of the line, having gone, toward
the close of the action, to assist the *Bellona*, became
fast on the same shoal. Nelson left the *Elephant*,
soon after she took the ground, to follow Lindholm.
The heat of action was over; and that kind of feeling
which the surrounding scene of havoc was so well fitted

to produce, pressed heavily upon his exhausted spirits.
The sky had suddenly become overcast; white flags
were waving from the mastheads of so many shattered
ships—the slaughter had ceased, but the grief was to
come; for the account of the dead was not yet made
up, and no man could tell for what friends he might
have to mourn. The very silence which follows the
cessation of such a battle becomes a weight upon the
heart at first, rather than a relief; and though the work
of mutual destruction was at an end, the *Danbrog* was,
at this time, drifting about in flames; presently she
blew up; while our boats, which had put off in all
directions to assist her, were endeavouring to rescue
her devoted crew, few of whom could be saved. The
fate of these men, after the gallantry which they had
displayed, particularly affected Nelson : for there was
nothing in this action of that indignation against the
enemy, and that impression of retributive justice,
which, at the Nile, had given a sterner temper to his
mind, and a sense of austere delight, in beholding the
vengeance of which he was the appointed minister.
The Danes were an honourable foe; they were of English mould as well as English blood; and now that the
battle had ceased, he regarded them rather as brethren
than as enemies. There was another reflection also
which mingled with these melancholy thoughts, and
predisposed him to receive them. He was not here
master of his own movements, as at Egypt; he had
won the day by disobeying his orders; and, in so far
as he had been successful, had convicted the commander-in-chief of an error in judgment. " Well,"
said he, as he left the *Elephant*, " I have fought contrary to orders, and I shall, perhaps, be hanged.
Never mind : let them ! "

This was the language of a man who, while he is
giving utterance to an uneasy thought, clothes it half
in jest, because he half repents that it has been disclosed. His services had been too eminent on that
day, his judgment too conspicuous, his success too

signal, for any commander, however jealous of his
own authority, or envious of another's merits, to express anything but satisfaction and gratitude, which
Sir Hyde heartily felt, and sincerely expressed.   It
was speedily agreed that there should be a suspension
of hostilities for four-and-twenty hours, that all the
prizes should be surrendered, and the wounded Danes
carried on shore.   There was a pressing necessity for
this : for the Danes, either from too much confidence
in the strength of their position, and the difficulty of
the channel; or supposing that the wounded might
be carried to shore during the action, which was
found totally impracticable; or, perhaps, from the
confusion which the attack excited, had provided no
surgeons : so that, when our men boarded the captured ships, they found many of the mangled and
mutilated Danes bleeding to death for want of proper
assistance—a scene, of all others, the most shocking
to a brave man's feelings.

The boats of Sir Hyde's division were actively
employed all night in bringing out the prizes, and
in getting afloat the ships which were on shore.   At
daybreak, Nelson, who had slept in his own ship,
the *St. George*, rowed to the *Elephant*, and his delight
in finding her afloat seemed to give him new life.
There he took a hasty breakfast, praising the men for
their exertions, and then pushed off to the prizes,
which had not yet been removed.   The *Zealand*, 74,
the last which struck, had drifted on the shoal under
the Trekroner; and relying, as it seems, upon the
protection which that battery might have afforded,
refused to acknowledge herself captured; saying, that
though it was true her flag was not to be seen, her
pendant was still flying.   Nelson ordered one of our
brigs and three longboats to approach her, and rowed
up himself to one of the enemy's ships to communicate with the commodore.   This officer proved to be
an old acquaintance, whom he had known in the West
Indies : so he invited himself on board; and, with

o 52

that urbanity, as well as decision, which always characterised him, urged his claim to the *Zealand* so well that it was admitted. The men from the boats lashed a cable round her bowsprit, and the gun-vessel towed her away. It is affirmed, and probably with truth, that the Danes felt more pain at beholding this than at all their misfortunes on the preceding day; and one of the officers, Commodore Steen Bille, went to the Trekroner Battery, and asked the commander why he had not sunk the *Zealand* rather than suffer her thus to be carried off by the enemy.

This was indeed a mournful day for Copenhagen. It was Good Friday; but the general agitation, and the mourning which was in every house, made all distinction of days be forgotten. There were, at that hour, thousands in that city who felt, and more, perhaps, who needed, the consolations of Christianity, but few or none who could be calm enough to think of its observances. The English were actively employed in refitting their own ships, securing the prizes, and distributing the prisoners; the Danes, in carrying on shore and disposing of the wounded and the dead. It had been a murderous action. Our loss, in killed and wounded, was nine hundred and fifty-three: part of this slaughter might have been spared. The commanding officer of the troops on board one of our ships asked where his men should be stationed? He was told that they could be of no use; that they were not near enough for musketry, and were not wanted at the guns; they had, therefore, better go below. This, he said, was impossible,—it would be a disgrace that could never be wiped away. They were, therefore, drawn up upon the gangway, to satisfy this cruel point of honour; and there, without the possibility of annoying the enemy, they were mown down! The loss of the Danes, including prisoners, amounted to about six thousand. The negotiations, meantime, went on; and it was agreed that Nelson should have an interview with the prince

the following day. Hardy and Freemantle landed
with him. This was a thing as unexampled as the
other circumstances of the battle. A strong guard
was appointed to escort him to the palace—as much
for the purpose of security as of honour. The populace, according to the British account, showed a
mixture of admiration, curiosity, and displeasure, at
beholding that man in the midst of them, who had
inflicted such wounds upon Denmark. But there
were neither acclamations nor murmurs. "The
people," says a Dane, "did not degrade themselves
with the former, nor disgrace themselves with the
latter : the admiral was received as one brave enemy
ever ought to receive another—he was received with
respect." The preliminaries of the negotiation were
adjusted at this interview. During the repast which
followed, Nelson, with all the sincerity of his character, bore willing testimony to the valour of his
foes. He told the prince that he had been in a
hundred and five engagements, but that this was the
most tremendous of all. "The French," he said,
"fought bravely; but they could not have stood for
one hour the fight which the Danes had supported
for four." He requested that Villemoes might be
introduced to him; and, shaking hands with the
youth, told the prince that he ought to be made an
admiral. The prince replied : "If, my lord, I am
to make all my brave officers admirals, I should have
no captains or lieutenants in my service."

The sympathy of the Danes for their countrymen
who had bled in their defence was not weakened by
distance of time or place in this instance. Things
needful for the service, or the comfort of the wounded,
were sent in profusion to the hospitals, till the superin-
tendents gave public notice that they could receive no
more. On the third day after the action the dead were
buried in the naval churchyard. The ceremony was
made as public and as solemn as the occasion
required : such a procession had never before been

seen in that, or, perhaps, in any other city. A public monument was erected upon the spot where the slain were gathered together. A subscription was opened on the day of the funeral for the relief of the sufferers, and collections in aid of it made throughout all the churches in the kingdom. This appeal to the feelings of the people was made with circumstances which gave it full effect. A monument was raised in the midst of the church, surmounted by the Danish colours : young maidens, dressed in white, stood round it, with either one who had been wounded in the battle or the widow and orphans of some one who had fallen : a suitable oration was delivered from the pulpit, and patriotic hymns and songs were afterwards performed. Medals were distributed to all the officers, and to the men who had distinguished themselves. Poets and painters vied with each other in celebrating a battle, which, disastrous as it was, had yet been honourable to their country : some, with pardonable sophistry, represented the advantage of the day as on their own side. One writer discovered a more curious, but less disputable ground of satisfaction, in the reflection that Nelson, as may be inferred from his name, was of Danish descent, and his actions, therefore, the Dane argued, were attributable to Danish valour.

The negotiation was continued during the five following days ; and, in that interval, the prizes were disposed of, in a manner which was little approved by Nelson. Six line of battle ships and eight praams had been taken. Of these, the *Holstein*, 64, was the only one which was sent home. The *Zealand* was a finer ship : but the *Zealand* and all the others were burnt, and their brass battering cannon sunk with the hulls in such shoal water, that, when the fleet returned from Revel, they found the Danes, with craft over the wrecks, employed in getting the guns up again. Nelson, though he forbore from any public expression of displeasure at seeing the proofs

and trophies of his victory destroyed, did not forget
to represent to the Admiralty the case of those who
were thus deprived of their prize-money. "Whether,"
said he to Earl St. Vincent, "Sir Hyde Parker may
mention the subject to you, I know not, for he is
rich, and does not want it: nor is it, you will believe
me, any desire to get a few hundred pounds that
actuates me to address this letter to you, but justice
to the brave officers and men who fought on that
day. It is true our opponents were in hulks and
floats, only adapted for the position they were in:
but that made our battle so much the harder, and
victory so much the more difficult to obtain. Believe
me, I have weighed all circumstances; and, in my
conscience, I think that the king should send a
gracious message to the House of Commons for a
gift to this fleet: for what must be the natural feelings of the officers and men belonging to it, to see
their rich commander-in-chief burn all the fruits of
their victory, which, if fitted up, and sent to England
(as many of them might have been, by dismantling
part of our fleet), would have sold for a good round
sum."

On the 9th Nelson landed again to conclude the
terms of the armistice. During its continuance the
armed ships and vessels of Denmark were to remain
in their then actual situation, as to armament, equipment, and hostile position; and the treaty of armed
neutrality, as far as related to the co-operation of
Denmark, was suspended. The prisoners were to be
sent on shore, an acknowledgment being given for
them, and for the wounded also, that they might be
carried to Great Britain's credit in the account of
war, in case hostilities should be renewed. The
British fleet was allowed to provide itself with all
things requisite for the health and comfort of its
men. A difficulty arose respecting the duration of
the armistice. The Danish Commissioners fairly
stated their fears of Russia; and Nelson, with that

frankness which sound policy and the sense of power
seem often to require as well as justify in diplomacy,
told them his reason for demanding a long term was,
that he might have time to act against the Russian
fleet, and then return to Copenhagen. Neither party
would yield upon this point, and one of the Danes
hinted at the renewal of hostilities. "Renew hostilities!" cried Nelson to one of his friends—for
he understood French enough to comprehend what
was said, though not to answer it in the same
language. "Tell him we are ready at a moment!—
ready to bombard this very night!" The conference,
however, proceeded amicably on both sides; and as
the commissioners could not agree upon this head,
they broke up, leaving Nelson to settle it with the
prince. A levee was held forthwith in one of the
state rooms; a scene well suited for such a consultation, for all these rooms had been stripped of their
furniture in fear of a bombardment. To a bombardment also Nelson was looking at this time; fatigue,
and anxiety, and vexation at the dilatory measures
of the commander-in-chief, combined to make him
irritable; and as he was on his way to the prince's
dining-room, he whispered to the officer on whose
arm he was leaning, "Though I have only one eye,
I can see that all this will burn well." After dinner
he was closeted with the prince, and they agreed
that the armistice should continue fourteen weeks,
and that, at its termination, fourteen days' notice
should be given before the recommencement of
hostilities.

An official account of the battle was published by
Olfert Fischer, the Danish commander-in-chief, in
which it was asserted that our force was greatly
superior; nevertheless, that two of our ships of the
line had struck, that the others were so weakened,
and especially Lord Nelson's own ship, as to fire only
single shots for an hour before the end of the action;
and that this hero himself, in the middle and very

heat of the conflict, sent a flag of truce on shore to
propose a cessation of hostilities. For the truth of
this account the Dane appealed to the prince, and all
those who, like him, had been eye-witnesses of the
scene. Nelson was exceedingly indignant at such
a statement, and addressed a letter in confutation
of it to the adjutant-general, Lindholm, thinking this
incumbent upon him for the information of the prince,
since His Royal Highness had been appealed to as a
witness. "Otherwise," said he, "had Commodore
Fischer confined himself to his own veracity, I should
have treated his official letter with the contempt it
deserved, and allowed the world to appreciate the
merits of the two contending officers." After pointing out and detecting some of the misstatements in
the account, he proceeds : "As to his nonsense about
victory, His Royal Highness will not much credit
him. I sunk, burnt, captured, or drove into the
harbour the whole line of defence to the southward
of the Crown Islands. He says he is told that two
British ships struck. Why did he not take possession
of them? I took possession of his as fast as they
struck. The reason is clear—that he did not believe
it : he must have known the falsity of the report.
He states that the ship in which I had the honour
to hoist my flag fired latterly only single guns. It
is true : for steady and cool were my brave fellows,
and did not wish to throw away a single shot. He
seems to exult that I sent on shore a flag of truce.
You know, and His Royal Highness knows, that the
guns fired from the shore could only fire through the
Danish ships which had surrendered ; and that, if I
fired at the shore, it could only be in the same
manner. God forbid that I should destroy an unresist-
ing Dane ! When they became my prisoners, I became their protector."

This letter was written in terms of great asperity
against the Danish commander. Lindholm replied in
a manner every way honourable to himself. He vin-

dicated the commodore in some points, and excused
him in others, reminding Nelson that every commander-in-chief was liable to receive incorrect reports.   With a natural desire to represent the action
in the most favourable light to Denmark, he took into
the comparative strength of the two parties the ships
which were aground, and which could not get into
action; and omitted the Trekroner, and the batteries
upon Amak Island.   He disclaimed all idea of claim-
ing as a victory " what, to every intent and purpose,"
said he, " was a defeat—but not an inglorious one.
As to your lordship's motive for sending a flag of
truce, it never can be misconstrued; and your subsequent conduct has sufficiently shown that humanity
is always the companion of true valour.   You have
done more; you have shown yourself a true friend to
the re-establishment of peace and good harmony between this country and Great Britain.   It is, therefore, with the sincerest esteem I shall always feel myself attached to your lordship."   Thus handsomely
winding up his reply, he soothed and contented Nelson, who, drawing up a memorandum of the comparative force of the two parties for his own satisfaction, assured Lindholm that if the commodore's statement had been in the same manly and honourable
strain he would have been the last man to have noticed
any little inaccuracies which might get into a commander-in-chief's public letter.

For the battle of Copenhagen Nelson was raised to
the rank of Viscount—an inadequate mark of reward
for services so splendid, and of such paramount importance to the dearest interests of England.   There
was, however, some prudence in dealing out honours
to him step by step : had he lived long enough, he
would have fought his way up to a dukedom.

CHAPTER VIII

WHEN Nelson informed Earl St. Vincent that the armistice had been concluded, he told him also, without reserve, his own discontent at the dilatoriness and indecision which he witnessed, and could not remedy. "No man," said he, "but those who are on the spot can tell what I have gone through, and do suffer. I make no scruple in saying that I would have been at Revel fourteen days ago! that, without this armistice, the fleet would never have gone but by order of the Admiralty, and with it, I dare say, we shall not go this week. I wanted Sir Hyde to let me at least go and cruise off Carlscrona, to prevent the Revel ships from getting in. I said I would not go to Revel, to take any of those laurels which I was sure he would reap there. Think for me, my dear lord; and if I have deserved well, let me return: if ill, for Heaven's sake supersede me, for I cannot exist in this state."

Fatigue, incessant anxiety, and a climate little suited to one of a tender constitution, which had now for many years been accustomed to more genial latitudes, made him, at this time, seriously determine upon returning home. "If the northern business were not settled," he said, "they must send more admirals; for the keen air of the north had cut him to the heart." He felt the want of activity and decision in the commander-in-chief more keenly; and this affected his spirits, and, consequently, his health, more than the inclemency of the Baltic. Soon after the armistice was signed, Sir Hyde proceeded to the eastward, with such ships as were fit for service, leaving Nelson to follow with the rest as soon as those which had received slight damages should be repaired and the rest sent to England. In passing between the isles of Amak and Saltholm most of the ships touched the ground, and some of them stuck fast for a while: no serious injury, however, was

sustained.   It was intended to act against the Russians
first, before the breaking up of the frost should enable
them to leave Revel; but learning, on the way, that
the Swedes had put to sea to effect a junction with
them, Sir Hyde altered his course, in hopes of intercepting this part of the enemy's force.   Nelson had,
at this time, provided for the more pressing emergencies of the service, and prepared, on the 18th, to
follow the fleet.   The *St. George* drew too much
water to pass the channel between the isles without
being lightened : the guns were therefore taken out
and put on board an American vessel : a contrary
wind, however, prevented Nelson from moving, and
on that same evening, while he was thus delayed, information reached him of the relative situation of the
Swedish and British fleets, and the probability of an
action.   The fleet was nearly ten leagues distant, and
both wind and current contrary : but it was not possible that Nelson could wait for a favourable season
under such an expectation.   He ordered his boat immediately, and stepped into it.   Night was setting in
—one of the cold spring nights of the North—and it
was discovered, soon after they had left the ship,
that in their haste they had forgotten to provide him
with a boat cloak.   He, however, forbade them to
return for one : and when one of his companions
offered his own greatcoat, and urged him to make use
of it, he replied, " I thank you very much—but, to
tell you the truth, my anxiety keeps me sufficiently
warm at present."

    " Do you think," said he, presently, " that our
fleet has quitted Bornholm?   If it has, we must follow
it to Carlscrona."   About midnight he reached it,
and once more got on board the *Elephant*.   On the
following morning the Swedes were discovered : but
they, as soon as they perceived the English approaching, retired, and took shelter in Carlscrona, behind
the batteries on the island at the entrance of that
port.   Sir Hyde sent in a flag of truce, stating that

Denmark had concluded an armistice, and requiring an explicit declaration from the Court of Sweden, whether it would adhere to, or abandon, the hostile measures which it had taken against the rights and interests of Great Britain. The commander, Vice-Admiral Cronstadt, replied, " that he could not answer a question which did not come within the particular circle of his duty, but that the king was then at Malmoe, and would soon be at Carlscrona." Gustavus shortly afterwards arrived, and an answer was then returned to this effect : " That His Swedish Majesty would not for a moment fail to fulfil, with fidelity and sincerity, the engagements he had entered into with his allies ; but he would not refuse to listen to equitable proposals, made by deputies furnished with proper authority by the King of Great Britain to the united northern powers." Satisfied with this answer, and with the known disposition of the Swedish court, Sir Hyde sailed for the Gulf of Finland : but he had not proceeded far before a despatch boat, from the Russian ambassador at Copenhagen, arrived, bringing intelligence of the death of the Emperor Paul ; and that his successor, Alexander, had accepted the offer made by England to his father of terminating the dispute by a convention ; the British admiral was, therefore, required to desist from all further hostilities.

It was Nelson's maxim, that, to negotiate with effect, force should be at hand, and in a situation to act. The fleet, having been reinforced from England, amounted to eighteen sail of the line ; and the wind was fair for Revel. There he would have sailed immediately, to place himself between that division of the Russian fleet and the squadron at Cronstadt, in case this offer should prove insincere. Sir Hyde, on the other hand, believed that the death of Paul had effected all which was necessary. The manner of that death, indeed, rendered it apparent that a change of policy would take place in the cabinet of Petersburgh

—but Nelson never trusted anything to the uncertain events of time which could possibly be secured by promptitude or resolution. It was not, therefore, without severe mortification that he saw the commander-in-chief return to the coast of Zealand and anchor in Kioge Bay—there to wait patiently for what might happen. There the fleet remained till despatches arrived from home, on the 5th of May, recalling Sir Hyde and appointing Nelson commander-in-chief.

Nelson wrote to Earl St. Vincent that he was unable to hold this honourable station. Admiral Graves also was so ill as to be confined to his bed, and he entreated that some person might come out and take the command. "I will endeavour," said he, "to do my best while I remain; but, my dear lord, I shall either soon go to heaven, I hope, or must rest quiet for a time. If Sir Hyde were gone, I would now be under sail." On the day when this was written he received news of his appointment. Not a moment was now lost. His first signal, as commander-in-chief, was to hoist in all launches, and prepare to weigh; and on the 7th he sailed from Kioge. Part of his fleet was left at Bornholm to watch the Swedes, from whom he required and obtained an assurance that the British trade in the Cattegat and in the Baltic should not be molested; and saying how unpleasant it would be to him if anything should happen which might, for a moment, disturb the returning harmony between Sweden and Great Britain, he apprised them that he was not directed to abstain from hostilities should he meet with the Swedish fleet at sea. Meantime, he himself, with ten sail of the line, two frigates, a brig and a schooner, made for the Gulf of Finland. Paul, in one of the freaks of his tyranny, had seized upon all the British effects in Russia, and even considered British subjects as his prisoners. "I will have all the English shipping and property restored," said Nelson, "but I will do nothing violently—neither commit my country, nor suffer Russia to mix the affairs of Denmark or Sweden with the detention of our ships." The wind was fair, and carried him, in four days, to Revel Roads. But the bay had been clear of firm ice on the 29th of April, while the English were lying idly at Kioge. The Russians had cut through the ice in the mole, six feet thick, and their whole squadron had sailed from Cronstadt on the third. Before that time it had lain at the mercy of the English. "Nothing," Nelson said, "if it had been right to make the attack, could have saved one ship of them in two hours after our entering the bay."

It so happened that there was no cause to regret the opportunity which had been lost, and Nelson immediately put the intentions of Russia to the proof. He sent on shore, to say that he came with friendly views, and was ready to return a salute. On their part the salute was delayed, till a message was sent to them to inquire for what reason; and the officer, whose neglect had occasioned the delay, was put under arrest. Nelson wrote to the emperor, proposing to wait on him personally and congratulate him on his accession, and urging the immediate release of British subjects and restoration of British property.

The answer arrived on the 16th. Nelson, meantime, had exchanged visits with the governor, and the most friendly intercourse had subsisted between the ships and the shore. Alexander's ministers, in their reply, expressed their surprise at the arrival of a British fleet in a Russian port, and their wish that it should return; they professed, on the part of Russia, the most friendly disposition towards Great Britain, but declined the personal visit of Lord Nelson, unless he came in a single ship. There was a suspicion implied in this which stung Nelson, and he said the Russian ministers would never have written thus if their fleet had been at Revel. He wrote an immediate reply, expressing what he felt; he told the court of Petersburgh, " that the word of a British admiral, when given in explanation of any part of his conduct, was as sacred as that of any sovereign's in Europe." And he repeated, " that, under other circumstances, it would have been his anxious wish to have paid his personal respects to the emperor, and signed, with his own hand, the act of amity between the two countries." Having despatched this, he stood out to sea immediately, leaving a brig to bring off the provisions which had been contracted for, and to settle the accounts. " I hope all is right," said he, writing to our ambassador at Berlin; " but seamen are but bad negotiators, for we put to issue in five minutes what diplomatic forms would be five months doing."

On his way down the Baltic, however, he met the Russian Admiral Tchitchagof, whom the emperor, in reply to Sir Hyde's overtures, had sent to communicate personally with the British commander-in-chief. The reply was such as had been wished and expected; and these negotiators going, seaman-like, straight to their object, satisfied each other of the friendly intentions of their respective Governments. Nelson then anchored off Rostock, and there he received an answer to his last despatch from Revel, in which the Russian court expressed their regret that there should have been any misconception between them, informed him that the British vessels which Paul had detained were ordered to be liberated, and invited him to Petersburgh in whatever mode might be most agreeable to himself. Other honours awaited him: the Duke of Mecklenburgh Strelitz, the queen's brother, came to visit him on board his ship; and towns, from the inland parts of Mecklenburgh, sent deputations with their public books of record, that they might have the name of Nelson in them, written by his own hand.

From Rostock the fleet returned to Kioge Bay. Nelson saw that the temper of the Danes towards England was such as naturally arose from the chastisement which they had so recently received. " In this nation," said he, " we shall not be forgiven for

having the upper hand of them : I only thank God we
have, or they would try to humble us to the dust.''
He saw also that the Danish Cabinet was completely
subservient to France: a French officer was, at this
time, the companion and counsellor of the Crown
Prince; and things were done in such open violation
of the armistice, that Nelson thought a second inflic-
tion of vengeance would soon be necessary. He wrote
to the Admiralty requesting a clear and explicit reply
to his inquiry, Whether the commander-in-chief was
at liberty to hold the language becoming a British
admiral?—''Which very probably,'' said he, '' if I
am here, will break the armistice, and set Copenhagen
in a blaze. I see everything which is dirty and mean
going on, and the Prince Royal at the head of it.
Ships have been masted, guns taken on board, floating batteries prepared—and, except hauling out and
completing their rigging, everything has been done
in defiance of the treaty. My heart burns at seeing
the word of a prince, nearly allied to our good king,
so falsified; but his conduct is such that he will lose
his kingdom if he goes on, for Jacobins rule in Denmark. I have made no representations yet, as it
would be useless to do so until I have the power of
correction. All I beg, in the name of the future commander-in-chief, is, that the orders may be clear; for
enough is done to break twenty treaties, if it should
be wished, or to make the Prince Royal humble himself before British generosity.''

Nelson was not deceived in his judgment of the
Danish Cabinet, but the battle of Copenhagen had
crippled its power. The death of the Czar Paul had
broken the confederacy; and that Cabinet, therefore,
was compelled to defer, till a more convenient season,
the indulgence of its enmity towards Great Britain.
Soon afterwards, Admiral Sir Charles Maurice Pole
arrived to take the command. The business, military
and political, had by that time been so far completed
that the presence of the British fleet soon became no

longer necessary. Sir Charles, however, made the
short time of his command memorable by passing the
Great Belt, for the first time, with line of battle ships,
working through the channel against adverse winds.
When Nelson left the fleet, this speedy termination of
the expedition, though confidently expected, was not
certain; and he, in his unwillingness to weaken the
British force, thought at one time of traversing Jut-
land in his boat, by the canal, to Tonningen on the
Eyder, and finding his way home from thence. This
intention was not executed; but he returned in a brig,
declining to accept a frigate—which few admirals
would have done, especially if, like him, they suffered
from sea-sickness in a small vessel. On his arrival at
Yarmouth the first thing he did was to visit the hospital, and see the men who had been wounded in the
late battle—that victory which had added new glory
to the name of Nelson, and which was of more importance even than the battle of the Nile to the
honour and strength and security of England.

He had not been many weeks on shore before he
was called upon to undertake a service for which no
Nelson was required. Buonaparte, who was now
first consul, and in reality sole ruler of France, was
making preparations, upon a great scale, for invading
England: but his schemes in the Baltic had been
baffled; fleets could not be created as they were
wanted; and his armies, therefore, were to come over
in gun-boats and such small craft as could be rapidly
built or collected for the occasion. From the former
Governments of France such threats have only been
matter of insult and policy: in Buonaparte they were
sincere—for this adventurer, intoxicated with success,
already began to imagine that all things were to be
submitted to his fortune. We had not, at that time,
proved the superiority of our soldiers over the French,
and the unreflecting multitude were not to be persuaded that an invasion could only be effected by
numerous and powerful fleets. A general alarm was

excited; and, in condescension to this unworthy feeling, Nelson was appointed to a command, extending from Orfordness to Beachy Head, on both shores :—a sort of service, he said, for which he felt no other ability than what might be found in his zeal.

To this service, however, such as it was, he applied with his wonted alacrity; and having hoisted his flag in the *Medusa* frigate, went to reconnoitre Boulogne—the point from which it was supposed the great attempt would be made, and which the French, in fear of an attack themselves, were fortifying with all care. He approached near enough to sink two of their floating batteries and destroy a few gunboats which were without the pier : what damage was done within could not be ascertained. " Boulogne," he said, " was certainly not a very pleasant place that morning; but," he added, " it is not my wish to injure the poor inhabitants, and the town is spared as much as the nature of the service will admit." Enough was done to show the enemy that they could not, with impunity, come outside their own ports. Nelson was satisfied, by what he saw, that they meant to make an attempt from this place, but that it was impracticable; for the least wind W.N.W. and they were lost. The ports of Flushing and Flanders were better points : there we could not tell by our eyes what means of transport were provided. From thence, therefore, if it came forth at all, the expedition would come : " And what a forlorn undertaking ! " said he. " Consider cross-tides, etc. As for rowing, that is impossible. It is perfectly right to be prepared for a mad Government; but, with the active force which has been given me, I may pronounce it almost impracticable."

That force had been got together with an alacrity which has seldom been equalled. On the 28th of July we were, in Nelson's own words, literally at the foundation of our fabric of defence; and twelve days afterwards we were so prepared on the enemy's coast that he did not believe they could get three miles from their ports. The *Medusa*, returning to our own shores, anchored in the rolling ground of Harwich; and, when Nelson wished to get to the Nore in her, the wind rendered it impossible to proceed there by the usual channel. In haste to be at the Nore, remembering that he had been a tolerable pilot for the mouth of the Thames in his younger days, and thinking it necessary that he should know all that could be known of the navigation, he requested the maritime surveyor of the coast, Mr. Spence, to get him into the Swin, by any channel : for neither the pilots which he had on board nor the Harwich ones would take charge of the ship. No vessel drawing more than fourteen feet had ever before ventured over the Naze. Mr. Spence, however, who had surveyed the channel, carried her safely through. The channel has since been called Nelson's, though he himself wished it to be named after the *Medusa* : his name needed no new memorial.

Nelson's eye was upon Flushing. "To take possession of that place," he said, "would be a week's expedition for four or five thousand troops." This, however, required a consultation with the Admiralty; and, that something might be done meantime, he resolved upon attacking the Flotilla in the mouth of Boulogne harbour, owning, at the same time, that this boat-warfare was not exactly congenial to his feelings. Into Helvoet or Flushing he should be happy to lead, if Government turned their thoughts that way. "While I serve," said he, "I will do it actively, and to the very best of my abilities. I require nursing like a child," he added; "my mind carries me beyond my strength, and will do me up,— but such is my nature."

The attack was made by the boats of the squadron in five divisions, under Captains Somerville, Parker, Cotgrave, Jones, and Conn. The previous essay had taught the French the weak parts of their position; and they had omitted no means of strengthening it, and of guarding against the expected attempt. The

boats put off about half-an-hour before midnight;
but, owing to the darkness, and the tide and half-tide,
which must always make night attacks so uncertain
on the coasts of the channel, the divisions separated.
One could not arrive at all; another not till near daybreak. The others made their attack gallantly, but
the enemy were fully prepared : every vessel was defended by long poles, headed with iron spikes, project-
ing from their sides; strong nettings were braced up
to their lower yards; they were moored by the bottom
to the shore, and chained one to another; they were
strongly manned with soldiers, and protected by land
batteries, and the shore was lined with troops. Many
were taken possession of; and, though they could not
have been brought out, would have been burnt, had
not the French resorted to a mode of offence which
they have often used, but which no other people have
ever been wicked enough to employ. The moment
the firing ceased on board one of their own vessels,
they fired upon it from the shore, perfectly regardless
of their own men.

The commander of one of the French divisions
acted like a generous enemy. He hailed the boats as
they approached, and cried out, in English : " Let me
advise you, my brave Englishmen, to keep your distance : you can do nothing here; and it is only use-
lessly shedding the blood of brave men to make the
attempt." The French official account boasted of the
victory. " The combat," it said, " took place in
sight of both countries; it was the first of the kind,
and the historian would have cause to make this re-
mark." They guessed our loss at four or five hundred—it amounted to one hundred and seventy-two.
In his private letters to the Admiralty Nelson affirmed
that had our force arrived as he intended, it was not
all the chains in France which could have prevented
our men from bringing off the whole of the vessels.
There had been no error committed, and never did
Englishmen display more courage. Upon this point

Nelson was fully satisfied; but he said he should never bring himself again to allow any attack wherein he was not personally concerned, and that his mind suffered more than if he had had a leg shot off in the affair. He grieved particularly for Captain Parker—an excellent officer, to whom he was greatly attached, and who had an aged father looking to him for assistance. His thigh was shattered in the action; and the wound proved mortal, after some weeks of suffering and manly resignation. During this interval Nelson's anxiety was very great. "Dear Parker is my child," said he; "for I found him in distress." And when he received the tidings of his death, he replied: "You will judge of my feelings: God's will be done. I beg that his hair may be cut off and given me; it shall be buried in my grave. Poor Mr. Parker! What a son has he lost! If I were to say I was content, I should lie; but I shall endeavour to submit with all the fortitude in my power. His loss has made a wound in my heart which time will hardly heal."

He now wished to be relieved from this service. The country, he said, had attached a confidence to his name which he had submitted to, and therefore had cheerfully repaired to the station; but this boat business, though it might be part of a great plan of invasion, could never be the only one, and he did not think it was a command for a vice-admiral. It was not that he wanted a more lucrative situation, for, seriously indisposed as he was, and low-spirited from private considerations, he did not know, if the Mediterranean were vacant, that he should be equal to undertake it. Just at this time the peace of Amiens was signed. Nelson rejoiced that the experiment was made, but was well aware that it was an experiment; he saw what he called the misery of peace, unless the utmost vigilance and prudence were exerted: and he expressed, in bitter terms, his proper indignation at the manner in which the mob of London welcomed the French general who brought the ratification, saying, " that they made him ashamed of his country."

He had purchased a house and estate at Merton, in Surrey, meaning to pass his days there in the society of Sir William and Lady Hamilton. This place he had never seen, till he was now welcomed there by the friends to whom he had so passionately devoted himself, and who were not less sincerely attached to him. The place, and everything which Lady Hamilton had done to it, delighted him; and he declared that the longest liver should possess it all. The depression of spirits under which he had long laboured, arose from the disquietude in which this connection had involved him—a connection which it was not possible his father could behold without sorrow and displeasure. Mr. Nelson, however, was soon convinced that the attachment, which Lady Nelson regarded with natural jealousy and resentment, did not in reality pass the bounds of ardent and romantic admiration : a passion which the manners and accomplishments of Lady Hamilton, fascinating as they were, would not have been able to excite if they had not been accompanied by more uncommon intellectual endowments, and by a character which, both in its strength and in its weakness, resembled his own. It did not, therefore, require much explanation to reconcile him to his son—an event the more essential to Nelson's happiness, because, a few months afterwards, the good old man died, at the age of seventy-nine.

Soon after the conclusion of peace, tidings arrived of our final and decisive successes in Egypt : in consequence of which, the Common Council voted their thanks to the army and navy for bringing the campaign to so glorious a conclusion. When Nelson, after the action of Cape St. Vincent, had been entertained at a City feast, he had observed to the Lord Mayor, " that, if the City continued its generosity, the navy would ruin them in gifts." To which the

Lord Mayor replied, putting his hand upon the admiral's shoulder: "Do you find victories and we will find rewards." Nelson, as he said, had kept his word—had doubly fulfilled his part of the contract—but no thanks had been voted for the battle of Copenhagen; and feeling that he and his companions in that day's glory had a fair and honourable claim to this reward, he took the present opportunity of addressing a letter to the Lord Mayor, complaining of the omission and the injustice. "The smallest services," said he, "rendered by the army or navy to the country, have been always noticed by the great city of London, with one exception—the glorious second of April—a day when the greatest dangers of navigation were overcome, and the Danish force, which they thought impregnable, totally taken or destroyed, by the consummate skill of our commanders, and by the undaunted bravery of as gallant a band as ever defended the rights of this country. For myself, if I were only personally concerned, I should bear the stigma, attempted to be now first placed upon my brow, with humility. But, my lord, I am the natural guardian of the fame of the officers of the navy, army, and marines, who fought and so profusely bled, under my command, on that day. Again, I disclaim for myself more merit than naturally falls to a successful commander; but when I am called upon to speak of the merits of the captains of His Majesty's ships, and of the officers and men, whether seamen, marines, or soldiers, whom I that day had the happiness to command, I then say, that never was the glory of this country upheld with more determined bravery than on that occasion—and, if I may be allowed to give an opinion as a Briton, then I say, that more important service was never rendered to our king and country. It is my duty, my lord, to prove to the brave fellows, my companions in danger, that I have not failed, at every proper place, to represent, as well as I am able, their bravery and meritorious conduct."

Another honour of greater import was withheld from the conquerors. The king had given medals to those captains who were engaged in the battles of the 1st of June, of Cape St. Vincent, of Camperdown, and of the Nile. Then came the victory at Copenhagen, which Nelson truly called the most difficult achievement, the hardest fought battle, the most glorious result that ever graced the annals of our country. He, of course, expected the medal; and, in writing to Earl St. Vincent, said : " He longed to have it, and would not give it up to be made an English duke." The medal, however, was not given : " For what reason," said Nelson, " Lord St. Vincent best knows "—words plainly implying a suspicion that it was withheld by some feeling of jealousy; and that suspicion estranged him during the remaining part of his life from one who had, at one time, been essentially, as well as sincerely, his friend, and of whose professional abilities he ever entertained the highest opinion.

The happiness which Nelson enjoyed in the society of his chosen friends was of no long continuance. Sir William Hamilton, who was far advanced in years, died early in 1803. He expired in his wife's arms, holding Nelson by the hand; and almost in his last words left her to his protection, requesting him that he would see justice done her by the Government, as he knew what she had done for her country. He left him her portrait in enamel, calling him his dearest friend, the most virtuous, loyal, and truly brave character he had ever known. The codicil, containing this bequest, concluded with these words : " God bless him, and shame fall on those who do not say, Amen." Sir William's pension of £1,200 a year ceased with his death. Nelson applied to Mr. Addington in Lady Hamilton's behalf, stating the important service which she had rendered to the fleet at Syracuse : and Mr. Addington, it is said, acknowledged that she had a just claim upon the gratitude of

the country. This barren acknowledgment was all
that was obtained; but a sum, equal to the pension
which her husband had enjoyed, was settled on her by
Nelson, and paid in monthly payments during his life.
A few weeks after this event the war was renewed;
and the day after His Majesty's message to Parliament, Nelson departed to take the command of the
Mediterranean fleet.

He took his station immediately off Toulon, and
there, with incessant vigilance, waited for the coming out of the enemy. When he had been fourteen
months thus employed, he received a vote of thanks
from the City of London for his skill and perseverance in blockading that port so as to prevent the
French from putting to sea. Nelson had not forgotten the wrong which the City had done to the
Baltic fleet by their omission, and did not lose the
opportunity which this vote afforded of recurring to
that point. "I do assure your Lordship," said he,
in answer to the Lord Mayor, "that there is not that
man breathing who sets a higher value upon the
thanks of his fellow-citizens of London than myself;
but I should feel as much ashamed to receive them for
a particular service, marked in the resolution, if I
felt that I did not come within that line of service, as
I should feel hurt at having a great victory passed
over without notice. I beg to inform your Lordship
that the port of Toulon has never been blockaded by
me—quite the reverse. Every opportunity has been
offered the enemy to put to sea: for it is there that
we hope to realise the hopes and expectations of our
country." Nelson then remarked, that the junior
flag-officers of his fleet had been omitted in this vote
of thanks, and his surprise at the omission was expressed with more asperity, perhaps, than an offence
so entirely and manifestly unintentional deserved;
but it arose from that generous regard for the feelings
as well as interests of all who were under his command, which made him as much beloved in the

fleets of Britain as he was dreaded in those of the enemy.

Never was any commander more beloved. He governed men by their reason and their affections : they knew that he was incapable of caprice or tyranny ; and they obeyed him with alacrity and joy, because he possessed their confidence as well as their love. " Our Nel," they used to say, " is as brave as a lion, and as gentle as a lamb." Severe discipline he detested, though he had been bred in a severe school : he never inflicted corporal punishment if it were possible to avoid it, and when compelled to enforce it, he, who was familiar with wounds and death, suffered like a woman. In his whole life Nelson was never known to act unkindly towards an officer. If he was asked to prosecute one for ill-behaviour, he used to answer : " That there was no occasion for him to ruin a poor devil, who was sufficiently his own enemy to ruin himself." But in Nelson there was more than the easiness and humanity of a happy nature : he did not merely abstain from injury : his was an active and watchful bene-volence, ever desirous not only to render justice, but to do good. During the peace he had spoken in Parliament upon the abuses respecting prize-money, and had submitted plans to Government for more easily manning the navy, and preventing desertion from it, by bettering the condition of the seamen. He proposed that their certificates should be regis-tered, and that every man who had served, with a good character, five years in war, should receive a bounty of two guineas annually after that time, and of four guineas after eight years. " This," he said, " might, at first sight, appear an enormous sum for the state to pay ; but the average life of a seaman is, from hard service, finished at forty-five : he cannot, therefore, enjoy the annuity many years ; and the interest of the money saved by their not deserting would go far to pay the whole expense."

To his midshipmen he ever showed the most
winning kindness, encouraging the diffident, temper-
ing the hasty, counselling and befriending both.
"Recollect," he used to say, "that you must be a
seaman to be an officer; and also, that you cannot
be a good officer without being a gentleman." A
lieutenant wrote to him, to say that he was dissatisfied
with his captain. Nelson's answer was in that spirit
of perfect wisdom and perfect goodness which regulated his whole conduct toward those who were under
his command. "I have just received your letter, and
I am truly sorry that any difference should arise
between your captain, who has the reputation of
being one of the bright officers of the service, and
yourself, a very young man, and a very young officer,
who must naturally have much to learn : therefore the
chance is that you are perfectly wrong in the disagree-
ment. However, as your present situation must be
very disagreeable, I will certainly take an early opportunity of removing you, provided your conduct to
your present captain be such that another may not
refuse to receive you." The gentleness and benignity
of his disposition never made him forget what was
due to discipline. Being on one occasion applied to,
to save a young officer from a court-martial which
he had provoked by his misconduct, his reply was :
"That he would do everything in his power to oblige
so gallant and good an officer as Sir John Warren,"
in whose name the intercession had been made : "But
what," he added, "would he do if he were here? —
Exactly what I have done, and am still willing to
do. The young man must write such a letter of con-
trition as would be an acknowledgment of his great
fault; and with a sincere promise, if his captain will
intercede to prevent the impending court-martial,
never to so misbehave again. On his captain's
inclosing me such a letter, with a request to cancel
the order for the trial, I might be induced to do it :
but the letters and reprimand will be given in the

public order-book of the fleet, and read to all the
officers. The young man has pushed himself forward
to notice, and he must take the consequence. It was
upon the quarter-deck, in the face of the ship's company, that he treated his captain with contempt; and
I am in duty bound to support the authority and
consequence of every officer under my command. A
poor ignorant seaman is for ever punished for contempt to *his* superiors."

A dispute occurred in the fleet, while it was off
Toulon, which called forth Nelson's zeal for the
rights and interests of the navy. Some young artillery officers, serving on board the bomb vessels,
refused to let their men perform any other duty but
what related to the mortars. They wished to have it
established that their corps was not subject to the
captain's authority. The same pretensions were
made in the Channel fleet about the same time; and
the artillery rested their claims to separate and independent authority on board, upon a clause in the Act,
which they interpreted in their favour. Nelson took
up the subject with all the earnestness which its importance deserved. "There is no real happiness in
this world," said he, writing to Earl St. Vincent, as
First Lord. "With all content and smiles around
me, up start these artillery boys (I understand they
are not beyond that age), and set us at defiance,
speaking in the most disrespectful manner of the navy
and its commanders. I know you, my dear Lord, so
well, that with your quickness the matter would have
been settled, and perhaps some of them been broke.
I am, perhaps, more patient, but, I do assure you, not
less resolved, if my plan of conciliation is not attended
to. You and I are on the eve of quitting the theatre
of our exploits; but we hold it to our successors
never, while we have a tongue to speak or a hand to
write, to allow the navy to be, in the smallest degree,
injured in its discipline by our conduct." To Trowbridge he wrote in the same spirit. "It is the old

history, trying to do away the Act of Parliament:
but I trust they will never succeed, for when they do,
farewell to our naval superiority. We should be
prettily commanded! Let them once gain the step
of being independent of the navy on board a ship, and
they will soon have the other, and command us. But,
thank God! my dear Trowbridge, the king himself
cannot do away the Act of Parliament. Although my
career is nearly run, yet it would embitter my future
days and expiring moments to hear of our navy being
sacrificed to the army." As the surest way of preventing such disputes, he suggested that the navy
should have its own corps of artillery; and a corps of
marine artillery was accordingly established.

Instead of lessening the power of the commander,
Nelson would have wished to see it increased: it was
absolutely necessary, he thought, that merit should
be rewarded at the moment, and that the officers of
the fleet should look up to the commander-in-chief for
their reward. He himself was never more happy than
when he could promote those who were deserving
of promotion. Many were the services which he thus
rendered unsolicited, and frequently the officer, in
whose behalf he had interested himself with the
Admiralty, did not know to whose friendly interference he was indebted for his good fortune. He
used to say, " I wish it to appear as a God-send."
The love which he bore the navy made him promote
the interests, and honour the memory, of all who
had added to its glories. " The near relations of
brother-officers," he said, " he considered as legacies
to the service." Upon mention being made to him of
a son of Rodney by the Duke of Clarence, his reply
was : " I agree with your Royal Highness most
entirely that the son of a Rodney ought to be the
protégé of every person in the kingdom, and particularly of the sea officers. Had I known that there
had been this claimant, some of my own lieutenants
must have given way to such a name, and he should

have been placed in the *Victory* : she is full, and I have twenty on my list; but, whatever numbers I have, the name of Rodney must cut many of them out.'' Such was the proper sense which Nelson felt of what was due to splendid services and illustrious names. His feelings toward the brave men who had served with him are shown by a note in his diary, which was probably not intended for any other eye than his own.—'' Nov. 7. I had the comfort of making an old *Agamemnon*, George Jones, a gunner, into the *Chameleon* brig.''

When Nelson took the command, it was expected that the Mediterranean would be an active scene. Nelson well understood the character of the perfidious Corsican, who was now sole tyrant of France; and knowing that he was as ready to attack his friends as his enemies, knew, therefore, that nothing could be more uncertain than the direction of the fleet from Toulon, whenever it should put to sea : '' It had as many destinations,'' he said, '' as there were countries.'' The momentous revolutions of the last ten years had given him ample matter for reflection, as well as opportunities for observation : the film was cleared from his eyes; and now, when the French no longer went abroad with the cry of liberty and equality, he saw that the oppression and misrule of the powers which had been opposed to them had been the main causes of their success, and that those causes would still prepare the way before them. Even in Sicily, where, if it had been possible longer to blind himself, Nelson would willingly have seen no evil, he perceived that the people wished for a change, and acknowledged that they had reason to wish for it. In Sardinia the same burden of misgovernment was felt; and the people, like the Sicilians, were impoverished by a government so utterly incompetent to perform its first and most essential duties, that it did not protect its own coasts from the Barbary pirates. He would fain have had us purchase this island (the finest in the Mediterranean) from its sovereign, who did not receive £5,000 a year from it, after its wretched establishment was paid. There was reason to think that France was preparing to possess herself of this important point, which afforded our fleet facilities for watching Toulon, not to be obtained elsewhere. An expedition was preparing at Corsica for the purpose; and all the Sardes, who had taken part with revolutionary France, were ordered to assemble there. It was certain that if the attack were made, it would succeed. Nelson thought that the only means to prevent Sardinia from becoming French was to make it English, and that half a million would give the king a rich price, and England a cheap purchase. A better, and therefore a wiser policy, would have been to exert our influence in removing the abuses of the Government; for foreign dominion is always, in some degree, an evil, and allegiance neither can nor ought to be made a thing of bargain and sale. Sardinia, like Sicily, and Corsica, is large enough to form a separate state. Let us hope that these islands may, ere long, be made free and independent. Freedom and independence will bring with them industry and prosperity; and wherever these are found, arts and letters will flourish, and the improvement of the human race proceed.

The proposed attack was postponed. Views of wider ambition were opening upon Buonaparte, who now almost undisguisedly aspired to make himself master of the continent of Europe; and Austria was preparing for another struggle, to be conducted as weakly, and terminated as miserably, as the former. Spain, too, was once more to be involved in war by the policy of France, that perfidious Government having in view the double object of employing the Spanish resources against England, and exhausting them, in order to render Spain herself finally its prey. Nelson, who knew that England and the Peninsula ought to be in alliance for the common interest of both, frequently expressed his hopes that Spain might resume her natural rank among the nations. "We ought," he said, "by mutual consent, to be the very best friends, and both to be ever hostile to France." But he saw that Buonaparte was meditating the destruction of Spain; and that, while the wretched court of Madrid professed to remain neutral, the appearances of neutrality were scarcely preserved. An order of the year 1771, excluding British ships of war from the Spanish ports, was revived and put in force, while French privateers from these very ports annoyed the British trade, carried their prizes in, and sold them even at Barcelona. Nelson complained of this to the captain-general of Catalonia, informing him that he claimed, for every British ship or squadron, the right of lying, as long as it pleased, in the ports of Spain, while that right was allowed to other powers. To the British ambassador he said: "I am ready to make large allowances for the miserable situation Spain has placed herself in; but there is a certain line beyond which I cannot submit to be treated with disrespect. We have given up French vessels taken within gunshot of the Spanish shore, and yet French vessels are permitted to attack our ships from the Spanish shore. Your Excellency may assure the Spanish Government, that in whatever place the Spaniards allow the French to attack us, in that place I shall order the French to be attacked."

During this state of things, to which the weakness of Spain, and not her will, consented, the enemy's fleet did not venture to put to sea. Nelson watched it with unremitting and almost unexampled perseverance. The station off Toulon he called his home. "We are in the right fighting trim," said he; "let them come as soon as they please. I never saw a fleet, altogether, so well officered and manned: would to God the ships were half as good! The finest ones in the service would soon be destroyed by such terrible weather. I know well enough, that if I were

to go into Malta I should save the ships during this
bad season : but, if I am to watch the French, I must
be at sea; and, if at sea, must have bad weather :
and if the ships are not fit to stand bad weather, they
are useless.'' Then only he was satisfied, and at ease,
when he had the enemy in view. Mr. Elliot, our
minister at Naples, seems, at this time, to have proposed to send a confidential Frenchman to him with
information. '' I should be very happy,'' he replied,
'' to receive authentic intelligence of the destination
of the French squadron, their route, and time of
sailing. Anything short of this is useless; and I
assure your Excellency, that I would not, upon any
consideration, have a Frenchman in the fleet, except
as a prisoner. I put no confidence in them. You
think yours good; the queen thinks the same : I
believe they are all alike. Whatever information you
can get me, I shall be very thankful for; but not a
Frenchman comes here. Forgive me, but my mother
hated the French.''

M. Latouche Treville, who had commanded at Boulogne, commanded now at Toulon. '' He was sent
for on purpose,'' said Nelson, '' as *he beat me* at Boulogne, to beat me again : but he seems very loath to
try.'' One day, while the main body of our fleet was
out of sight of land, Rear-Admiral Campbell, recon-
noitring with the *Canopus*, *Donegal*, and *Amazon*,
stood in close to the port; and M. Latouche, taking
advantage of a breeze which sprung up, pushed out,
with four ships of the line and three heavy frigates,
and chased him about four leagues. The Frenchman, delighted at having found himself in so novel a
situation, published a boastful account, affirming that
he had given chase to the whole British fleet, and that
Nelson had fled before him ! Nelson thought it due
to the Admiralty to send home a copy of the *Victory*'s
log upon this occasion. '' As for himself,'' he said,
'' if his character was not established by that time
for not being apt to run away, it was not worth his

while to put the world right." "If this fleet gets
fairly up with M. Latouche," said he to one of his
correspondents, "his letter, with all his ingenuity,
must be different from his last. We had fancied that
we chased him into Toulon; for, blind as I am, I
could see his water-line, when he clued his topsails up,
shutting in Sepet. But, from the time of his meeting
Captain Hawker, in the *Isis*, I never heard of his
acting otherwise than as a poltroon and a liar. Contempt is the best mode of treating such a miscreant."
In spite, however, of contempt, the impudence of this
Frenchman half angered him. He said to his
brother : " You will have seen Latouche's letter; how
he chased me, and how I ran. I keep it : and if I take
him, by God he shall eat it."

Nelson, who used to say that in sea affairs nothing
is impossible and nothing improbable, feared the
more that this Frenchman might get out and elude
his vigilance, because he was so especially desirous of
catching him, and administering to him his own lying
letter in a sandwich. M. Latouche, however, escaped
him in another way. He died, according to the
French papers, in consequence of walking so often
up to the signal-posts upon Sepet, to watch the
British fleet. "I always pronounced that would be
his death," said Nelson. "If he had but come out
and fought me, it would, at least, have added ten
years to my life." The patience with which he had
watched Toulon, he spoke of, truly, as a perseverance
at sea which had never been surpassed. From May,
1803, to August, 1805, he himself went out of his ship
but three times : each of those times was upon the
king's service, and neither time of absence exceeded
an hour. The weather had been so unusually severe,
that, he said, the Mediterranean seemed altered. It
was his rule never to contend with the gales, but
either run to the southward to escape their violence,
or furl all the sails, and make the ships as easy as
possible. The men, though he said flesh and blood

Q 52

could hardly stand it, continued in excellent health, which he ascribed, in great measure, to a plentiful supply of lemons and onions. For himself, he thought he could only last till the battle was over. One battle more it was his hope that he might fight. " However," said he, " whatever happens, I have run a glorious race." He was afraid of blindness, and this was the only evil which he could not contemplate without unhappiness. More alarming symptoms he regarded with less apprehension, describing his own " shattered carcass " as in the worst plight of any in the fleet : and he says, " I have felt the blood gushing up the left side of my head, and the moment it covers the brain, I am fast asleep." The fleet was in worse trim than the men, but when he compared it with the enemy's, it was with a right English feeling. " The French fleet yesterday," said he, in one of his letters, " was to appearance in high feather, and as fine as paint could make them,—but when they may sail, or where they may go, I am very sorry to say is a secret I am not acquainted with. Our weather-beaten ships, I have no fear, will make their sides like a plum-pudding."

Hostilities at length commenced between Great Britain and Spain. That country, whose miserable Government made her subservient to France, was once more destined to lavish her resources and her blood in furtherance of the designs of a perfidious ally. The immediate occasion of the war was the seizure of four treasure-ships by the English. The act was perfectly justifiable, for those treasures were intended to furnish means for France; but the circumstances which attended it were as unhappy as they were un-foreseen. Four frigates had been despatched to inter-cept them. They met with an equal force. Resist-ance, therefore, became a point of honour on the part of the Spaniards, and one of their ships soon blew up, with all on board. Had a stronger squadron been sent, this deplorable catastrophe might have been spared—a catastrophe which excited not more indignation in Spain than it did grief in those who were its unwilling instruments, in the English Government, and in the English people. On the 5th of October this unhappy affair occurred, and Nelson was not apprised of it till the 12th of the ensuing month. He had, indeed, sufficient mortification at the breaking out of the Spanish war—an event which, it might reasonably have been supposed, would amply enrich the officers of the Mediterranean, and repay them for the severe and unremitting duty on which they had been so long employed. But of this harvest they were deprived; for Sir John Orde was sent with a small squadron, and a separate command, to Cadiz. Nelson's feelings were never wounded so deeply as now. " I had thought," said he, writing in the first flow and freshness of indignation; " I fancied,—but, nay; it must have been a dream, an idle dream,—yet, I confess it, I *did* fancy that I had done my country service; and thus they use me !—And under what circumstances, and with what pointed aggravation ! Yet, if I know my own thoughts, it is not for myself, or on my own account chiefly, that I feel the sting and the disappointment. No ! it is for my brave officers; for my noble-minded friends and comrades. Such a gallant set of fellows ! Such a band of brothers ! My heart swells at the thought of them."

War between Spain and England was now declared ; and on the 18th of January the Toulon fleet, having the Spaniards to co-operate with them, put to sea. Nelson was at anchor off the coast of Sardinia, where the Madelena islands form one of the finest harbours in the world, when, at three in the afternoon of the 19th, the *Active* and *Seahorse* frigates brought this long-hoped-for intelligence. They had been close to the enemy at ten on the preceding night, but lost sight of them in about four hours. The fleet immediately unmoored and weighed, and at six in the evening ran through the strait between Biche and Sardinia—a pas-

sage so narrow, that the ships could only pass one at
a time, each following the stern lights of its leader.
From the position of the enemy, when they were last
seen, it was inferred that they must be bound round
the southern end of Sardinia.   Signal was made the
next morning to prepare for battle.   Bad weather
came on, baffling the one fleet in its object, and the
other in its pursuit.   Nelson beat about the Sicilian
seas for ten days, without obtaining any other information   of   the   enemy   than   that   one   of   their
ships   had   put   into Ajaccio   dismasted;   and   having   seen   that   Sardinia,   Naples,   and   Sicily   were
safe,   believing   Egypt   to   be   their   destination,   for
Egypt he ran.   The disappointment and   distress
which he had experienced in his former pursuit of the
French through the same seas were now renewed:
but Nelson, while he endured these anxious and unhappy feelings, was still consoled by the same confidence as on the former occasion, that, though his
judgment might be erroneous, under all circumstances
he was right in having formed it.   " I have consulted
no man," said he to the Admiralty; "therefore the
whole blame of ignorance in forming my judgment
must rest with me.   I would allow no man to take
from me an atom of my glory had I fallen in with the
French fleet; nor do I desire any man to partake any
of the responsibility.   All is mine, right or wrong."
Then, stating the grounds upon which he had proceeded, he added : " At this moment of sorrow I
still feel I have acted right."   In the same spirit he
said to Sir Alexander Ball : " When I call to remembrance all the circumstances, I approve, if nobody
else does, of my own conduct."

Baffled thus, he bore up for Malta, and met intelligence from Naples that the French, having been dispersed in a gale, had put back to Toulon.   From the
same quarter he learnt that a great number of saddles
and muskets had been embarked; and this confirmed
him in his opinion that Egypt was their destination.

That they should have put back in consequence of
storms, which he had weathered, gave him a consol-
ing sense of British superiority. " These gentlemen," said he, " are not accustomed to a Gulf of
Lyons' gale: we have buffeted them for one-and-
twenty months, and not carried away a spar." He,
however, who had so often braved these gales, was
now, though not mastered by them, vexatiously
thwarted and impeded: and on February 27th he was
compelled to anchor in Pulla Bay, in the Gulf of
Cagliari. From the 21st of January the fleet had
remained ready for battle, without a bulkhead up,
night or day. He anchored here, that he might not be
driven to leeward. As soon as the weather moderated
he put to sea again; and, after again beating about
against contrary winds, another gale drove him to
anchor in the Gulf of Palma, on the 8th of March.
This he made his rendezvous; he knew that the
French troops still remained embarked, and wishing
to lead them into a belief that he was stationed upon
the Spanish coast, he made his appearance off Barcelona with that intent. About the end of the month
he began to fear that the plan of expedition was abandoned; and sailing once more towards his old station
off Toulon, on the 4th of April he met the *Phœbe*, with
news that Villeneuve had put to sea on the last of
March with eleven ships of the line, seven frigates,
and two brigs. When last seen, they were steering
toward the coast of Africa. Nelson first covered the
channel between Sardinia and Barbary, so as to
satisfy himself that Villeneuve was not taking the
same route for Egypt which Gantheaume had taken
before him, when he attempted to carry reinforcements there. Certain of this, he bore up on the 7th
for Palermo, lest the French should have passed to
the north of Corsica, and he despatched cruisers in
all directions. On the 11th he felt assured that they
were not gone down the Mediterranean; and sending
off frigates to Gibraltar, to Lisbon, and to Admiral

Cornwallis, who commanded the squadron off Brest, he endeavoured to get to the westward, beating against westerly winds. After five days, a neutral gave intelligence that the French had been seen off Cape de Gatte on the 7th. It was soon afterwards ascertained that they had passed the Straits of Gibraltar on the day following; and Nelson, knowing that they might already be half-way to Ireland or Jamaica, exclaimed that he was miserable. One gleam of comfort only came across him in the reflection that his vigilance had rendered it impossible for them to undertake any expedition in the Mediterranean.

Eight days after this certain intelligence had been obtained, he describes his state of mind thus forcibly, in writing to the Governor of Malta : " My good fortune, my dear Ball, seems flown away. I cannot get a fair wind, or even a side wind. Dead foul !—Dead foul !—But my mind is fully made up what to do when I leave the Straits, supposing there is no certain account of the enemy's destination. I believe this ill-luck will go near to kill me; but, as these are times for exertion, I must not be cast down, whatever I may feel." In spite of every exertion which could be made by all the zeal and all the skill of British seamen, he did not get in sight of Gibraltar till the 30th of April; and the wind was then so adverse, that it was impossible to pass the Gut. He anchored in Mazari Bay, on the Barbary shore; obtained supplies from Tetuan; and when, on the 5th, a breeze from the eastward sprang up at last, sailed once more, hoping to hear of the enemy from Sir John Orde, who commanded off Cadiz, or from Lisbon. " If nothing is heard of them," said he to the Admiralty, " I shall probably think the rumours which have been spread are true, that their object is the West Indies ; and, in that case, I think it my duty to follow them,— or to the Antipodes, should I believe that to be their destination." At the time when this resolution was

taken, the physician of the fleet had ordered him to
return to England before the hot months.

Nelson had formed his judgment of their destination, and made up his mind accordingly, when
Donald Campbell, at that time an Admiral in the
Portuguese service, the same person who had given
important tidings to Earl St. Vincent of the movements of that fleet from which he won his title, a
second time gave timely and momentous intelligence
to the flag of his country. He went on board the
Victory, and communicated to Nelson his certain
knowledge that the combined Spanish and French
fleets were bound for the West Indies. Hitherto all
things had favoured the enemy. While the British
commander was beating up against strong southerly
and westerly gales, they had wind to their wish from
the N.E.; and had done in nine days what he was a
whole month in accomplishing. Villeneuve, finding
the Spaniards at Carthagena were not in a state of
equipment to join him, dared not wait, but hastened
on to Cadiz. Sir John Orde necessarily retired at his
approach. Admiral Gravina, with six Spanish ships
of the line and two French, came out to him, and they
sailed without a moment's loss of time. They had
about three thousand French troops on board, and
fifteen hundred Spanish :—six hundred were under
orders, expecting them at Martinique, and one
thousand at Guadaloupe. General Lauriston commanded the troops. The combined fleet now consisted
of eighteen sail of the line, six forty-four gun frigates,
one of twenty-six guns, three corvettes, and a brig.
They were joined afterwards by two French line of
battle ships, and one forty-four. Nelson pursued them
with ten sail of the line and three frigates. " Take
you a Frenchman apiece," said he to his captains,
" and leave me the Spaniards :—when I haul down
my colours I expect you to do the same,—and not
till then."

The enemy had five-and-thirty days' start ; but he

calculated that he should gain eight or ten days upon
them by his exertions. May 15th he made Madeira,
and on June 4th reached Barbadoes, whither he had
sent despatches before him; and where he found
Admiral Cochrane, with two ships, part of our
squadron on those seas being at Jamaica. He found
here also accounts that the combined fleets had been
seen from St. Lucia on the 28th, standing to the
southward, and that Tobago and Trinidad were their
objects. This Nelson doubted; but he was alone in
his opinion, and yielded it with these foreboding
words : " If your intelligence proves false, you lose
me the French fleet." Sir William Myers offered to
embark here with two thousand troops; they were
taken on board, and the next morning he sailed for
Tobago. Here accident confirmed the false intelligence which had, whether from intention or error,
misled him. A merchant at Tobago, in the general
alarm, not knowing whether this fleet was friend or
foe, sent out a schooner to reconnoitre, and acquaint
him by signal. The signal which he had chosen happened to be the very one which had been appointed
by Colonel Shipley of the engineers, to signify that
the enemy were at Trinidad; and, as this was at the
close of day, there was no opportunity of discovering
the mistake. An American brig was met with about
the same time; the master of which, with that pro-
pensity to deceive the English and assist the French
in any manner, which has been but too common
among his countrymen, affirmed, that he had been
boarded off Granada a few days before by the French,
who were standing towards the Bocas of Trinidad.
This fresh intelligence removed all doubts. The ships
were cleared for action before daylight, and Nelson
entered the Bay of Paria on the 7th, hoping and expecting to make the mouths of the Orinoco as famous
in the annals of the British navy as those of the Nile.
Not an enemy was there; and it was discovered that
accident and artifice had combined to lead him so

far to leeward, that there could have been little hope of fetching to windward of Granada for any other fleet. Nelson, however, with skill and exertions never exceeded, and almost unexampled, bore for that island.

Advices met him on the way that the combined fleets, having captured the Diamond Rock, were then at Martinique, on the 4th, and were expected to sail that night for the attack of Granada. On the 9th Nelson arrived off that island; and there learnt that they had passed to leeward of Antigua the preceding day, and taken a homeward-bound convoy. Had it not been for false information, upon which Nelson had acted reluctantly, and in opposition to his own judgment, he would have been off Port Royal just as they were leaving it, and the battle would have been fought on the spot where Rodney defeated De Grasse. This he remembered in his vexation; but he had saved the colonies, and above two hundred ships laden for Europe, which would else have fallen into the enemy's hands; and he had the satisfaction of knowing that the mere terror of his name had effected this, and had put to flight the allied enemies, whose force nearly doubled that before which they fled. That they were flying back to Europe he believed, and for Europe he steered in pursuit on the 13th, having disembarked the troops at Antigua, and taking with him the *Spartiate,* 74 :—the only addition to the squadron with which he was pursuing so superior a force. Five days afterwards the *Amazon* brought intelligence that she had spoke a schooner who had seen them, on the evening of the 15th, steering to the N., and, by computation, eighty-seven leagues off. Nelson's diary at this time denotes his great anxiety, and his perpetual and all-observing vigilance.—" June 21. Midnight, nearly calm, saw three planks, which I think came from the French fleet. Very miserable, which is very foolish." On the 17th of July he came in sight of Cape St. Vincent, and steered for Gibral-

tar.—" July 18th," his diary says, " Cape Spartel in
sight, but no French fleet, nor any information about
them. How sorrowful this makes me! but I cannot
help myself." The next day he anchored at Gibraltar; and on the 20th, says he, " I went on shore for
the first time since June 16th, 1803; and from having
my foot out of the *Victory*, two years, wanting ten
days."

Here he communicated with his old friend Collingwood, who, having been detached with a squadron,
when the disappearance of the combined fleets, and
of Nelson in their pursuit, was known in England,
had taken his station off Cadiz. He thought that
Ireland was the enemy's ultimate object,—that they
would now liberate the Ferrol squadron, which was
blocked up by Sir Robert Calder,—call for the Rochefort ships, and then appear off Ushant with three
or four-and-thirty sail; there to be joined by the Brest
fleet. With this great force he supposed they would
make for Ireland,—the real mark and bent of all their
operations: and their flight to the West Indies, he
thought, had been merely undertaken to take off Nelson's force, which was the great impediment to their
undertaking.

Collingwood was gifted with great political pene-
tration. As yet, however, all was conjecture concerning the enemy; and Nelson having victualled and
watered at Tetuan, stood for Ceuta on the 24th, still
without information of their course. Next day intelligence arrived that the *Curieux* brig had seen them
on the 19th, standing to the northward. He proceeded off Cape St. Vincent, rather cruising for
intelligence than knowing whither to betake himself:
and here a case occurred, that more than any other
event in real history resembles those whimsical proofs
of sagacity which Voltaire, in his Zadig, has bor-
rowed from the Orientals. One of our frigates spoke
an American, who, a little to the westward of the
Azores, had fallen in with an armed vessel, appearing

to be a dismasted privateer, deserted by her crew, which had been run on board by another ship, and had been set fire to; but the fire had gone out. A log-book, and a few seamen's jackets, were found in the cabin; and these were brought to Nelson. The log-book closed with these words : " Two large vessels in the W.N.W."; and this led him to conclude that the vessel had been an English privateer, cruising off the Western Islands. But there was in this book a scrap of dirty paper, filled with figures. Nelson, immediately upon seeing it, observed that the figures were written by a Frenchman; and, after studying this for a while, said, " I can explain the whole. The jackets are of French manufacture, and prove that the privateer was in possession of the enemy. She had been chased and taken by the two ships that were seen in the W.N.W. The prize-master, going on board in a hurry, forgot to take with him his reckoning : there is none in the log-book; and the dirty paper contains her work for the number of days since the privateer last left Corvo : with an unaccounted-for run, which I take to have been the chase, in his endeavour to find out her situation by back reckonings. By some mismanage-ment, I conclude, she was run on board of by one of the enemy's ships, and dismasted. Not liking delay (for I am satisfied that those two ships were the advanced ones of the French squadron), and fancying we were close at their heels, they set fire to the vessel, and abandoned her in a hurry. If this explana-tion be correct, I infer from it that they are gone more to the northward; and more to the northward I will look for them." This course accordingly he held, but still without success. Still persevering, and still disappointed, he returned near enough to Cadiz to ascertain that they were not there; traversed the Bay of Biscay; and then, as a last hope, stood over for the north-west coast of Ireland, against adverse winds, till on the evening of the 12th of August, he learnt that they had not been heard of there. Frustrated thus in

all his hopes, after a pursuit, to which, for its extent,
rapidity, and perseverance, no parallel can be produced, he judged it best to reinforce the Channel fleet
with his squadron, lest the enemy, as Collingwood
apprehended, should bear down upon Brest with their
whole collected force. On the 15th he joined Admiral
Cornwallis off Ushant. No news had yet been
obtained of the enemy; and on the same evening he
received orders to proceed, with the *Victory* and
Superb, to Portsmouth.

CHAPTER IX

AT Portsmouth, Nelson, at length, found news of
the combined fleet. Sir Robert Calder, who had been
sent out to intercept their return, had fallen in with
them on the 22nd of July, sixty leagues west of Cape
Finisterre. Their force consisted of twenty sail of
the line, three fifty-gun ships, five frigates, and two
brigs; his, of fifteen line of battle ships, two frigates,
a cutter, and a lugger. After an action of four hours
he had captured an 84 and a 74, and then thought it
necessary to bring-to the squadron, for the purpose of
securing their prizes. The hostile fleets remained in
sight of each other till the 26th, when the enemy bore
away. The capture of two ships from so superior a
force would have been considered as no inconsider-
able victory a few years earlier; but Nelson had
introduced a new era in our naval history, and the
nation felt, respecting this action, as he had felt on
a somewhat similar occasion. They regretted that
Nelson, with his eleven ships, had not been in Sir
Robert Calder's place; and their disappointment was
generally and loudly expressed.
Frustrated as his own hopes had been, Nelson had

yet the high satisfaction of knowing that his judgment had never been more conspicuously approved, and that he had rendered essential service to his country by driving the enemy from those islands, where they expected there could be no force capable of opposing them. The West India merchants in London, as men whose interests were more immediately benefited, appointed a deputation to express their thanks for his great and judicious exertions. It was now his intention to rest awhile from his labours, and recruit himself, after all his fatigues and cares, in the society of those whom he loved. All his stores were brought up from the *Victory*; and he found in his house at Merton the enjoyment which he had anticipated. Many days had not elapsed before Captain Blackwood, on his way to London with despatches, called on him at five in the morning. Nelson, who was already dressed, exclaimed, the moment he saw him : "I am sure you bring me news of the French and Spanish fleets ! I think I shall yet have to beat them ! " They had refitted at Vigo, after the indecisive action with Sir Robert Calder; then proceeded to Ferrol, brought out the squadron from thence, and with it entered Cadiz in safety. " Depend on it, Blackwood," he repeatedly said, " I shall yet give M. Villeneuve a drubbing." But, when Blackwood had left him, he wanted resolution to declare his wishes to Lady Hamilton and his sisters, and endeavoured to drive away the thought. " He had done enough," he said; " let the man trudge it who has lost his budget ! " His countenance belied his lips; and as he was pacing one of the walks in the garden, which he used to call the quarter-deck, Lady Hamilton came up to him, and told him she saw he was uneasy. He smiled, and said : " No, he was as happy as possible; he was surrounded by his family, his health was better since he had been on shore, and he would not give sixpence to call the king his uncle." She replied that she did not believe him,—that she

knew he was longing to get at the combined fleets,—
that he considered them as his own property,—that he
would be miserable if any man but himself did the
business, and that he ought to have them, as the price
and reward of his two years' long watching, and his
hard chase. "Nelson," said she, "however we may
lament your absence, offer your services;—they will
be accepted, and you will gain a quiet heart by it: you
will have a glorious victory, and then you may return
here and be happy." He looked at her with tears in
his eyes—"Brave Emma!—Good Emma!—If there
were more Emmas, there would be more Nelsons."

His services were as willingly accepted as they
were offered; and Lord Barham, giving him the list
of the navy, desired him to choose his own officers.
"Choose yourself, my lord," was his reply: "the
same spirit actuates the whole profession: you cannot
choose wrong." Lord Barham then desired him to
say what ships, and how many, he would wish, in
addition to the fleet which he was going to command,
and said they should follow him as soon as each was
ready. No appointment was ever more in unison with
the feelings and judgment of the whole nation. They,
like Lady Hamilton, thought that the destruction of
the combined fleets ought properly to be Nelson's
work: that he, who had been

> "Half around the sea-girt ball,
> The hunter of the recreant Gaul."

ought to reap the spoils of the chase, which he had
watched so long, and so perseveringly pursued.

Unremitting exertions were made to equip the ships
which he had chosen, and especially to refit the *Victory*, which was once more to bear his flag. Before
he left London he called at his upholsterer's, where
the coffin, which Captain Hallowell had given him,
was deposited; and desired that its history might be
engraven upon the lid, saying, it was highly probable
that he might want it on his return. He seemed, in-

deed, to have been impressed with an expectation
that he should fall in the battle. In a letter to his
brother, written immediately after his return, he had
said: " We must not talk of Sir Robert Calder's
battle—I might not have done so much with my small
force. If I had fallen in with them, you might probably have been a lord before I wished; for I know
they meant to make a dead set at the *Victory*." Nelson had once regarded the prospect of death with
gloomy satisfaction: it was when he anticipated the
upbraidings of his wife, and the displeasure of his
venerable father. The state of his feelings now was
expressed, in his private journal, in these words:
" Friday night (Sept. 13), at half-past ten, I drove
from dear, dear Merton, where I left all which I hold
dear in this world, to go to serve my king and country. May the great God, whom I adore, enable me
to fulfil the expectations of my country! and, if it is
His good pleasure that I should return, my thanks will
never cease being offered up to the throne of His
mercy. If it is His good providence to cut short my
days upon earth, I bow with the greatest submission;
relying that He will protect those so dear to me, whom
I may leave behind! His will be done! Amen!
Amen! Amen!"

Early on the following morning he reached Portsmouth; and, having despatched his business on shore,
endeavoured to elude the populace by taking a by-
way to the beach; but a crowd collected in his train,
pressing forward to obtain a sight of his face;—many
were in tears, and many knelt down before him, and
blessed him as he passed. England has had many
heroes, but never one who so entirely possessed the
love of his fellow-countrymen as Nelson. All men
knew that his heart was as humane as it was fearless;
that there was not in his nature the slightest alloy of
selfishness or cupidity; but that, with perfect and entire devotion, he served his country with all his heart,
and with all his soul, and with all his strength; and,

therefore, they loved him as truly and as fervently
as he loved England. They pressed upon the para-
pet to gaze after him when his barge pushed off, and
he was returning their cheers by waving his hat. The
sentinels, who endeavoured to prevent them from tres-
passing upon this ground, were wedged among the
crowd; and an officer, who, not very prudently upon
such an occasion, ordered them to drive the people
down with their bayonets, was compelled speedily to
retreat; for the people would not be debarred from
gazing, till the last moment, upon the hero, the darling
hero of England.

He arrived off Cadiz on the 29th of September,—his
birthday. Fearing that, if the enemy knew his force,
they might be deterred from venturing to sea, he kept
out of sight of land, desired Collingwood to fire no
salute and hoist no colours, and wrote to Gibraltar, to
request that the force of the fleet might not be inserted
there in the *Gazette*. His reception in the Mediterranean fleet was as gratifying as the farewell of his
countrymen at Portsmouth: the officers, who came on
board to welcome him, forgot his rank as commander
in their joy at seeing him again. On the day of his
arrival, Villeneuve received orders to put to sea the
first opportunity. Villeneuve, however, hesitated when
he heard that Nelson had resumed the command. He
called a council of war; and their determination was,
that it would not be expedient to leave Cadiz, unless
they had reason to believe themselves stronger by one-
third than the British force. In the public measures
of this country secrecy is seldom practicable, and seldom attempted: here, however, by the precautions of
Nelson and the wise measures of the Admiralty, the
enemy were for once kept in ignorance; for, as the
ships appointed to reinforce the Mediterranean fleet
were despatched singly—each as soon as it was ready
—their collected number was not stated in the news-
papers, and their arrival was not known to the enemy.
But the enemy knew that Admiral Louis, with six

sail, had been detached for stores and water to Gibraltar. Accident also contributed to make the French admiral doubt whether Nelson himself had actually taken the command. An American, lately arrived from England, maintained that it was impossible, for he had seen him only a few days before in London, and, at that time, there was no rumour of his going again to sea.

The station which Nelson had chosen was some fifty or sixty miles to the west of Cadiz, near Cape St. Mary's. At this distance he hoped to decoy the enemy out, while he guarded against the danger of being caught with a westerly wind near Cadiz, and driven within the Straits. The blockade of the port was rigorously enforced; in hopes that the combined fleet might be forced to sea by want. The Danish vessels, therefore, which were carrying provisions from the French ports in the bay, under the name of Danish property, to all the little ports from Ayamonte to Algeziras, from whence they were conveyed in coasting boats to Cadiz, were seized. Without this proper exertion of power, the blockade would have been rendered nugatory, by the advantage thus taken of the neutral flag. The supplies from France were thus effectually cut off. There was now every indication that the enemy would speedily venture out: officers and men were in the highest spirits at the prospect of giving them a decisive blow, such, indeed, as would put an end to all further contest upon the seas. Theatrical amusements were performed every evening in most of the ships, and *God Save the King* was the hymn with which the sports concluded. " I verily believe," said Nelson (writing on the 6th of October), " that the country will soon be put to some expense on my account; either a monument, or a new pension and honours; for I have not the smallest doubt but that a very few days, almost hours, will put us in battle. The success no man can ensure; but for the fighting them, if they can be got at, I pledge

R ⁵²

myself.—The sooner the better : I don't like to have
these things upon my mind."

At this time he was not without some cause of
anxiety : he was in want of frigates—the eyes of the
fleet—as he always called them :—to the want of
which, the enemy before were indebted for their
escape, and Buonaparte for his arrival in Egypt. He
had only twenty-three ships—others were on the way
—but they might come too late; and, though Nelson
never doubted of victory, mere victory was not what
he looked to—he wanted to annihilate the enemy's
fleet. The Carthagena squadron might effect a junction with this fleet on the one side; and, on the other,
it was to be expected that a similar attempt would be
made by the French from Brest;—in either case, a
formidable contingency to be apprehended by the
blockading force. The Rochefort squadron did push
out, and had nearly caught the *Agamemnon* and
l'Aimable, in their way to reinforce the British admiral.
Yet Nelson at this time weakened his own fleet. He
had the unpleasant task to perform of sending home
Sir Robert Calder, whose conduct was to be made the
subject of a court-martial, in consequence of the
general dissatisfaction which had been felt and expressed at his imperfect victory. Sir Robert Calder,
and Sir John Orde, Nelson believed to be the only two
enemies whom he had ever had in his profession ;—
and, from that sensitive delicacy which distinguished
him, this made him the more scrupulously anxious
to show every possible mark of respect and kindness
to Sir Robert. He wished to detain him till after
the expected action; when the services which he might
perform, and the triumphant joy which would be excited, would leave nothing to be apprehended from an
inquiry into the previous engagement. Sir Robert,
however, whose situation was very painful, did not
choose to delay a trial, from the result of which he
confidently expected a complete justification : and Nelson, instead of sending him home in a frigate, insisted

on his returning in his own ninety-gun ship, ill as
such a ship could at that time be spared. Nothing
could be more honourable than the feeling by which
Nelson was influenced, but, at such a crisis, it ought
not to have been indulged.

On the 9th Nelson sent Collingwood what he called,
in his diary, the Nelson-touch. " I send you," said
he, " my plan of attack, as far as a man dare venture
to guess at the very uncertain position the enemy may
be found in : but it is to place you perfectly at ease
respecting my intentions, and to give full scope to
your judgment for carrying them into effect. We
can, my dear Coll, have no little jealousies. We have
only one great object in view, that of annihilating our
enemies, and getting a glorious peace for our country.
No man has more confidence in another than I have
in you ; and no man will render your services more
justice than your very old friend Nelson and Bronté."
The order of sailing was to be the order of battle : the
fleet in two lines, with an advanced squadron of eight
of the fastest sailing two-deckers. The second in
command, having the entire direction of his line, was
to break through the enemy, about the twelfth ship
from their rear : he would lead through the centre, and
the advanced squadron was to cut off three or four
ahead of the centre. This plan was to be adapted to
the strength of the enemy, so that they should always
be one-fourth superior to those whom they cut off.
Nelson said, " That his admirals and captains, knowing his precise object to be that of a close and decisive
action, would supply any deficiency of signals, and act
accordingly. In case signals cannot be seen or clearly
understood, no captain can do wrong if he places his
ship alongside that of an enemy." One of the last
orders of this admirable man was, that the name and
family of every officer, seaman, and marine, who might
be killed or wounded in action, should be, as soon as
possible, returned to him, in order to be transmitted
to the chairman of the Patriotic Fund, that the case

might be taken into consideration, for the benefit of the sufferer or his family.

About half-past nine in the morning of the 19th, the *Mars*, being the nearest to the fleet of the ships which formed the line of communication with the frigates in shore, repeated the signal that the enemy were coming out of port. The wind was at this time very light, with partial breezes, mostly from the S.S.W. Nelson ordered the signal to be made for a chase in the south-east quarter. About two, the repeating ships announced that the enemy were at sea. All night the British fleet continued under all sail, steering to the south-east. At daybreak they were in the entrance of the Straits, but the enemy were not in sight. About seven, one of the frigates made signal that the enemy were bearing north. Upon this the *Victory* hove to; and shortly afterwards Nelson made sail again to the northward. In the afternoon the wind blew fresh from the south-west, and the English began to fear that the foe might be forced to return to port. A little before sunset, however, Blackwood, in the *Euryalus*, telegraphed that they appeared determined to go to the westward,—'' And that,'' said the admiral in his diary, '' they shall not do, if it is in the power of Nelson and Bronté to prevent them.'' Nelson had signified to Blackwood, that he depended upon him to keep sight of the enemy. They were observed so well, that all their motions were made known to him; and, as they wore twice, he inferred that they were aiming to keep the port of Cadiz open, and would retreat there as soon as they saw the British fleet : for this reason he was very careful not to approach near enough to be seen by them during the night. At daybreak the combined fleets were distinctly seen from the *Victory's* deck, formed in a close line of battle ahead, on the starboard tack, about twelve miles to leeward, and standing to the south. Our fleet consisted of twenty-seven sail of the line and four frigates; theirs of thirty-three, and seven large frigates. Their superiority was greater in size, and weight of metal, than in numbers. They had four thousand troops on board; and the best riflemen who could be procured, many of them Tyrolese, were dispersed through the ships. Little did the Tyrolese, and little did the Spaniards, at that day, imagine what horrors the wicked tyrant whom they served was preparing for their country!

Soon after daylight Nelson came upon deck. The 21st of October was a festival in his family; because on that day his uncle, Captain Suckling, in the *Dreadnought*, with two other line of battle ships, had beaten off a French squadron of four sail of the line and three frigates. Nelson, with that sort of superstition from which few persons are entirely exempt, had more than once expressed his persuasion that this was to be the day of his battle also; and he was well pleased at seeing his prediction about to be verified. The wind was now from the west,—light breezes, with a long heavy swell. Signal was made to bear down upon the enemy in two lines; and the fleet set all sail. Collingwood, in the *Royal Sovereign*, led the lee-line of thirteen ships; the *Victory* led the weather-line of fourteen. Having seen that all was as it should be, Nelson retired to his cabin, and wrote this prayer:—

" May the Great God, whom I worship, grant to my country, and for the benefit of Europe in general, a great and glorious victory; and may no misconduct in any one tarnish it; and may humanity after victory be the predominant feature in the British fleet! For myself individually, I commit my life to Him that made me, and may His blessing alight on my endeavours for serving my country faithfully! To Him I resign myself, and the just cause which is intrusted to me to defend. Amen, Amen, Amen."

Having thus discharged his devotional duties, he annexed, in the same diary, the following remarkable writing:—

" *October 21st, 1805.—Then in sight of the combined
fleets of France and Spain, distant about ten
miles*

" Whereas the eminent services of Emma Hamilton,
widow of the Right Honourable Sir William Hamilton, have been of the very greatest service to my
king and country, to my knowledge, without ever
receiving any reward from either our king or country :

" First, That she obtained the King of Spain's
letter, in 1796, to his brother, the King of Naples,
acquainting him of his intention to declare war against
England : from which letter the ministry sent out
orders to the then Sir John Jervis to strike a stroke,
if opportunity offered, against either the arsenals of
Spain or her fleets. That neither of these was done
is not the fault of Lady Hamilton ; the opportunity
might have been offered.

" Secondly : The British fleet under my command
could never have returned the second time to Egypt,
had not Lady Hamilton's influence with the Queen
of Naples caused letters to be wrote to the governor of
Syracuse, that he was to encourage the fleet's being
supplied with everything, should they put into any
port in Sicily. We put into Syracuse, and received
every supply ; went to Egypt, and destroyed the
French fleet.

" Could I have rewarded these services, I would not
now call upon my country ; but as that has not been
in my power, I leave Emma Lady Hamilton, therefore,
a legacy to my king and country, that they will give
her an ample provision to maintain her rank in life.

" I also leave to the beneficence of my country my
adopted daughter, Horatia Nelson Thompson ; and
I desire she will use in future the name of Nelson only.

" These are the only favours I ask of my king and
country, at this moment when I am going to fight
their battle. May God bless my king and country,

and all those I hold dear ! My relations it is needless to mention : they will, of course, be amply provided for.

" NELSON AND BRONTÉ."

" Witness { Henry Blackwood.
        { T. M. Hardy."

The child, of whom this writing speaks, was believed to be his daughter, and so, indeed, he called her the last time that he pronounced her name. She was then about five years old, living at Merton, under Lady Hamilton's care. The last minutes which Nelson passed at Merton were employed in praying over this child as she lay sleeping. A portrait of Lady Hamilton hung in his cabin; and no Catholic ever beheld the picture of his patron-saint with devouter reverence. The undisguised and romantic passion with which he regarded it amounted almost to superstition ; and when the portrait was now taken down, in clearing for action, he desired the men who removed it to " take care of his guardian angel." In this manner he frequently spoke of it, as if he believed there were a virtue in the image. He wore a miniature of her also next his heart. Blackwood went on board the *Victory* about six. He found him in good spirits, but very calm; not in that exhilaration which he had felt upon entering into battle at Aboukir and Copenhagen ; he knew that his own life would be particularly aimed at, and seems to have looked for death with almost as sure an expectation as for victory. His whole attention was fixed upon the enemy. They tacked to the northward, and formed their line on the larboard tack; thus bringing the shoals of Trafalgar and St. Pedro under the lee of the British, and keeping the port of Cadiz open for themselves. This was judiciously done : and Nelson, aware of all the advantages which it gave them, made signal to prepare to anchor.

Villeneuve was a skilful seaman; worthy of serving

a better master and a better cause. His plan of defence was as well conceived, and as original, as the plan of attack. He formed the fleet in a double line, every alternate ship being about a cable's length to windward of her second ahead and astern. Nelson, certain of a triumphant issue to the day, asked Blackwood what he should consider as a victory. That officer answered, that, considering the handsome way in which battle was offered by the enemy, their apparent determination for a fair trial of strength, and the situation of the land, he thought it would be a glorious result if fourteen were captured. He replied : " I shall not be satisfied with less than twenty." Soon afterwards he asked him if he did not think there was a signal wanting. Captain Blackwood made answer that he thought the whole fleet seemed very clearly to understand what they were about. These words were scarcely spoken before that signal was made, which will be remembered as long as the language, or even the memory, of England shall endure—Nelson's last signal :—" England expects every man to do his duty ! " It was received throughout the fleet, with a shout of answering acclamation, made sublime by the spirit which it breathed and the feeling which it expressed. " Now," said Lord Nelson, " I can do no more. We must trust to the Great Disposer of all events, and the justice of our cause. I thank God for this great opportunity of doing my duty."

He wore that day, as usual, his admiral's frock coat, bearing on the left breast four stars of the different orders with which he was invested. Ornaments which rendered him so conspicuous a mark for the enemy, were beheld with ominous apprehensions by his officers. It was known that there were riflemen on board the French ships, and it could not be doubted but that his life would be particularly aimed at. They communicated their fears to each other; and the surgeon, Mr. Beatty, spoke to the chaplain, Dr. Scott, and to Mr. Scott, the public secretary, desiring that some person would entreat him to change his dress, or cover the stars : but they knew that such a request would highly displease him. "In honour I gained them," he had said when such a thing had been hinted to him formerly, "and in honour I will die with them." Mr. Beatty, however, would not have been deterred by any fear of exciting his displeasure, from speaking to him himself upon a subject in which the weal of England as well as the life of Nelson was concerned, but he was ordered from the deck before he could find an opportunity. This was a point upon which Nelson's officers knew that it was hopeless to remonstrate or reason with him; but both Blackwood, and his own captain, Hardy, represented to him how advantageous to the fleet it would be for him to keep out of action as long as possible; and he consented at last to let the *Leviathan* and the *Téméraire,* which were sailing abreast of the *Victory,* be ordered to pass ahead. Yet even here the last infirmity of this noble mind was indulged; for these ships could not pass ahead if the *Victory* continued to carry all her sail; and so far was Nelson from shortening sail, that it was evident he took pleasure in pressing on, and rendering it impossible for them to obey his own orders. A long swell was setting into the Bay of Cadiz : our ships, crowding all sail, moved majestically before it, with light winds from the south-west. The sun shone on the sails of the enemy; and their well-formed line, with their numerous three-deckers, made an appearance which any other assailants would have thought formidable; but the British sailors only admired the beauty and the splendour of the spectacle; and, in full confidence of winning what they saw, remarked to each other, what a fine sight yonder ships would make at Spithead !

The French admiral, from the *Bucentaure,* beheld the new manner in which his enemy was advancing, Nelson and Collingwood each leading his line; and, pointing them out to his officers, he is said to have

exclaimed, that such conduct could not fail to be successful. Yet Villeneuve had made his own dispositions
with the utmost skill, and the fleets under his command waited for the attack with perfect coolness.
Ten minutes before twelve they opened their fire.
Eight or nine of the ships immediately ahead of the
Victory, and across her bows, fired single guns at her,
to ascertain whether she was yet within their range.
As soon as Nelson perceived that their shot passed
over him, he desired Blackwood and Captain Prowse,
of the *Sirius*, to repair to their respective frigates;
and, on their way, to tell all the captains of the line
of battle ships that he depended on their exertions;
and that, if by the prescribed mode of attack they
found it impracticable to get into action immediately,
they might adopt whatever they thought best, provided it led them quickly and closely alongside an
enemy. As they were standing on the front of the
poop, Blackwood took him by the hand, saying, he
hoped soon to return and find him in possession of
twenty prizes. He replied : " God bless you, Blackwood ! I shall never see you again."

Nelson's column was steered about two points more
to the north than Collingwood's, in order to cut off
the enemy's escape into Cadiz : the lee-line, therefore,
was first engaged. " See," cried Nelson, pointing to
the *Royal Sovereign,* as she steered right for the
centre of the enemy's line, cut through it astern of
the *Santa Anna*, three-decker, and engaged her at the
muzzle of her guns on the starboard side : " see how
that noble fellow, Collingwood, carries his ship into
action ! " Collingwood, delighted at being first in the
heat of the fire, and knowing the feelings of his commander and old friend, turned to his captain, and
exclaimed, " Rotherham, what would Nelson give to
be here ! " Both these brave officers, perhaps, at this
moment thought of Nelson with gratitude, for a circumstance which had occurred on the preceding day.
Admiral Collingwood, with some of the captains, hav-

ing gone on board the *Victory* to receive instructions,
Nelson inquired of him where his captain was? and
was told, in reply, that they were not upon good terms
with each other. "Terms!" said Nelson;—"good
terms with each other!" Immediately he sent a boat
for Captain Rotherham; led him, as soon as he
arrived, to Collingwood, and saying, " Look, yonder
are the enemy!" bade them "shake hands like Englishmen."

The enemy continued to fire a gun at a time at the
Victory, till they saw that a shot had passed through
her main-topgallant-sail; then they opened their
broadsides, aiming chiefly at her rigging, in the hope
of disabling her before she could close with them.
Nelson, as usual, had hoisted several flags, lest one
should be shot away. The enemy showed no colours
till late in the action, when they began to feel the
necessity of having them to strike. For this reason,
the *Santissima Trinidad*, Nelson's old acquaintance,
as he used to call her, was distinguishable only by her
four decks; and to the bow of this opponent he
ordered the *Victory* to be steered. Meantime an
incessant raking fire was kept up upon the *Victory*.
The admiral's secretary was one of the first who fell:
he was killed by a cannon-shot, while conversing with
Hardy. Captain Adair, of the marines, with the help
of a sailor, endeavoured to remove the body from
Nelson's sight, who had a great regard for Mr. Scott;
but he anxiously asked, "Is that poor Scott that's
gone?" and being informed that it was indeed so,
exclaimed, "Poor fellow!" Presently a double-
headed shot struck a party of marines, who were
drawn up on the poop, and killed eight of them : upon
which Nelson immediately desired Captain Adair to
disperse his men round the ship, that they might not
suffer so much from being together. A few minutes
afterwards a shot struck the fore brace bits on the
quarter-deck, and passed between Nelson and Hardy,
a splinter from the bit tearing off Hardy's buckle and

bruising his foot. Both stopped, and looked anxiously
at each other, each supposing the other to be wounded.
Nelson then smiled, and said, "This is too warm
work, Hardy, to last long."

The *Victory* had not yet returned a single gun:
fifty of her men had been by this time killed or
wounded, and her main-topmast, with all her studding
sails and their booms, shot away. Nelson declared
that, in all his battles, he had seen nothing which surpassed the cool courage of his crew on this occasion.
At four minutes after twelve she opened her fire
from both sides of her deck. It was not possible to
break the enemy's line without running on board one
of their ships: Hardy informed him of this, and
asked which he would prefer. Nelson replied: "Take
your choice, Hardy, it does not signify much." The
master was then ordered to put the helm to port, and
the *Victory* ran on board the *Redoutable*, just as her
tiller ropes were shot away. The French ship received
her with a broadside; then instantly let down her
lower-deck ports, for fear of being boarded through
them, and never afterwards fired a great gun during
the action. Her tops, like those of all the enemy's
ships, were filled with riflemen. Nelson never placed
musketry in his tops; he had a strong dislike to the
practice, not merely because it endangers setting fire
to the sails, but also because it is a murderous sort of
warfare, by which individuals may suffer, and a commander, now and then, be picked off, but which never
can decide the fate of a general engagement.

Captain Harvey, in the *Temeraire*, fell on board
the *Redoutable* on the other side. Another enemy
was in like manner on board the *Temeraire*: so that
these four ships formed as compact a tier as if they
had been moored together, their heads lying all the
same way. The lieutenants of the *Victory*, seeing
this, depressed their guns of the middle and lower
decks, and fired with a diminished charge, lest the
shot should pass through, and injure the *Temeraire*.

And because there was danger that the *Redoutable* might take fire from the lower-deck guns, the muzzles of which touched her side when they were run out, the fireman of each gun stood ready with a bucket of water, which, as soon as the gun was discharged, he dashed into the hole made by the shot. An incessant fire was kept up from the *Victory* from both sides; her larboard guns playing upon the *Bucentaure* and the huge *Santissima Trinidad.*

It had been part of Nelson's prayer that the British fleet might be distinguished by humanity in the victory which he expected. Setting an example himself, he twice gave orders to cease firing upon the *Redoutable,* supposing that she had struck, because her great guns were silent; for, as she carried no flag, there was no means of instantly ascertaining the fact. From this ship, which he had thus twice spared, he received his death. A ball fired from her mizen-top, which, in the then situation of the two vessels, was not more than fifteen yards from that part of the deck where he was standing, struck the epaulette on his left shoulder,—about a quarter after one, just in the heat of the action. He fell upon his face, on the spot which was covered with his poor secretary's blood. Hardy, who was a few steps from him, turning round, saw three men raising him up. "They have done for me at last, Hardy," said he. "I hope not!" cried Hardy. "Yes," he replied; "my back bone is shot through." Yet even now, not for a moment losing his presence of mind, he observed, as they were carrying him down the ladder, that the tiller ropes, which had been shot away, were not yet replaced, and ordered that new ones should be rove immediately :—then, that he might not be seen by the crew, he took out his handkerchief, and covered his face and his stars.—Had he but concealed these badges of honour from the enemy, England, perhaps, would not have had cause to receive with sorrow the news of the battle of Trafalgar.

The cockpit was crowded with wounded and dying men, over whose bodies he was with some difficulty conveyed, and laid upon a pallet in the midshipmen's berth. It was soon perceived, upon examination, that the wound was mortal. This, however, was concealed from all, except Captain Hardy, the chaplain, and the medical attendants. He himself being certain, from the sensation in his back, and the gush of blood which he felt momently within his breast, that no human care could avail him, insisted that the surgeon should leave him, and attend to those to whom he might be useful : " For," said he, " you can do nothing for me." All that could be done was to fan him with paper, and frequently to give him lemonade, to alleviate his intense thirst. He was in great pain, and expressed much anxiety for the event of the action, which now began to declare itself. As often as a ship struck the crew of the *Victory* hurraed ; and at every hurra a visible expression of joy gleamed in the eyes, and marked the countenance, of the dying hero. But he became impatient to see Captain Hardy ; and as that officer, though often sent for, could not leave the deck, Nelson feared that some fatal cause prevented him, and repeatedly cried : " Will no one bring Hardy to me? He must be killed ! He is surely dead ! "—An hour and ten minutes elapsed, from the time when Nelson received his wound, before Hardy could come to him. They shook hands in silence ; Hardy in vain struggling to suppress the feelings of that most painful and yet sublimest moment. " Well, Hardy," said Nelson, " how goes the day with us ? "—" Very well," replied Hardy ; " ten ships have struck, but five of their van have tacked, and show an intention of bearing down upon the *Victory*. I have called two or three of our fresh ships round, and have no doubt of giving them a drubbing."—" I hope," said Nelson, " none of our ships have struck? " Hardy answered, " There was no fear of that." Then, and not till then, Nelson spoke of himself. " I am a dead man, Hardy," said he; "I am going fast:—it will be all over with me soon. Come nearer to me. Let my dear Lady Hamilton have my hair, and all other things belonging to me." Hardy observed, that he hoped Mr. Beatty could yet hold out some prospect of life. "Oh no!" he replied; "it is impossible. My back is shot through. Beatty will tell you so." Captain Hardy then, once more, shook hands with him; and, with a heart almost bursting, hastened upon deck.

By this time all feeling below the breast was gone, and Nelson, having made the surgeon ascertain this, said to him: "You know I am gone. I know it. I feel something rising in my breast"—putting his hand on his left side—"which tells me so." And upon Beatty's inquiring whether his pain was very great, he replied, "So great, that he wished he was dead. Yet," said he, in a lower voice, "one would like to live a little longer too!" And after a few minutes, in the same under-tone, he added: "What would become of poor Lady Hamilton if she knew my situation!" Next to his country she occupied his thoughts. Captain Hardy, some fifty minutes after he had left the cockpit, returned; and, again taking the hand of his dying friend and commander, congratulated him on having gained a complete victory. How many of the enemy were taken he did not know, as it was impossible to perceive them distinctly—but fourteen or fifteen at least. "That's well," cried Nelson; "but I bargained for twenty." And then, in a stronger voice, he said, "Anchor, Hardy; anchor." Hardy, upon this, hinted that Admiral Collingwood would take upon himself the direction of affairs. "Not while I live, Hardy!" said the dying Nelson, ineffectually endeavouring to raise himself from the bed: "do you anchor." His previous order for preparing to anchor had shown how clearly he foresaw the necessity of this. Presently, calling Hardy back, he said to him, in a low voice, "Don't throw me overboard"; and he desired that he might be buried by his parents, unless it should please the king to order otherwise. Then, reverting to private feelings : " Take care of my dear Lady Hamilton, Hardy ; take care of poor Lady Hamilton.—Kiss me, Hardy," said he. Hardy knelt down, and kissed his cheek : and Nelson said, " Now I am satisfied. Thank God, I have done my duty." Hardy stood over him in silence for a moment or two, then knelt again, and kissed his forehead. " Who is that ? " said Nelson ; and being informed, he replied, " God bless you, Hardy." And Hardy then left him—for ever.

Nelson now desired to be turned upon his right side, and said : " I wish I had not left the deck ; for I shall soon be gone." Death was, indeed, rapidly approaching. He said to the chaplain : " Doctor, I have *not* been a *great* sinner " ; and, after a short pause, " Remember that I leave Lady Hamilton, and my daughter Horatia, as a legacy to my country." His articulation now became difficult ; but he was distinctly heard to say, " Thank God, I have done my duty ! " These words he had repeatedly pronounced ; and they were the last words he uttered. He expired at thirty minutes after four,—three hours and a quarter after he had received his wound.

Within a quarter of an hour after Nelson was wounded, above fifty of the *Victory's* men fell by the enemy's musketry. They, however, on their part, were not idle ; and it was not long before there were only two Frenchmen left alive in the mizentop of the *Redoutable.* One of them was the man who had given the fatal wound : he did not live to boast of what he had done. An old quartermaster had seen him fire ; and easily recognised him, because he wore a glazed cocked hat and a white frock. This quarter-master, and two midshipmen, Mr. Collingwood and Mr. Pollard, were the only persons left on the *Victory's* poop ; the two midshipmen kept firing at the top, and he supplied them with cartridges. One

of the Frenchmen, attempting to make his escape
down the rigging, was shot by Mr. Pollard, and fell
on the poop. But the old quartermaster, as he cried
out, "That's he, that's he," and pointed at the other,
who was coming forward to fire again, received a
shot in his mouth, and fell dead. Both the midshipmen then fired, at the same time, and the fellow
dropped in the top. When they took possession of
the prize, they went into the mizentop, and found him
dead; with one ball through his head, and another
through his breast.

The *Redoutable* struck within twenty minutes
after the fatal shot had been fired from her. During
that time she had been twice on fire,—in her fore-
chains and in her forecastle. The French, as they had
done in other battles, made use, in this, of fireballs
and other combustibles—implements of destruction
which other nations, from a sense of honour and
humanity, have laid aside—which add to the sufferings
of the wounded, without determining the issue of the
combat—which none but the cruel would employ, and
which never can be successful against the brave.
Once they succeeded in setting fire, from the *Redoubt-
able,* to some ropes and canvas on the *Victory*'s
booms. The cry ran through the ship, and reached
the cockpit; but even this dreadful cry produced no
confusion : the men displayed that perfect self-
possession in danger by which English seamen are
characterised; they extinguished the flames on board
their own ship, and then hastened to extinguish them
in the enemy, by throwing buckets of water from the
gangway. When the *Redoutable* had struck, it was
not practicable to board her from the *Victory*; for,
though the two ships touched, the upper works of
both fell in so much, that there was a great space
between their gangways; and she could not be
boarded from the lower or middle decks, because her
ports were down. Some of our men went to

S 52

Lieutenant Quilliam, and offered to swim under her
bows and get up there; but it was thought unfit to
hazard brave lives in this manner.

What our men would have done from gallantry,
some of the crew of the *Santissima Trinidad* did to
save themselves. Unable to stand the tremendous fire
of the *Victory*, whose larboard guns played against
this great four-decker, and not knowing how else to
escape them, nor where else to betake themselves for
protection, many of them leapt overboard, and swam
to the *Victory*; and were actually helped up her side
by the English during the action. The Spaniards
began the battle with less vivacity than their unworthy
allies, but they continued it with greater firmness.
The *Argonauta* and *Bahama* were defended till they
had each lost about four hundred men; the *San Juan
Nepomuceno* lost three hundred and fifty. Often as
the superiority of British courage has been proved
against France upon the seas, it was never more
conspicuous than in this decisive conflict. Five of our
ships were engaged muzzle to muzzle with five of the
French. In all five the Frenchmen lowered their
lower-deck ports, and deserted their guns; while our
men continued deliberately to load and fire, till they
had made the victory secure.

Once, amidst his sufferings, Nelson had expressed
a wish that he were dead; but immediately the spirit
subdued the pains of death, and he wished to live a
little longer; doubtless that he might hear the com-
pletion of the victory which he had seen so gloriously
begun. That consolation—that joy—that triumph,
was afforded him. He lived to know that the victory
was decisive; and the last guns which were fired at
the flying enemy were heard a minute or two before
he expired. The ships which were thus flying were
four of the enemy's van, all French, under Rear-
Admiral Dumanoir. They had borne no part in the
action; and now, when they were seeking safety in
flight, they fired not only into the *Victory* and *Royal*

Sovereign as they passed, but poured their broadsides into the Spanish captured ships; and they were seen to back their top-sails, for the purpose of firing with more precision. The indignation of the Spaniards at this detestable cruelty from their allies, for whom they had fought so bravely and so profusely bled, may well be conceived. It was such, that when, two days after the action, seven of the ships which had escaped into Cadiz came out, in hopes of retaking some of the disabled prizes, the prisoners in the *Argonauta,* in a body, offered their services to the British prize-master, to man the guns against any of the French ships: saying, that if a Spanish ship came alongside, they would quietly go below; but they requested that they might be allowed to fight the French, in resentment for the murderous usage which they had suffered at their hands. Such was their earnestness, and such the implicit confidence which could be placed in Spanish honour, that the offer was accepted, and they were actually stationed at the lower-deck guns. Dumanoir and his squadron were not more fortunate than the fleet from whose destruction they fled,—they fell in with Sir Richard Strachan, who was cruising for the Rochefort squadron, and were all taken. In the better days of France, if such a crime could then have been committed, it would have received an exemplary punishment from the French Government; under Buonaparte, it was sure of impunity, and, perhaps, might be thought deserving of reward. But, if the Spanish court had been independent, it would have become us to have delivered Dumanoir and his captains up to Spain, that they might have been brought to trial, and hanged in sight of the remains of the Spanish fleet.

The total British loss in the battle of Trafalgar amounted to 1,587. Twenty of the enemy struck,— unhappily the fleet did not anchor, as Nelson, almost with his dying breath, had enjoined,—a gale came on from the south-west; some of the prizes went down,

some went on shore; one effected its escape into
Cadiz; others were destroyed; four only were saved,
and those by the greatest exertions. The wounded
Spaniards were sent ashore, an assurance being given
that they should not serve till regularly exchanged;
and the Spaniards, with a generous feeling, which
would not, perhaps, have been found in any other
people, offered the use of their hospitals for our
wounded, pledging the honour of Spain that they
should be carefully attended there. When the storm
after the action drove some of the prizes upon the
coast, they declared that the English, who were thus
thrown into their hands, should not be considered as
prisoners of war; and the Spanish soldiers gave up
their own beds to their shipwrecked enemies. The
Spanish vice-admiral, Alava, died of his wounds.
Villeneuve was sent to England, and permitted to
return to France. The French Government say that
he destroyed himself on the way to Paris, dreading
the consequences of a court-martial; but there is every
reason to believe that the tyrant, who never acknowledged the loss of the battle of Trafalgar, added
Villeneuve to the numerous victims of his murderous
policy.

It is almost superfluous to add that all the honours
which a grateful country could bestow were heaped
upon the memory of Nelson. His brother was made
an earl, with a grant of £6,000 per year; £10,000
were voted to each of his sisters; and £100,000 for
the purchase of an estate. A public funeral was
decreed, and a public monument. Statues and monuments also were voted by most of our principal cities.
The leaden coffin, in which he was brought home,
was cut in pieces, which were distributed as relics of
Saint Nelson,—so the gunner of the *Victory* called
them,—and when, at his interment, his flag was about
to be lowered into the grave, the sailors who assisted
at the ceremony, with one accord rent it in pieces, that
each might preserve a fragment while he lived.

The death of Nelson was felt in England as something more than a public calamity : men started at the intelligence, and turned pale, as if they had heard of the loss of a dear friend. An object of our admiration and affection, of our pride and of our hopes, was suddenly taken from us; and it seemed as if we had never, till then, known how deeply we loved and reverenced him. What the country had lost in its great naval hero—the greatest of our own, and of all former times—was scarcely taken into the account of grief. So perfectly, indeed, had he performed his part, that the maritime war, after the battle of Trafalgar, was considered at an end; the fleets of the enemy were not merely defeated, but destroyed; new navies must be built, and a new race of seamen reared for them, before the possibility of their invading our shores could again be contemplated. It was not, therefore, from any selfish reflection upon the magnitude of our loss that we mourned for him : the general sorrow was of a higher character. The people of England grieved that funeral ceremonies, public monuments, and posthumous rewards, were all which they could now bestow upon him, whom the king, the legislature, and the nation, would alike have delighted to honour; whom every tongue would have blessed; whose presence in every village through which he might have passed would have wakened the church bells, have given school-boys a holiday, have drawn children from their sports to gaze upon him, and "old men from the chimney corner," to look upon Nelson ere they died. The victory of Trafalgar was celebrated, indeed, with the usual forms of rejoicing, but they were without joy; for such already was the glory of the British navy, through Nelson's surpassing genius, that it scarcely seemed to receive any addition from the most signal victory that ever was achieved upon the seas; and the destruction of this mighty fleet, by which all the maritime schemes of France were totally frustrated, hardly appeared to add to our security or strength; for, while Nelson was living to watch the combined squadrons of the enemy, we felt ourselves as secure as now, when they were no longer in existence.

There was reason to suppose from the appearances upon opening the body, that, in the course of nature, he might have attained, like his father, to a good old age. Yet he cannot be said to have fallen prematurely whose work was done; nor ought he to be lamented, who died so full of honours, and at the height of human fame. The most triumphant death is that of the martyr; the most awful, that of the martyred patriot; the most splendid, that of the hero in the hour of victory: and if the chariot and the horses of fire had been vouchsafed for Nelson's translation, he could scarcely have departed in a brighter blaze of glory. He has left us, not indeed his mantle of inspiration, but a name and an example, which are at this hour inspiring hundreds of the youth of England: a name which is our pride, and an example which will continue to be our shield and our strength. Thus it is that the spirits of the great and the wise continue to live and to act after them: verifying, in this sense, the language of the old mythologist:

Τοι μεν δαιμονες εισι, Διος μεγαλου δια βουλας
Εσθλοι, επιχθονιοι, φυλακες θνητων ανθρωπων.

THE END.

INDEX

The following abbreviations have been used for nationalities: B. (British), Da. (Danish), Fr. (French), Sp. (Spanish). The letter L after the name of a ship indicates line-of-battle ship.

EVERYMAN'S LIBRARY: A Selected List

BIOGRAPHY

Baxter, Richard (1615–91).
THE AUTOBIOGRAPHY OF RICHARD BAXTER. 868
Boswell, James (1740–95). *See* Johnson.
Brontë, Charlotte (1816–55).
LIFE, 1857. By *Mrs Gaskell*. Introduction by *May Sinclair*. (*See also* Fiction.) 318
Burns, Robert (1759–96).
LIFE, 1828. By *J. G. Lockhart* (1794–1854). With Introduction by *Prof. James Kinsley*, M.A., PH.D. (*See also* Poetry and Drama.) 156
Byron, Lord (1788–1824).
LETTERS. Edited by *R. G. Howarth*, B.LITT., and with an Introduction by *André Maurois*. (*See also* Poetry and Drama.) 931
Canton, William (1845–1926).
A CHILD'S BOOK OF SAINTS, 1898. (*See also* Essays.) 61
Cellini, Benvenuto (1500–71).
THE LIFE OF BENVENUTO CELLINI, written by himself. Translated by *Anne Macdonell*. Introduction by *William Gaunt*. 51
Cowper, William (1731–1800).
SELECTED LETTERS. Edited, with Introduction, by *W. Hadley*, M.A. 774
(*See also* Poetry and Drama.)

Dickens, Charles (1812–70).
LIFE, 1874. By *John Forster* (1812–76). Introduction by *G. K. Chesterton*. 2 vols.
(*See also* Fiction.) 781–2

Evelyn, John (1620–1706).
DIARY. Edited by *William Bray*, 1819. Intro. by *G. W. E. Russell*. 2 vols. 220–1
Fox, George (1624–91).
JOURNAL, 1694. Revised by *Norman Penney*, with Account of Fox's last years. Introduction by *Rufus M. Jones*. 754
Franklin, Benjamin (1706–90).
AUTOBIOGRAPHY, 1817. With Introduction and Account of Franklin's later life by *W. Macdonald*. Reset new edition (1949), with a newly compiled Index. 316
Goethe, Johann Wolfgang von (1749–1832).
LIFE, 1855. By *G. H. Lewes* (1817–78). Introduction by *Havelock Ellis*. Index.
(*See also* Poetry and Drama.) 269
Hudson, William Henry (1841–1922).
FAR AWAY AND LONG AGO, 1918. Intro. by *John Galsworthy*. 956
Johnson, Samuel (1709–84).
LIVES OF THE ENGLISH POETS, 1781. Introduction by *Mrs L. Archer-Hind*. 2 vols.
(*See also* Essays, Fiction.) 770–1
BOSWELL'S LIFE OF JOHNSON, 1791. A new edition (1949), with Introduction by *S. C. Roberts*, M.A., LL.D., and a 30-page Index by Alan Dent. 2 vols. 1–2
Keats, John (1795–1821).
LIFE AND LETTERS, 1848. By *Lord Houghton* (1809–85). Introduction by *Robert Lynd*. Note on the letters by Lewis Gibbs. (*See also* Poetry and Drama.) 801
Lamb, Charles (1775–1834).
LETTERS. New edition (1945) arranged from the Complete Annotated Edition of the Letters. 2 vols. (*See also* Essays and Belles-Lettres, Fiction.) 342–3
Napoleon Buonaparte (1769–1821).
HISTORY OF NAPOLEON BUONAPARTE, 1829. By *J. G. Lockhart* (1794–1854). 3
(*See also* Essays and Belles-Lettres.)
Nelson, Horatio, Viscount (1758–1805).
LIFE, 1813. By *Robert Southey* (1774–1843). (*See also* Essays.) 52
Outram, General Sir James (1803–63), 'the Bayard of India.'
LIFE, 1903. Deals with important passages in the history of India in the nineteenth century. By *L. J. Trotter* (1827–1912). 396
Pepys, Samuel (1633–1703).
DIARY. Newly edited (1953), with modernized spelling, by *John Warrington*, from the edition of Mynors Bright (1875–9). 3 vols. 53–5
Plutarch (46?–120).
LIVES OF THE NOBLE GREEKS AND ROMANS. Dryden's edition, 1683–6. Revised, with Introduction, by *A. H. Clough* (1819–61). 3 vols. 407–9
Rousseau, Jean Jacques (1712–78).
CONFESSIONS, 1782. 2 vols. Complete and unabridged English translation. New Introduction by *Prof. R. Niklaus*, B.A., PH.D., of Exeter University. 859–60
(*See also* Essays, Theology and Philosophy.)
Scott, Sir Walter (1771–1832).
LOCKHART'S LIFE OF SCOTT. An abridgement by *J. G. Lockhart* himself from the original 7 volumes. New Introduction by *W. M. Parker*, M.A. 39

Swift, Jonathan (1667–1745).
  JOURNAL TO STELLA, 1710–13. Deciphered by *J. K. Moorhead*. Introduction by *Sir
  Walter Scott*. Sir Walter Scott's essay 'Swift, Stella and Vanessa' is included.   757
                                                          (*See also* Essays, Fiction.)
Walpole, Horace (1717–97).
  SELECTED LETTERS. Edited, with Introduction, by *W. Hadley*, M.A.   775
Wellington, Arthur Wellesley, Duke of (1769–1852).
  LIFE, 1862. By *G. R. Gleig* (1796–1888).   341

CLASSICAL

Aeschylus (525–455 B.C.).
  PLAYS. Translated into English Verse by *G. M. Cookson*. New Introduction by
  John Warrington, and notes on each play.   62
Aristophanes (450?–385? B.C.).
  THE COMEDIES. Translated by *J. Hookham Frere*, etc. Edited, with Introduction,
  by *J. P. Maine* and *J. H. Frere*. 2 vols.   (*Vol. 1 temporarily out of print.*) 516
Aristotle (384–322 B.C.).
  POLITICS and THE ATHENIAN CONSTITUTION. Edited and translated by *John
  Warrington*.   605
  METAPHYSICS. Edited and translated by *John Warrington*. Introduction by *Sir
  David Ross*, K.B.E., M.A., D.LITT.   1000
Caesar, Julius (102?–44 B.C.).
  WAR COMMENTARIES. 'The Gallic Wars' and 'The Civil War.' Newly translated
  and edited by *John Warrington*.   702
Cicero, Marcus Tullius (106–43 B.C.).
  THE OFFICES (translated by *Thomas Cockman*, 1699); LAELIUS, ON FRIENDSHIP;
  CATO, ON OLD AGE; AND SELECT LETTERS (translated by *W. Melmoth*, 1753). With
  Note on Cicero's Character by De Quincey. Introduction by *John Warrington*. 345
Demetrius (fl. late first century A.D.). (*See under* Aristotle.)
Demosthenes (384–322 B.C.). (*See under* Oratory, p. 11.)
Epictetus (*b. c.* A.D. 60).
  MORAL DISCOURSES. THE ENCHIRIDION AND FRAGMENTS. Translated by *Elizabeth
  Carter* (1717–1806). Edited by *W. H. D. Rouse*, M.A.   404
Euripides (484?–407 B.C.).
  PLAYS. New Introduction by *John Warrington*. Translated by *A. S. Way*, D.LITT.
  2 vols.   63, 271
Herodotus (484?–425? B.C.).
  HISTORY. The 'History' deals with the period covering the Persian invasion of
  Greece, 492–480 B.C. Rawlinson's Translation, additional notes and Introduction,
  by *E. H. Blakeney*. 2 vols. (*Vol. II temporarily out of print.*)   405–6
Homer (? ninth century B.C.).
  ILIAD. New verse translation by *S. O. Andrew* and *Michael Oakley*.   453
  ODYSSEY. The new verse translation (first published 1953) by *S. O. Andrew*.
  Introduction by *John Warrington*.   454
Juvenal (*c.* A.D. 50–*c.* 130).
  SATIRES: with THE SATIRES OF PERSIUS. Introduction by *Prof. H. J. Rose*, M.A.,
  F.B.A. William Gifford Translation, 1802. Revised by *John Warrington*.   997
Lucretius (*c.* 99?–50? B.C.).
  ON THE NATURE OF THINGS. Metrical Translation by *W. E. Leonard*.   750
Ovid (43 B.C.–A.D. 18).
  SELECTED WORKS. Chosen by *J. C.* and *M. J. Thornton*. Selections from the
  Metamorphoses, Heroical Epistles, the *Festivals*, the *Ibis*, and his epistles written in
  exile: also his *Art of Love*.   955
Persius (34–62). See Juvenal.
Plato (427–347 B.C.).
  THE REPUBLIC. Translated, with an Introduction, by *A. D. Lindsay*, C.B.E., LL.D.
  The greatest achievement of the Greek intellect in philosophy.   64
  SOCRATIC DISCOURSES OF PLATO AND XENOPHON. Introduction by *A. D. Lindsay*,
  C.B.E., LL.D.   457
  THE LAWS. The last of Plato's dialogues is here printed in the A. E. Taylor (1869–
  1945) Translation.   275
Sophocles (496?–406 B.C.).
  DRAMAS. This volume contains the seven surviving dramas.   114
Thucydides (*c.* 460–401 B.C.).
  HISTORY OF THE PELOPONNESIAN WAR. Translation by *Richard Crawley*. Intro-
  duction by *John Warrington*. Index and five plans.   455
Virgil (70–19 B.C.).
  AENEID. Verse translation by *Michael Oakley*. Introduction by *E. M. Forster*. 161
  ECLOGUES AND GEORGICS. Verse Translation by *T. F. Royds*. The 'Eclogues' were
  inspired by Theocritus; the 'Georgics' describe a countryman's life.   222
Xenophon (430?–360? B.C.). (*See under* Plato.)

2

ESSAYS AND BELLES-LETTRES

5

Manzoni, Alessandro (1785–1873).
    THE BETROTHED (*I Promessi Sposi*, 1840, rev. ed.). Translated (1951) from the
    Italian by *Archibald Colquhoun*, who also adds a preface.   999
Marryat, Frederick (1792–1848).
    MR MIDSHIPMAN EASY. New Introduction by *Oliver Warner*.   82
    THE SETTLERS IN CANADA, 1844. Introduction by *Oliver Warner*.   370
Maugham, W. Somerset (*b.* 1874).
    CAKES AND ALE, 1930. The finest novel of the author's inter-war period.   932
Maupassant, Guy de (1850–93).
    SHORT STORIES. Translated by *Marjorie Laurie*. Intro. by *Gerald Gould*.   907
Melville, Herman (1819–91).
    MOBY DICK, 1851. Intro. by *Prof. Sherman Paul*.   179
    TYPEE, 1846; and BILLY BUDD (*published* 1924). South Seas adventures. New
    Introduction by *Milton R. Stern*.   180
Meredith, George (1828–1909).
    THE ORDEAL OF RICHARD FEVEREL, 1859. Introduction by *Robert Sencourt*. 916
Mickiewicz, Adam (1798–1855).
    PAN TADEUSZ, 1834. Translated into English prose, with Introduction, by *Prof.
    G. R. Noyes*. Poland's epic of Napoleonic wars.   842
Modern Short Stories. Selected by *John Hadfield*. Twenty stories.   954
Moore, George (1852–1933).
    ESTHER WATERS, 1894. The story of Esther Waters, the servant girl who 'went
    wrong.' Introduction by *C. D. Medley*.   933
Mulock [Mrs Craik], Maria (1826–87).
    JOHN HALIFAX, GENTLEMAN, 1856. Introduction by *J. Shaylor*.   123
Pater, Walter (1839–94).
    MARIUS THE EPICUREAN, 1885. Introduction by *Osbert Burdett*.   903
Poe, Edgar Allan (1809–49).
    TALES OF MYSTERY AND IMAGINATION. Introduction by *Padraic Colum*.   336
                                 (*See also* Poetry and Drama.)
Priestley, J. B. (*b.* 1894).
    ANGEL PAVEMENT, 1931. A finely conceived novel of London.   938
Quiller-Couch, Sir Arthur (1863–1944).
    HETTY WESLEY, 1903. Introduction by the author.   (*See also* Essays.) 864
Radcliffe, Mrs Ann (1764–1823).
    THE MYSTERIES OF UDOLPHO, 1794. Intro. by *R. A. Freeman*. 2 vols.   865–6
Reade, Charles (1814–84).
    THE CLOISTER AND THE HEARTH, 1861. Introduction by *Swinburne*.   29
Richardson, Samuel (1689–1761).
    PAMELA, 1740. Introduction by *George Saintsbury*. 2 vols.   683–4
    CLARISSA, 1747–8. Introduction by *Prof. W. L. Phelps*. 4 vols.   882–5
Russian Short Stories. Translated, with Introduction, by *Rochelle S. Townsend*. Stories
    by Pushkin, Gogol, Tolstoy, Korolenko, Chehov, Chirikov, Andreyev, Kuprin,
    Gorky, Sologub.   758
Scott, Sir Walter (1771–1832).
    The following Waverley Novels each contain an Introduction, biographical and
    bibliographical, based upon Lockhart's *Life*:
    THE ANTIQUARY, 1816. Introduction by *W. M. Parker*, M.A.   126
    THE BRIDE OF LAMMERMOOR, 1819. A romance of life in East Lothian, 1695. New
    Introduction by *W. M. Parker*, M.A.   129
    GUY MANNERING, 1815. A mystery story of the time of George III. New Intro-
    duction by *W. M. Parker*, M.A.   133
    THE HEART OF MIDLOTHIAN, 1818. Period of the Porteous Riots, 1736. New Intro-
    duction by *W. M. Parker*, M.A.   134
    IVANHOE, 1820. A romance of the days of Richard I.   16
    KENILWORTH, 1821. The tragic story of Amy Robsart, in Elizabeth I's time. New
    Preface and Glossary by *W. M. Parker*, M.A.   135
    OLD MORTALITY, 1817. Battle of Bothwell Bridge, 1679. New Introduction by
    W. M. Parker, M.A.   137
    QUENTIN DURWARD, 1823. A tale of adventures in fifteenth-century France. New
    Introduction by *W. M. Parker*, M.A.   140
    REDGAUNTLET, 1824. A tale of adventure in Cumberland, about 1763. New Intro-
    duction by *W. M. Parker*, M.A.   141
    ROB ROY, 1818. A romance of the Rebellion of 1715.   142
    THE TALISMAN, 1825. Richard Cœur-de-Lion and the Third Crusade, 1191. New
    Preface by *W. M. Parker*, M.A.   (*See also* Biography.) 144
Shchedrin (M. E. Saltykov, 1826–92).
    THE GOLOVLYOV FAMILY. Translated by *Natalie Duddington*. Introduction by
    Edward Garnett.   908
Shelley, Mary Wollstonecraft (1797–1851).
    FRANKENSTEIN, 1818. With Mary Shelley's own Preface.   616
Shorter Novels.
    Vol. I: ELIZABETHAN. Introduction by *George Saintsbury* and Notes by *Philip
    Henderson*. Contains: Deloney's 'Jack of Newberie' and 'Thomas of Reading';
    Nashe's 'The Unfortunate Traveller'; Green's 'Carde of Fancie.'   824

Voltaire, François Marie Arouet de (1694–1778).
CANDIDE, AND OTHER TALES. Smollett's translation, edited by *J. C. Thornton*. 936
(*See also* History.)
Walpole, Hugh Seymour (1884–1941).
MR PERRIN AND MR TRAILL, 1911. 918
Wells, Herbert George (1866–1946).
ANN VERONICA, 1909. Introduction by *A. J. Hoppé*. 997
THE WHEELS OF CHANCE, 1896; and THE TIME MACHINE, 1895. 915
Wilde, Oscar.
THE PICTURE OF DORIAN GRAY, 1891. (*See* Poetry and Drama.)
Woolf, Virginia (1882–1941).
TO THE LIGHTHOUSE, 1927. Introduction by *D. M. Hoare*, PH.D. 949
Zola, Émile (1840–1902).
GERMINAL, 1885. Translated, with an Introduction, by *Havelock Ellis*. 897

HISTORY

Anglo-Saxon Chronicle. Translated and Edited by *G. N. Garmonsway*, F.R.HIST.SOC.
Foreword by *Prof. Bruce Dickins*. 624
Bede, the Venerable (673–735).
THE ECCLESIASTICAL HISTORY OF THE ENGLISH NATION. Translated by *John Stevens*, revised by *J. A. Giles*, with notes by *L. C. Jane*. Introduction by *Prof. David Knowles*, O.S.B., M.A., LITT.D., F.B.A., F.S.A. 479
Carlyle, Thomas (1795–1881).
THE FRENCH REVOLUTION, 1837. Introduction by *Hilaire Belloc*. 2 vols. 31–2
(*See also* Biography, Essays.)
Chesterton, Cecil (1879–1918). A HISTORY OF THE U.S.A., 1917. Edited by *Prof. D. W. Brogan*, M.A. 965
Creasy, Sir Edward (1812–78).
FIFTEEN DECISIVE BATTLES OF THE WORLD, FROM MARATHON TO WATERLOO, 1852. With Diagrams and Index. New Introduction by *Audrey Butler*, M.A. (OXON.). 300
Gibbon, Edward (1737–94).
THE DECLINE AND FALL OF THE ROMAN EMPIRE, 1776–88. Notes by *Oliphant Smeaton*. Intro. by *Christopher Dawson*. Complete text in 6 vols. 434–6, 474–6
Green, John Richard (1837–83).
A SHORT HISTORY OF THE ENGLISH PEOPLE, 1874. Introduction by *L. C. Jane*. English history from 607 to 1873. Continued by: 'A Political and Social Survey from 1815 to 1915,' by *R. P. Farley*, and revised to 1950. 727–8
Holinshed, Raphael (*d.* 1580?).
HOLINSHED'S CHRONICLE AS USED IN SHAKESPEARE'S PLAYS, 1578. Introduction by *Prof. Allardyce Nicoll* and *Josephine Nicoll*. 800
Joinville, Jean de. *See* Villehardouin.
Lützow, Count Franz von (1849–1916).
BOHEMIA: AN HISTORICAL SKETCH, 1896. Introduction by *President T. G. Masaryk*. H. A. Piehler covers events from 1879 to 1938. 432
Macaulay, Thomas Babington, Baron (1800–59).
THE HISTORY OF ENGLAND. The complete text in four volumes, which together contain 2,450 pages. Introduction by *Douglas Jerrold*. 34–7
(*See also* Essays.)
Maine, Sir Henry (1822–88).
ANCIENT LAW, 1861. Introduction by *Prof. J. H. Morgan*. 734
Mommsen, Theodor (1817–1903).
HISTORY OF ROME, 1856. Translated by *W. P. Dickson*, LL.D. Introduction by *Edward A. Freeman*. 4 vols. (Vols. III and IV only.) 544–5
Motley, John (1814–77).
THE RISE OF THE DUTCH REPUBLIC, 1856. Intro. by *V. R. Reynolds*. 3 vols. 86–8
Paston Letters, The, 1418–1506. 2 vols. A selection. 752–3
Prescott, William Hickling (1796–1859).
HISTORY OF THE CONQUEST OF MEXICO, 1843. 2 vols. 397–8
Stanley, Arthur (1815–81).
LECTURES ON THE HISTORY OF THE EASTERN CHURCH, 1861. Introduction by *A. J. Grieve*, M.A. 251
Thierry, Augustin (1795–1856).
THE NORMAN CONQUEST, 1825. Introduction by *J. A. Price*, B.A. 2 vols. (*Vol. I temporarily out of print.*) 198–9
Villehardouin, Geoffrey de (1160?–1213?), and **Joinville, Jean, Sire de** (1224–1317).
MEMOIRS OF THE CRUSADES. Translated, with an Introduction, by *Sir Frank T. Marzials*. 333
Voltaire, François Marie Arouet de (1694–1778).
THE AGE OF LOUIS XIV, 1751. Translation by *Martyn P. Pollack*.
(*See also* Fiction.) 780

ORATORY

British Orations. The 1960 edition of this selection of British historical speeches contains selections from four of the most famous of Sir Winston Churchill's World War II speeches. 714

Burke, Edmund (1729–97).
SPEECHES AND LETTERS ON AMERICAN AFFAIRS. New Introduction by the *Very Rev. Canon Peter McKevitt*, PH.D. (*See also* Essays and Belles-Lettres.) 340

Demosthenes (384–322 B.C.).
THE CROWN, AND OTHER ORATIONS. Translated with an Appendix on Athenian economics by *C. Rann Kennedy.* Introduction by *John Warrington.* 546

Lincoln, Abraham (1809–65).
SPEECHES AND LETTERS, 1832–65. A new selection edited with an Introduction by *Paul M. Angle.* Chronology of Lincoln's life and index. 206

POETRY AND DRAMA

Anglo-Saxon Poetry. English poetry between A.D. 650 and 1000, from 'Widsith' and 'Beowulf' to the battle-pieces of 'Brunanburh' and 'Maldon.' Selected and translated by *Prof. R. K. Gordon,* M.A. Reset, and revised by the translator, 1954. 794

Arnold, Matthew (1822–88).
COMPLETE POEMS. Introduction by *R. A. Scott-James.* 334

Ballads, A Book of British. Introduction and Notes by *R. Brimley Johnson.* Ballads from the earliest times to those of Yeats and Kipling. 572

Beaumont, Francis (1584–1616), and **Fletcher, John** (1579–1625).
SELECT PLAYS. Introduction by *Prof. G. P. Baker.* 'The Knight of the Burning Pestle,' 'The Maid's Tragedy,' 'A King and No King,' 'The Faithful Shepherdess.' 'The Wild Goose Chase,' 'Bonduca,' with a glossary. 506

Blake, William (1757–1827).
POEMS AND PROPHECIES. Edited, with special Introduction, by *Max Plowman.* 792

Brontë, Emily.
POEMS. (*See* Fiction.)

Browning, Robert (1812–89).
POEMS AND PLAYS, 1833–64. With a new Introduction by *John Bryson,* M.A., dealing with the four-volume Everyman Browning set. 2 vols. Volume III, containing *The Ring and the Book,* Browning's long dramatic poem (No. 502), is temporarily out of print. 41–2
POEMS, 1871–90. Introduction by *M. M. Bozman.* 964

Burns, Robert (1759–96).
POEMS AND SONGS. A very full selection and a very accurate text of Burns's copious lyrical output. Edited and introduced by *Prof. James Kinsley,* M.A., PH.D. 94
(*See also* Biography.)

Byron, George Gordon Noel, Lord (1788–1824).
THE POETICAL AND DRAMATIC WORKS. 3 vols. Edited with a Preface by *Guy Pocock* (*See also* Biography.) 486–8

Century. A CENTURY OF HUMOROUS VERSE, 1850–1950. Edited by *Roger Lancelyn Green,* M.A., B.LITT. 813

Chaucer, Geoffrey (c. 1343–1400).
CANTERBURY TALES. New standard text edited by *A. C. Cawley,* M.A., PH.D., based on the Ellesmere Manuscript, with an ingenious system of glosses, page by page. 307
TROILUS AND CRISEYDE. Prepared by *John Warrington* from the Campsall Manuscript. 992

Coleridge, Samuel Taylor (1772–1834).
THE GOLDEN BOOK. (*See also* Essays, etc.) 43

Cowper, William (1731–1800).
POEMS. Intro. by *Hugh I'Anson Fausset.* (*See also* Biography.) 872

Dante Alighieri (1265–1321).
THE DIVINE COMEDY, first printed 1472. H. F. Cary's Translation, 1805–14. Edited, with Notes and Index, by *Edmund Gardner.* Foreword by *Prof. Mario Praz.* 308

De la Mare, Walter (1873–1956). (*See* Essays.)

Donne, John (1573–1631).
COMPLETE POEMS. Edited, with a revised Intro., by *Hugh I'Anson Fausset.* 867

Dryden, John (1631–1700).
POEMS. Edited by *Bonamy Dobrée,* O.B.E., M.A. 910

Eighteenth-century Plays. Edited by *John Hampden.* Includes Gay's 'Beggar's Opera,' Addison's 'Cato,' Rowe's 'Jane Shore,' Fielding's 'Tragedy of Tragedies, or, Tom Thumb the Great,' Lillo's 'George Barnwell,' Colman and Garrick's 'Clandestine Marriage,' and Cumberland's 'West Indian.' 818

English Galaxy of Shorter Poems, The. Chosen and Edited by *Gerald Bullett.* 959

English Religious Verse. Edited by *G. Lacey May.* An anthology from the Middle Ages to the present day, including some 300 poems by 150 authors. 937

Everyman, and Medieval Miracle Plays. New edition edited by *A. C. Cawley,* M.A., PH.D. Forewords to individual plays. 381

Fitzgerald, Edward (1809–83). See 'Persian Poems.'

11

Palgrave, Francis Turner (1824–97). *See* 'Golden Treasury of English Songs and Lyrics, The.'   96

Persian Poems. Selected and edited by *Prof. A. J. Arberry*, M.A., LITT.D., F.B.A.   996

Poe, Edgar Allan (1809–49).
  POEMS AND ESSAYS. Introduction by *Andrew Lang.*   (*See also* Fiction.) 791

Poems of our Time. An Anthology edited by *Richard Church*, C.B.E., *M. M. Bozman* and *Edith Sitwell*, D.LITT., D.B.E. Nearly 400 poems by about 130 poets.   981

Pope, Alexander (1688–1744).
  COLLECTED POEMS. Edited with Intro. (1956) by *Prof. Bonamy Dobrée*, O.B.E., M.A.   760

Restoration Plays. Introduction by *Edmund Gosse.* Includes Dryden's 'All for Love,' Wycherley's 'The Country Wife,' Congreve's 'The Way of the World,' Otway's 'Venice Preserved,' Farquhar's 'Beaux-Stratagem,' Vanbrugh's 'Provoked Wife.' Etherege's 'Man of Mode.'   604

Rossetti, Dante Gabriel (1828–82).
  POEMS AND TRANSLATIONS. Introduction by *E. G. Gardner.*   627

Shakespeare, William (1564–1616).
  A Complete Edition, based on Clark and Wright's Cambridge text, and edited by *Oliphant Smeaton.* With biographical Introduction, Chronological Tables and full Glossary. 3 vols.
      Comedies, 153; Histories, Poems and Sonnets, 154; Tragedies, 155

Shelley, Percy Bysshe (1792–1822).
  POETICAL WORKS. Introduction by *A. H. Koszul.* 2 vols.   257–8

Sheridan, Richard Brinsley (1751–1816).
  COMPLETE PLAYS. Introduction and notes by *Lewis Gibbs.*   95

Silver Poets of the Sixteenth Century. Edited by *Gerald Bullett.* The works of Sir Thomas Wyatt (1503–42), Henry Howard, Earl of Surrey (1517?–47), Sir Philip Sidney (1554–86), Sir Walter Ralegh (1552–1618) and Sir John Davies (1569–1626.)   985

Spenser, Edmund (1552–99).
  THE FAERIE QUEENE. Introduction by *Prof. J. W. Hales,* and Glossary. 2 vols. The reliable Morris text and glossary are used for this edition.   443–4
  THE SHEPHERD'S CALENDAR, 1579; and OTHER POEMS. Introduction by *Philip Henderson.*   879

Stevenson, Robert Louis (1850–94).
  POEMS. A CHILD'S GARDEN OF VERSES, 1885; UNDERWOODS, 1887; SONGS OF TRAVEL, 1896; and BALLADS, 1890, Introduction by *Ernest Rhys.*   768
       (*See also* Essays, Fiction, Travel.)

Swinburne, Algernon Charles (1837–1909).
  POEMS AND PROSE. A selection, edited with an Intro. by *Richard Church.*   961

Synge, J. M. (1871–1909).
  PLAYS, POEMS AND PROSE. Introduction by *Michaél Mac Liammóir.*   968

Tchekhov, Anton (1860–1904).
  PLAYS AND STORIES. 'The Cherry Orchard,' 'The Seagull,' 'The Wood Demon,' 'Tatyana Riepin' and 'On the Harmfulness of Tobacco' are included, as well as 13 of his best stories. The translation is by *S. S. Koteliansky.* Introduction by *David Magarshack.*   941

Tennyson, Alfred, Lord (1809–92).
  POEMS. A comprehensive edition (1950), with an Introduction by *Mildred Bozman.* 2 vols.   44, 626

Twenty-four One-Act Plays. Enlarged edition, new Introduction by *John Hampden.* Contains plays by T. S. Eliot, Sean O'Casey, Laurence Housman, W. B. Yeats, James Bridie, Noel Coward, Lord Dunsany, Wolf Mankowitz and others.   947

Webster, John (1580?–1625?), and **Ford, John** (1586–1639).
  SELECTED PLAYS. Introduction by *Prof. G. B. Harrison*, M.A., PH.D. In one volume: 'The White Devil,' 'The Duchess of Malfi,' 'The Broken Heart,' ''Tis Pity She's a Whore.'   899

Whitman, Walt (1819–92).
  LEAVES OF GRASS, 1855–92. New edition (1947) by *Dr Emory Holloway.*   573

Wilde, Oscar (1854–1900).
  PLAYS, PROSE WRITINGS, AND POEMS. Edited, with Introduction, by *Hesketh Pearson.* Including the two plays, 'The Importance of Being Earnest' and 'Lady Windermer's Fan'; his novel, 'The Picture of Dorian Gray'; the poem, 'The Ballad of Reading Gaol'; the essay, 'The Soul of Man,' etc.   858

Wordsworth, William (1770–1850).
  POEMS. Edited, with Introductory study, notes, bibliography and full index, by *Philip Wayne*, M.A.   203, 311, 998

REFERENCE

Reader's Guide to Everyman's Library. Compiled by *A. J. Hoppé.* This volume is a new compilation and gives in one alphabetical sequence the names of all the authors, titles and subjects in Everyman's Library and its supplementary series, Everyman's Reference Library and the Children's Illustrated Classics.   889

Many volumes formerly included in Everyman's Library reference section are now included in Everyman's Reference Library and are bound in larger format.

ROMANCE

Aucassin and Nicolette, with other Medieval Romances. Translated, with Introduction, by *Eugene Mason.*   497

Boccaccio, Giovanni (1313–75).
    DECAMERON, 1471. Translated by *J. M. Rigg*, 1903. Introduction by *Edward Hutton*, 2 vols. Unabridged.   845–6

Bunyan, John (1628–88).
    PILGRIM'S PROGRESS, Parts I and II, 1678–84. Reset edition. Introduction by *Prof. G. B. Harrison*, M.A., PH.D.   (*See also* Theology and Philosophy.) 204

Cervantes, Saavedra Miguel de (1547–1616).
    DON QUIXOTE DE LA MANCHA. Translated by *P. A. Motteux.* Notes by *J. G. Lockhart.* Introduction and supplementary Notes by *L. B. Walton*, M.A., B.LITT. 2 vols.   385–6

Chrétien de Troyes (fl. 12th cent.).
    ARTHURIAN ROMANCES ('Erec et Enide'; 'Cligés'; 'Yvain' and 'Lancelot'). Translated into prose, with Introduction, notes and bibliography, by *William Wistar Comfort.*   698

Kalevala, or The Land of Heroes. Translated from the Finnish by W. F. Kirby. 2 vols.   259–60

Mabinogion, The. Translated with Introduction by *Thomas Jones*, M.A., D.LITT., and *Gwyn Jones*, M.A.   97

Malory, Sir Thomas (fl. 1400?–70).
    LE MORTE D'ARTHUR. Introduction by *Sir John Rhys.* 2 vols.   45–6

Marie de France (12th century), LAYS OF, AND OTHER FRENCH LEGENDS. Eight of Marie's 'Lais' and two of the anonymous French love stories of the same period translated with an Introduction by *Eugene Mason.*   557

Njal's Saga. THE STORY OF BURNT NJAL (written about 1280–90). Translated from the Icelandic by *Sir G. W. Dasent* (1861). Introduction (1957) and Index by *Prof. Edward Turville-Petre*, B.LITT., M.A.   558

Rabelais, François (1494?–1553).
    THE HEROIC DEEDS OF GARGANTUA AND PANTAGRUEL, 1532–5. Introduction by *D. B. Wyndham Lewis.* 2 vols. A complete unabridged edition of Urquhart and Motteux's translation, 1653–94.   826–7

SCIENCE

Boyle, Robert (1627–91).
    THE SCEPTICAL CHYMIST, 1661. Introduction by *M. M. Pattison Muir.*   559

Darwin, Charles (1809–82).
    THE ORIGIN OF SPECIES, 1859. The sixth edition embodies Darwin's final additions and revisions. New Introduction (1956) by *W. R. Thompson*, F.R.S.   811

Eddington, Arthur Stanley (1882–1944).   (*See also* Travel and Topography.)
    THE NATURE OF THE PHYSICAL WORLD, 1928. Introduction by *Sir Edmund Whittaker*, F.R.S., O.M.   922

Euclid (fl. *c.* 330–*c.* 275 B.C.).
    THE ELEMENTS OF EUCLID. Edited by *Isaac Todhunter*, with Introduction by *Sir Thomas L. Heath*, K.C.B., F.R.S.   891

Faraday, Michael (1791–1867).
    EXPERIMENTAL RESEARCHES IN ELECTRICITY, 1839–55. With Plates and Diagrams, and an appreciation by *Prof. John Tyndall.*   576

Harvey, William (1578–1657).
    THE CIRCULATION OF THE BLOOD. Introduction by *Ernest Parkyn.*   262

Howard, John (1726?–90).
    THE STATE OF THE PRISONS, 1777. Intro. and Notes by *Kenneth Ruck.*   835

Marx, Karl (1818–83).
    CAPITAL, 1867. Translated by *Eden* and *Cedar Paul.* 2 vols. Introduction by *Prof. G. D. H. Cole.*   848–9

Mill, John Stuart (1806–73). *See* Wollstonecraft.

Owen, Robert (1771–1858).
    A NEW VIEW OF SOCIETY, 1813; and OTHER WRITINGS. Introduction by *G. D. H. Cole.*   799

Pearson, Karl (1857–1936).
    THE GRAMMAR OF SCIENCE, 1892.   939

Ricardo, David (1772–1823).
    THE PRINCIPLES OF POLITICAL ECONOMY AND TAXATION, 1817. Introduction by *Prof. Michael P. Fogarty*, M.A.   590

Smith, Adam (1723–90).
    THE WEALTH OF NATIONS, 1766. Intro. by *Prof. Edwin Seligman.* 2 vols. 412–13

White, Gilbert (1720–93).
    A NATURAL HISTORY OF SELBORNE, 1789. New edition (1949). Introduction and Notes by *R. M. Lockley.*   48

Wollstonecraft, Mary (1759–97), THE RIGHTS OF WOMAN, 1792; and Mill, John Stuart (1806–73), THE SUBJECTION OF WOMEN, 1869. New Introduction by *Pamela Frankau.*   825

THEOLOGY AND PHILOSOPHY

15

Robinson, Wade (1838–76).
   THE PHILOSOPHY OF ATONEMENT, AND OTHER SERMONS, 1875. Introduction by *F. B. Meyer.*   637

Rousseau, Jean Jacques (1712–78).
   THE SOCIAL CONTRACT, 1762; and OTHER ESSAYS. Introduction by *G. D. H. Cole.* (*See also* Biography, Essays.)   660

Saint Augustine (353–430).
   CONFESSIONS. Dr Pusey's Translation, 1838, with Introduction by *A. H. Armstrong*, M.A.   200
   THE CITY OF GOD. Complete text of John Healey's Elizabethan Translation, 1610. Edited by *R. V. G. Tasker*, M.A., B.D., with an Introduction by *Sir Ernest Barker.* 2 vols.   982–3

Saint Francis (1182–1226).
   THE LITTLE FLOWERS; THE MIRROR OF PERFECTION (by Leo of Assisi); and THE LIFE OF ST FRANCIS (by St Bonaventura). Introduction by *Thomas Okey.*   485

Spinoza, Benedictus de (1632–77).
   ETHICS, 1677; and ON THE CORRECTION OF THE UNDERSTANDING, 1687. Translated by *Andrew Boyle.* New Introduction by *T. S. Gregory.*   481

Swedenborg, Emanuel (1688–1772).
   THE TRUE CHRISTIAN RELIGION, 1771. New and unabridged translation by *F. Bayley.* Introduction by *Dr Helen Keller.* 960 pages.   893

Thomas à Kempis (1380?–1471).
   THE IMITATION OF CHRIST, 1471.   484

Thomas Aquinas (1225–74).
   SELECTED WRITINGS. Selected and edited by *Father M. C. D'Arcy.*   953

TRAVEL AND TOPOGRAPHY

Borrow, George (1803–81).
   THE BIBLE IN SPAIN, 1842. Introduction by *Edward Thomas.*   151
   WILD WALES: the People, Language and Scenery, 1862. Introduction by *David Jones*, C.B.E., the painter and Borrovian. (*See also* Fiction.) 49

Boswell, James (1740–95).
   JOURNAL OF A TOUR TO THE HEBRIDES WITH SAMUEL JOHNSON, 1786. Edited, with a new Introduction, by *Lawrence F. Powell*, M.A., HON. D.LITT.   387

Calderón de la Barca, Mme (1804–82).
   LIFE IN MEXICO, 1843. Introduction by *Manuel Romero De Terreros.*   664

Cobbett, William (1762–1835).
   RURAL RIDES, 1830. Introduction by *Asa Briggs*, M.A., B.SC. 2 vols.   638–9

Cook, James (1728–79).
   VOYAGES OF DISCOVERY. Edited by *John Barrow*, F.R.S., F.S.A. Introduction by *Guy Pocock*, M.A.   99

Crèvecœur, J. Hector St John de (1735–1813).
   LETTERS FROM AN AMERICAN FARMER, 1782. Intro. and Notes by *W. Barton Blake.*   640

Darwin, Charles (1809–82).
   THE VOYAGE OF THE 'BEAGLE,' 1839. (*See also* Science.) 104

Defoe, Daniel (1661?–1731).
   A TOUR THROUGH ENGLAND AND WALES, 1724–6. Intro. by *G. D. H. Cole.* 2 vols. (*See also* Fiction.) 820–1

Kinglake, Alexander (1809–91).
   EOTHEN, 1844. Introduction by *Harold Spender.*   337

Lane, Edward William (1801–76).
   MANNERS AND CUSTOMS OF THE MODERN EGYPTIANS, 1836. With a new Introduction by *Moursi Saad el-Din*, of the Egyptian Ministry of Education.   315

Park, Mungo (1771–1806).
   TRAVELS. Introduction (1954) by *Prof. Ronald Miller*, M.A., PH.D.   205

Polo, Marco (1254–1324).
   TRAVELS. Introduction by *John Masefield.*   306
   Portuguese Voyages, 1498–1663. Edited by *Charles David Ley.*   986

Stevenson, Robert Louis (1850–94).
   AN INLAND VOYAGE, 1878; TRAVELS WITH A DONKEY, 1879; and THE SILVERADO SQUATTERS, 1883. New Introduction by *M. R. Ridley*, M.A.   766
   (*See also* Essays, Poetry, Fiction.)

Stow, John (1525?–1605).
   THE SURVEY OF LONDON. The fullest account of Elizabethan London.   589

Wakefield, Edward Gibbon (1796–1862).
   A LETTER FROM SYDNEY, AND OTHER WRITINGS ON COLONIZATION. Introduction by *Prof. R. C. Mills.*   828

Waterton, Charles (1782–1865).
   WANDERINGS IN SOUTH AMERICA, 1825. Introduction by *Edmund Selous.*   772